Digital Learning Series

A Series by Post-Technology Educators

To the extent that education is the engagement of individual learners to knowledge, the Internet has changed everything because knowledge has moved to a new location. What is known by humankind is now located primarily on the Internet, and what is not there today will be soon.

The great migration of knowledge into cyberspace has kicked off a technological revolution in education. Teachers have marched off to computer classes. Librarians have been retrained as technology specialists. The "crayon set" can type before they're in kindergarten, and coding is a second language for the generation of kids now in high school. Millions of dollars have been spent wiring schools, and millions more are being spent reworking the wiring to broadcast the Internet to mobile receivers.

All the technological advances, both in equipment and user skills, have certainly been crucial to engaging knowledge on the Internet. But there is a further necessary component to the new education era introduced by the Internet. This book series swings the focus from the technology of connectivity to the digital form and substance of the knowledge engaged by learners on the Internet. Where is the information and how do we find it? In what form does it appear? How do we learn it? How do we teach it? These are real questions encountered every day in classroom teaching, independent study, and the preparation of online learning materials.

We can answer these questions by realizing that the interesting challenges today are no longer technical. True innovation is concerned with creating learning resources in the digital milieu. It is technically possible to link to almost anything on the Internet, but how do we choose what to link to in order to create an effective learning environment? Teaching and learning knowledge in its new location require tools that are *cognitively* new, though no longer *technically* so. How does interactive multimedia connected to a stunningly rich context web make learning grammar or geography or genetics different from studying these subjects in an isolated classroom or book? How can I implement the advantages and minimize the disadvantages in my own teaching and learning? These and many other such immediate and important questions arise once we become competent on the technical side.

The authors who have written books for this series are active participants in the challenges of engaging individual learners to the Internet, describing the reconnection to knowledge in our post-technology education world.

Judy Breck, Series Editor
New York City
September 2003

Digital Learning Series
Edited by Judy Breck

1. Jennifer Cordi. *Engaging Knowledge: The Inference of Internet Content Development and Its Meaning for Scientific Learning and Research.* 2004.
2. Noah Kravitz. *Teaching and Learning with Technology: Learning Where to Look.* 2004.
3. Judy Breck. *109 Ideas for Virtual Learning: How Open Content Will Help Close the Digital Divide.* 2006.

109 IDEAS FOR VIRTUAL LEARNING

How Open Content Will Help Close the Digital Divide

Judy Breck

Digital Learning Series, No. 3

ROWMAN & LITTLEFIELD EDUCATION
Lanham, Maryland • Toronto • Oxford
2006

KH

Published in the United States of America
by Rowman & Littlefield Education
A Division of Rowman & Littlefield Publishers, Inc.
A wholly owned subsidary of The Rowman & Littlefield Publishing Group, Inc.
4501 Forbes Boulevard, Suite 200, Lanham, Maryland 20706
www.rowmaneducation.com

PO Box 317
Oxford
OX2 9RU, UK

British Library Cataloguing in Publication Information Available

Library of Congress Cataloging-in-Publication Data

Breck, Judy, 1936-
    109 ideas for virtual learning : how open content will help close the digital
divide / Judy Breck.
        p.   cm.— (Digital learning series ; 3)
    ISBN 1-57886-372-4 (hardcover : alk. paper)—
    ISBN 1-57886-280-9 (pbk. : alk. paper)
    1. Teaching—Computer network resources.   2. Education—Computer
network resources.   3. Internet in education.   4. Computer managed
instruction.   I. Title: One hundred and nine ideas for virtual learning.
II. Title.   III. Series: Digital learning series ; no. 3.
LB1044.87.B726   2006
371.33′467′8—dc22   2005023028

∞ ™The paper used in this publication meets the minimum requirements of
American National Standard for Information Sciences—Permanence of
Paper for Printed Library Materials, ANSI/NISO Z39.48–1992.
Manufactured in the United States of America.

8/22/06

Dedicated to Anil Srivastava
Visionary of the connecting world

CONTENTS

SECTION 3: ACCESS

SECTION 4: AGGREGATION

SECTION 5: ADAPTING

SECTION 6: ACTION

PREFACE

The new network medium that is the subject of this book makes plain that what we know seldom proceeds in a tidy straight line. In addition to one line of thought, ideas are inevitably richly interfaced as a network of meaning.

This book is divided into six sections, following the traditional linear book format that lets the reader move along from one section to the next in a progression of ideas. A second organization format in this book suggests the network of ideas that gives us an understanding of the new primary home of what is known by humankind: the Internet. There are 109 small pieces of writing called "ideas." Each idea has meaning to add to the bigger picture of the emergence of global Golden Age of learning. There are 109 of these idea pieces simply because when I had written what I felt needed to be said, that is how many there were.

Many of the ideas can be read independently. A very timely and important subject introduced in Idea 3, and mentioned in other ideas as well, is open content for learning. This idea explains that learning content that is not free and open to all atrophies into irrelevance because network structure demands respect for open virtual knowledge. Idea 55 provides an overview of the burgeoning open content movement that is moving to the forefront of education.

The history of virtual learning content pouring into the Internet from 1997 to 2005 is a story that has seldom if ever been told. The cascade emerged quietly, and I was one of the few people at the time—or since—focused on the larger picture. Ideas 52 and 53 are my eyewitness account of what occured. Many excellent example websites are de-

scribed to give the reader a flavor of the wonderful knowledge that has
come online to become open and free.

Extending the ideas and spread throughout the book, 205 web pages
that illustrate what is being explained are named and described. These
examples from the new virtual knowledge ecology are listed in Appendix
2. They also can be accessed from my website GoldenSwamp.com on
the *Subject Sampler* page where they are listed under the number and
title of the ideas in the book. The websites named in these ideas are
easiest to visit in my *Subject Sampler* because you do not need to type
their URLs into your browser address bar. In the *Sampler*, you can click
the website titles to go directly to the pages on the Internet.

As I write this, I approach the last year of my seventh decade and find
myself pontificating about a golden era dawning in a world in which
most people seem to think things are going from bad to worse. I have
learned that there is wisdom and crucial energy in optimism. I have personal memories of the fading of a Great Depression, Allied victory in
World War II, the end of the polio that ravaged my generation, getting
through the Cold War with the world pretty much intact, the fall of the
Berlin Wall, and the emergence of a global medium by which everybody
will be able to communicate and to learn virtually anything. My optimism has not gone unrewarded.

What will be the next wonderful things? This book is about one of
them. Why should not all of our next generations be literate individuals
and knowledge whizzes in the subjects that interest them? I think it can
happen, and I think it will. In these pages I tell you why.

The book exists because of the support of a number of people. Anil
Srivastava is the rare sort of serial optimist without whom the world
would never improve, and I am grateful for his suggestion to write this
book. Without the confidence, support, and help of Rowman & Littlefield Education's leader Tom Koerner, I could not have done it.

John Seely Brown gave me the insight into the miminalization key to
emerging knowledge and added a compelling new dimension to the *109
Ideas* with what he explains in the foreword. I am very grateful to Howard Rheingold and Mike Smith for book cover comments.

There are people to whom I am in debt for encouragement to write
about my ideas. They include Greg Chotkowski, Lynda Weinman,
Debra Lesser, Nan Halperin, Richard Flynn, and my family.

Finally, as I wrote the accounts of HomeworkCentral.com, I was re-
minded that Peter van Roden rescued us from chaos, and my thanks to
him is overdue. He then gallantly led the first true general open content
for learning web collection through the crucial period when we were
able to understand and capture the new aggregation powers of the expanding Internet.

You might be wondering what could come to your rescue in education crisis, or entrapment in mediocrity, in a school, a district, a country,
or within your family. In these pages, I offer you the new and unstoppa-
ble advance of the knowledge aggregating in the expanding Internet. Be
of good cheer; grand change is coming as global learning is now emerging from the chaos of education.

The following 109 ideas guide us across the digital divide into a future
that places enlightenment into the hands of our children.

FOREWORD

It is hard not to open up any newspaper on any day and not read about the need for reinventing education. Tom Friedman in his seminal book, *The World Is Flat,* makes dramatically clear the competitive threat the USA faces from Asia in today's globalized knowledge economy, and none other than Bill Gates, CEO of Microsoft, calls for the reinvention of education for the twenty-first century. Yes, many of us have a gut feeling that somehow we must take a fresh approach to education in the twenty-first century. But taking a fresh approach requires new lenses to see the vast resources that could be marshaled to meet the challenges of not only reinventing education but also setting of the stage for creating a culture of learning.

Within this context, I opened up Judy Breck's manuscript, *109 Ideas for Virtual Learning: How Open Content Will Help Close the Digital Divide,* with great anticipation, and I was certainly not disappointed. Indeed, Judy instantly grasps the real potential of the networked (digital) age to open up an ecology of learning, opportunities for both formal and informal learning.

Let me dwell a moment on this powerful metaphor, an ecology of learning, founded not just on the vast information now readily accessible on the Internet but also the tools that amplify the social aspects of learning—learning in communities, learning with amateurs interacting with professionals, learning as a constantly expanding exploration of ideas. From my perspective, this helps reposition learning by doing into emphasizing learning from joining niche communities of similarly inclined folks who want to create, share, and build on each other's work.

Let me provide a couple of examples of the possibilities that have intrigued me. These examples stress the fact that the Internet is much more than just a vast repository of information. From my perspective (and Judy's), it is a social medium for the acquisition of knowledge and for collaborative learning. In fact, for all collaboration because real collaboration always involves learning.

To explore this potential a bit further, consider the open-source movement, where folks distributed all over the world come together on the Internet to build and constantly evolve complex software systems. The most famous example of this is the Linux operating system. Although the system itself and the governance model for building social capital around it are fascinating topics in their own right, I want to focus here on how this open-source movement acts as a learning resource for thousands of students wanting to master the practices of software programming. What has emerged is a new form of distributed, cognitive apprenticeship based on learning by doing, learning by joining a community of practice (through legitimate peripheral participation), and enculturation into the sensibilities and practices of the community. Key to this particular community is learning how to write code that can be easily read by others. One enters this community by working on peripheral projects—simple additions to existing code—that become open to peer review. You can get feedback; examine, test, and modify the code of others; see how the system evolves; witness or participate in commentary on projects; suggest new ideas of your own; and so on. Indeed, you are not just "learning-about," you are "learning-to-be."

Another example is Wikipedia, the vast, open-source encyclopedia emerging on the Internet. Currently, Wikipedia has more than one million articles in it and is being accessed more frequently than the *New York Times* online. It is a place where many of us turn first to find out information. As such, it has an obvious role in education by providing readily accessible and moderately trustworthy information for students of any age anywhere. But it plays a much more subtle role as an emerging form of cognitive apprenticeship. The way that Wikipedia works is that often a niche community of passionately inclined amateurs will take an initial stab at researching and writing up a topic of great interest to them. Then what tends to happen is that professionals and others with more highly specialized fragments of knowledge start to jump in and roll back and improve some of what was written. The process is always on-going, although for a particular topic, it does tend to converge to a stable, but living, document pretty quickly. Now consider this process as a platform for apprenticeship. The amateurs (and others who are watching and participating) get to see the practices of scholarship in action. They get to see (and participate in) the debates that emerge around the roll backs and so forth. Thus, the "apprentices" get to experience the practices of being a scholar.

Although this kind of accidental learning of a practice was never an intentional part of the Wikipedia project, it is an explicit part of some of the more focused projects developing on many of our campuses today. For example, the Decameron Web at Brown University has become a definitive site for scholars around the world to discuss Boccaccio's *Decameron,* a early novel in Italian literature. Although the primary participants are established scholars, it is also a site where graduate and undergraduate students can be legitimate peripheral participants, learning-to-be scholars, learning the practices of scholarship.

I have focused here mostly on extended forms of cognitive apprenticeship where the Internet can easily be seen to be an active medium fostering learning-by-doing, but nearly always with various kinds of social scaffolding to help create a reflective practicum. As such, this medium helps to provide a window into various ways of knowing. It also fosters productive inquiry—that is, that aspect of any activity where we are deliberately, though not always consciously, seeing what we need in order to do what we want to do.

Now, these examples do not constitute a radical transformation of learning—certainly not the kind of transformation that will help us prepare our students to be leaders of the twenty-first century. But they do help lay the foundation for something more radical and that is the shift from a supply/push theory of education to a demand/pull theory. The pedagogies of the twentieth century were aimed at doling out stocks of knowledge and skills for the student to hold in reserve until needed. My guess is that the twenty-first century will call for replacing stocks of knowledge with the ability to position oneself in flows of activities—where learning is both purposeful but also co-lateral. Shifting our attention from how to build stocks to how to participate in flows shifts us to thinking about learning ecologies where the constant cross-pollination of ideas and actions creates a vibrancy to learning.

In summary, the opportunities for new kinds of learning environments that take advantage of the Internet are nearly limitless. I have barely scratched the surface of the vast and rich array of examples provided by Judy in her book. Judy, more than anyone, grasps that the 'Net is as much a social medium as an informational medium. One without the other is hardly novel. But what is novel here is that by combining the social with the informational, we are creating a medium that affords both learning and knowing and that is our grand opportunity.

John Seely Brown
Former Chief Scientist, Xerox Corporation
Director Emeritus, Xerox PARC
Author (with Paul Duguid), *The Social Life of Information*
Author (with John Hagel), *The Only Sustainable Edge*

APPROACH

💡 1 THE MOST IMPORTANT IDEA

Some ideas have greatly changed human experience. When Europeans had rediscovered the Americas and then gradually comprehended what they had found, the idea of a new world emerged to set off transforming waves of further exploration and migration. When James Watson and Francis Crick recognized the double helix and realized that DNA encoded the information that directs the structure of living beings, that idea revolutionized entire sciences and led to the invention of new ones.

There is an idea about education that is just as huge as these two discoveries were. That transforming idea for education is this: The network, patterning structure of what a mind can know is mirrored in the network, patterning structure of the open Internet. That idea is not only theoretically elegant. It is so powerful that it has been a self-fulfilling prophecy: Over the past decade what is known by humankind has spontaneously nestled into the Internet and begun interconnecting itself there as an embedded cognitive network.

This online mirroring of knowledge structure is both static and dynamic, creating a venue of virtual learning within an ecology of virtual knowledge. Learning there is compelling and natural for the human mind. The result is not a learning method. Instead, learners can directly engage the interactive interface reflecting the interrelationships of what is known.

The European explorers did not create the Americas; the continents had been there for eons. Watson and Crick did not think up DNA; it

had been in each and every living cell since the beginning of cells themselves. The Americas and DNA were discovered.

It is equally true that thought and knowledge have always been network structures. Although not yet fully understood, the network structure of what we know strongly hints of integration with the biological
basis of the mind—the brain—which is a network of neurons connected
through synapses. What is very new is a global medium that can mirror
the network structure of knowledge: the Internet.

The Internet was sparked by universities early on, but its major development has been pushed by commercial forces, not education. I believe, though, that the greatest change the Internet will cause is the
solution of education woes and the achievement of global literacy and
learning. The paths blazed early on by explorers of the Americas as they
looked for gold were later trod by others to realize a new vision of
human liberty. Education is poised to benefit from the online world
built by other enterprises.

Seeing a great discovery when it first happens can be very hard to do.
Public awareness in the Old World that the Americas were vast new
lands took many decades. The larger idea of a New World took even
longer. DNA was appreciated more quickly but not immediately in
broad circles. A big part of the challenge of seeing a change is that our
language lags in forming words to describe it. The Europeans eventually
settled on a name for the new lands suggested by a cartographer after
he made some maps of coastal discoveries by minor explorer Amerigo
Vespucci. As for DNA, this grand discovery bears an opaque name derived from the highly unintuitive word deoxyribonucleic.

The most important Internet idea for learning does not yet have a
name. In the pages ahead, I will refer to the discovery for learning as the
virtual knowledge ecology. In Idea 80, I call the comprehensive virtual
network of what is known by humankind the *Grand Idea*. The name of
my website, GoldenSwamp.com, is a fanciful reference to the phenomenon of the emerging virtual ecology.

The pivotal word for comprehending that ecology is *network*. In the
winter of 2003, I was riding on a train, looking out a window, when the
network idea came into focus and its implications began flooding my
mind. It was a genuine eureka moment that altered my thinking on
many subjects. I had understood for several years that something amaz-

ing was going on with knowledge within the Internet, as I explain in Idea 35. At that moment on the train, I suddenly knew what it was: Knowledge behaves the way it does because it is embedded in a virtual network. The utterly nonrestrictive structure of a virtual network allows the bits of knowledge to interconnect freely, in every sort of static and dynamic pattern, to express unlimited nuances of meaning—doing something very much like what we do when we think.

In a virtual network structure, the connectivity of facts and ideas is not limited by the book or classroom in which it is embedded. It is not trapped in a curriculum or lesson plan or semester or degree plan. Instead, a network effect emerges as content rests and dances in a venue where only the meaning of any one bit determines to which other bits it reaches out and links. As bits connect, patterns emerge of various ideas and concepts.

The remainder of this Idea will outline the various sections of this book. Each section is a group of Ideas that provide background for understanding and taking advantage of the most important idea.

APPROACH

If we were to voyage by time machine back to ten years after Columbus first returned to report he had found land to the west, what approach could we take that would ignite the sweeping new idea that would change so very much in human affairs? How would we make it clear that Columbus had landed in a new world?

We would be limited to using early sixteenth-century tools and information—no laptops allowed. All we would be able to point to would be a lot of separate bits of evidence and assumptions from that evidence. That is the approach I have taken in this book, as I have written it about ten years after the tipping point that began the cascade into the Internet of what is known by humankind.

The problem with explaining a new and transforming idea is not that the people of the sixteenth century or of the twenty-first were or are lacking in intelligence and vision. The difficulty is simply that there is no previous example. The new worlds of the Americas and of the virtual knowledge ecology had no precedent. The ideas in this book approach what is happening from many different perspectives in the hope that the reader will join the discourse as this grand new intellectual adventure of the mirroring of what we know is explored by us all.

ATTITUDE

To appreciate the surprise of the virtual knowledge ecology, which has yet to be noticed in any significant way in education, it will help to keep in mind people like Christopher Columbus. In his case, he never figured out that more had happened than reaching some unidentifiable portion of the Far East. He never got past that assumption to realize he had landed in a massive new world. Certainly sailing west and reaching the Far East was a very big deal—but a very great deal more than that had happened. A pervasive attitude and preconception in the education establishment has been that the Internet knowledge is a new, and perhaps questionable, resource to be judged and managed by educators.

Although there has been nonstop discussion of the Internet and education, the network effect and the virtual knowledge ecology it causes are largely unmentioned. There are a withering number of Internet education promises, complaints, alarms, and confusions. The same sort of thing went on during the twelve years Columbus lived after his first visit to the Americas. He made a total of four voyages and died frustrated because he had not found the identifiable Far East. He did not come back from his voyages to proclaim he had found two great continents, which one day would be home to entire nations. As for DNA, five years after its discovery, I took a senior college zoology class where DNA was not even mentioned.

Even when a discovery is becoming understood, changing attitudes toward the way things are done is extremely hard. The saying goes that it is necessary to wait for the old high priests to die off before a really different something new can hold sway. Hopefully, we can get beyond that problem because what is at stake in understanding the new virtual knowledge ecology is the minds of our children.

I do not think the main problem is old priests, although there continues to be significant conscious or subconscious resistance within the education establishment to embracing the new ecology. At the least,

Internet critics have engulfed digital education in considerable confusion; something like thinking about the Far East instead of noticing a new world. Section 2 seeks to cut through those confusions that I think have kept us from seeing, much less appreciating, the virtual knowledge ecology.

To accept the re-centering of learning into the virtual knowledge ecology is to turn our backs on schools of thought as we know them. I, for one, have been active off and on for nearly fifty years in trying to make the schools we have better. For me, the possibility of trying something new seems liberating. The virtual knowledge ecology not only holds out that possibility, I think it demands that we now lift primary knowledge stewardship out of the schools.

The visceral reaction most of us have to even mentioning such a thing is alarm: Kids have to have schools! As you read the ideas in Section 2, you might see them as a rant against schools, and perhaps they are. I hope, though, that you will at least look through them, because they may help you temporarily set aside the education establishment Internet litany with which we have been programmed for many years. You may more easily see a new world and be spared ongoing misconceptions akin to mixing up the Far East with the Americas.

ACCESS

Two concepts fuel the theme and message of this book on Internet learning. The first one is that, in the 1990s, what is known by humankind appeared virtually within the network structure we call the Internet.

To assume the Internet is simply a new place to retrieve knowledge is not unintelligent. I heard one of the most intelligent and successful men of my generation take that position in a television interview in the fall of 2004. He said, "the Internet is just access," and that he prefers books, libraries, and other traditional resources. His comment implies that the knowledge that has migrated to the Internet is just sitting there, as it does in traditional resources. Even if that were all that had happened, it would be very good news because the Internet, and thus the knowledge, becomes available to more people every day.

For the man who dismissed the Internet as simply an alternative place to access knowledge, the problem is that what he would find in his preferred traditional places is now inferior to that located within the Internet. The knowledge available on the Internet is superior to versions in any other location. The Internet is the finest knowledge resource ever to exist. Ideas 40 and 78 set out the many reasons this is true. They describe how virtual knowledge is easier to access, more complete, frequently updated, often interactive, many times easier to understand, and increasingly most authoritative. The fellow who says he prefers traditional resources is limiting his access, not opting for equal access.

The ideas in Section 3 tell the story of the migration of knowledge to virtual simulation within the Internet and discuss samples of the best knowledge online.

AGGREGATION

The second phenomenon causing the most important Internet idea for learning that is the theme and message of this book was fully under way at the dawn of the twenty-first century because virtual knowledge was by then massively interacting within the network that interconnected it. That interaction is much bigger news than access to knowledge. As the knowledge aggregates online, the network effect causes a new virtual world, composed of what is known by humankind interconnecting cognitively and available to anyone connected to the Internet. In the open network where that virtual knowledge is located, it aggregates both statically and dynamically into patterns that emerge as new, enriched simulations of ideas that can only be found online. The ideas in Section 4 explore the development and mechanisms of this new virtual ecology of human knowledge and learning.

The gift of the most important Internet idea for learning is our new virtual knowledge ecology, where everything known by humankind abounds in its freshest and most complete and authoritative manifestation, interconnecting in context and bubbling up with emergent ideas that form the virtual knowledge ecology. That ecology, like what Columbus found, is a new world. Like DNA, it is a key to understanding and solving a basic human function, in this case learning.

ADAPTING

Section 5 presents ideas for retooling learning to suit the new knowledge location in the online virtual ecology. These ideas explore how various sectors are dealing with the need to adapt. The bad news is that, institutionally, the adaptation of education has not been pretty. The good news is that technology, cultures, and—most crucially—individual learners feel like they are coming home as their minds cozy up into the knowledge interfaced by the virtual knowledge ecology.

ACTION

Section 6 ideas suggests action. You may know a lot more about some of the areas discussed than I do. You will probably think of many other implications and suggestions, prompted by the great change in knowledge we are experiencing. I hope you will engage the visions the virtual knowledge ecology inspires and help to transform them into reality.

Hesitancy in much of education toward acting on the virtual knowledge ecology has kept education so far behind the times that it has become silly. The kids have already taken action. They go online when they want to really learn something. Most youngsters find their way into the open Internet outside of school, thinking of the virtual knowledge ecology as a place to really learn something, in contrast to the limited Internet access, incoherence, and boredom of school.

The generation born into the Internet era is growing increasingly intellectually disconnected at school because of the "keep out" signs there around the virtual knowledge ecology. As the youngest generations around the globe connect to the Internet in more numbers and with more powerful interfaces, the knowledge relevancy of traditional schools will fade away. Institutions that we may create to nurture and acculturate our children will change in ways we cannot yet visualize or understand.

The virtual knowledge ecology establishes a new and previously unimaginable relationship between human beings and what we know. We can all be intellectual creatures of this ecology, which we will relish as a state of nature for learning. The ideas that comprise this book sketch a quickening dawn of the global Golden Age of learning that lies ahead.

2 IDEAS IN COMMON

Recently, I was riding to Manhattan in the back seat of a private taxi I had hailed outside a school in Queens. The driver was a tall, handsome Middle Eastern looking man who appeared to be in his thirties. As we left the area of the school, I saw several men about his age on the sidewalk. They wore full-length white linen robes. Unlike my driver, who was clean-shaven and bare-headed, they all had long beards and white skullcaps.

"Are those guys Muslims?" I asked.

"Yes," he said and then fell silent.

I responded, "They didn't have turbans." To which he said nothing. I was afraid I had offended him somehow, and thought to myself that the turban comment was a dumb thing to say. Silently, I lectured myself about not saying silly things, especially about culturally sensitive matters to someone whose culture was not clear.

My mind wandered off out the window with my gaze as I enjoyed the ride through the streets of Queens. It was mid-afternoon on a beautiful June day. The borough was showing off its diversity, as all sorts of different looking people mingled on the streets. There are schools in Queens with kids from over forty countries.

The driver and I said nothing for at least fifteen minutes. Then quite suddenly, as we began our ascent up a ramp to the 59th Street Bridge, he said, "Where are you from?" I quickly said that I had grown up in West Texas but had lived in New York City for over half of my life. When I then asked him where he was from, he said Bangladesh. I asked how long he had been in America: eight years. Was he a citizen: yes.

He wanted to know how long my family had been here, and I tried to explain that most of my ancestors came to Massachusetts before 1700. He wanted to know where that was, and I explained it was above Connecticut—a place he would know as a New York taxi driver.

I was surprised very much by the questioning that came next. I do not recall exactly how he put it, but he was trying to find out about the discovery of America. Such an event was obviously at best a very hazy concept for him. Just as we crossed the middle of the bridge over the East River, I said to him: "Columbus sailed the ocean blue in fourteen hundred and ninety-two."

My tall, handsome, Bangladeshi-American driver grabbed a pencil and seemed to scribble on something next to him in the front seat. When I asked him why he wanted to know, he said he liked to know things like that. Then, he listened eagerly as I talked about the finding of the Americas by the Europeans, the coming of the Spanish and French first, the early settling by the Dutch in New York.

We continued the history lesson all the way up First Avenue. As we neared my apartment, I asked him if he had children, and he responded that he had a son who was only seven months old. As I got out of the car, I laughed and said he should memorize the 1492 rhyme about Columbus—that students had been doing that for a long time. "Oh, I will," he said with a smile, "I have it written down."

The question my driver asked me that surprised me most was when I first told him about Columbus. "How do we know that?" he asked in a puzzled tone when I told him Columbus sailed over here in 1492.

My fairly lame response was, "Don't worry, this is something we know for sure. It is well-established." That seemed to satisfy him. I did not get into the philosophical problems about the reality of knowing. I figured the date of Columbus's first landing in the Americas was not controversial historically. More importantly, I hoped it would give him something specific to tie into as he increases his useful knowledge of history.

I was surprised by my driver's question "How do we know?" because of the "we." I took it that he was asking this in a very perceptive broad way. The "we" would be humankind. There is, as Webster's says, something we can think of as "what is known" by us all—by humankind.

When my taxi driver was a young boy in Bangladesh, he seems not to have learned that Columbus had sailed the ocean blue in 1492. His access to knowledge may have been at best spotty, but maybe it was good. He might have had a teacher who knew about Columbus and told him. Perhaps there were books in his village or neighborhood school that offered the facts of the discovery of the Americas by the Europeans.

It is possible that he was told about Columbus at some point. He might even have learned the rhyme and later forgotten it. Perhaps he will not remember what I told him or will lose the version he wrote down. Or, maybe he did not even write it down and was just being polite. When I paid him for the ride, I asked him for a receipt, and he told me he did not have any paper so he could not give me one.

My driver's experience with knowledge has absolutely no effect on the knowledge itself. A deep and pervasive flaw in twentieth-century education has been the blurring of the line between process and substance. A strange woman in the backseat reciting a rhyme is a learning delivery process. The fact that Columbus landed in the Americas in 1492 is knowledge delivered by process. It is the sort of knowing substance Benjamin Franklin would have called useful knowledge. It fits within this definition from Webster's dictionary of *knowledge: the sum total of what is known: the whole body of truth, fact, information, principles, or other objects of cognition acquired by mankind.*[1]

The root meaning of pedagogy is leading a child to knowledge. Curricula, lesson plans, textbooks, classroom activities, and teachers are all kinds of or players in processes. The rhyme about Columbus is a form of process that conveys knowledge. Looking something up on the Internet is a process.

What is known by humankind is not process. Without any of the processes mentioned above, Columbus (almost certainly) crossed the Atlantic to the Americas in 1492, 2 + 2 = 4, and London is located on the Thames River.

The definition of knowledge given above says it is acquired. The mind of an individual student has learned the 1492 date, the sum of 2 + 2, and the location of London in order to acquire these particular bits of what is known by humankind. These bits of knowledge exist as part of what humankind has acquired, whether a student learns them or not.

The stunning change that the Internet has caused for education is that what is known by humankind now exists virtually in cyberspace. It is all there: the whole body of truth, fact, information, principles, or other objects of cognition our species has acquired. If my wireless laptop had been in the backseat of the taxi with me, I could have displayed the Columbus date on its screen and handed it to my driver. When his infant son is in grade school (or sooner), the boy will have his own mobile device with access to the whole body of knowledge acquired by humankind—which is the same stuff Ben Franklin and his philosophical friends termed *useful knowledge*.

The useful knowledge on the Internet is there virtually. In an older sense of the word, something that is virtual can mean that is it imaginary or hypothetical instead of actual. The computer era has led to this new meaning, now listed in Webster's, of the word *virtual: being on or simulated on a computer or computer network*.[2] Thus, a virtual knowledge ecology is an ecology of knowledge simulated online.

The statement that what is known by humankind is now accessible on the Internet simply means it has been simulated on the Internet, which is a computer network. When the Internet began, it first interfaced knowledge by simulating text, bringing online what could be printed in books and other formats. Images soon followed, then full multimedia— all of which included an interactivity with the computer user that had been absent in predigital media. Ideas 52 and 53 describe in some detail, and with examples for subjects and sources, the history of this migration of what is known onto the Internet.

Virtual learning is learning what is known by humankind simulated by computers and participating in the network ecology located there. That learning has thus far involved many kinds of process: self-instruction, online courses, being guided by a teacher, and other methods. So far, the education industry's primary practice has been to extract pieces out of the ecology, embed them in textbooks, presentations, and standards, and sell these products, mostly to schools.

There is, though, an unasked question: If the virtual knowledge ecology is spontaneously organizing what is known by following the same network laws that form the coherence of knowledge and thought, should there still be an enormous education industry that organizes and presents knowledge in other ways to students? That is a multibillion dollar question we should be addressing in education.

My answer is no. Education for acquiring what is known by humankind should be a process that releases learners to engage the virtual knowledge ecology. The education industry should redirect itself toward supplying that ecology with increasingly compelling open content for learning that simulates the natural networks inherent in the structure of knowledge itself and from which its meaning emerges.

⚐ 3 IDEAS ARE OPEN

If we look beyond education's many muddles of our day, there comes into view a marvelous place, teeming with our finest human knowledge. That knowledge is behaving spontaneously in new ways: dynamically and cognitively because it is embedded in a network. What is known by humankind and our interfacing with it are moving into a profoundly improved new era.

All of this is real. It is not theoretical. It is something that has happened because what is known by humankind appeared virtually in an open network venue, and that network structure mirrors the structure of knowledge that has been acquired by humankind. This marvel takes place because, in the network venue, knowledge itself can interact according to its meaning. The knowledge is not only better because we can access it, but also because of the fact that it has been relocated, onto the Internet. The Internet is a cognitively connective medium for knowledge—something we have not had in the past and are now just beginning to understand and appreciate.

The virtual knowledge ecology is the web of open content for learning that is amassing in something we call cyberspace. Cyberspace appeared in the later years of the twentieth century. You have your own little cyber habitat for information on your hard drive. Your mini-cyberspace is not the information stored in your computer. It appears when you start connecting things. When you relate numbers in a spreadsheet like Excel, those connections cause numeric results to emerge in the cyberspace in your hard drive. The phenomenal part is that the cells in the spreadsheet actually *create* information from the relationships between cells: C 34 + F 19 = the sum of the two numbers you enter into the two respective cells. Where did that sum come from? It emerged dynamically in the cyberspace used by the cells to connect and calculate. Accounting was revolutionized by the new phenomenon of information that could emerge in cyberspaces.

As the 1990s rolled on, cyberspace showed up big time, this time outside single computers. The growth of the Internet, and Tim Berners-Lee's invention of the World Wide Web within it, created an open global cyberspace into which potentially everyone on earth can be connected.

As Internet cyberspace grew larger and more welcoming (broader band), more and more information that had been located in its old haunts—printed materials, hard drives, disks, and human minds—entered cyberspace by morphing into digital simulations. All sorts of information became represented digitally: files, records, statistics, laws, lists, news, pornography, propaganda, resumes, catalogs, and on and on. Any bit could connect to any other bit.

Soon, the power to connect things in cyberspace began to change industries. Catalogs were connected to customers and to their credit cards, giving birth to e-commerce. Resumes were connected to employers who were hiring, and headhunting morphed into cyberhiring. A text string you typed in a box was connected for split nanoseconds to all the other text on the Internet, returning a list of places that had the same string, thus giving birth to search engines. As has been drummed into our heads by the anticyber folks, people who wanted to look at dirty pictures could connect to them, and pornography became a major cyber industry.

E-commerce, job-employer connecting, searching, porn, and many other virtual enterprises all coexist in cyberspace. Recently, the blogosphere swelled into a major occupant of cyberspace. The blogosphere consistes of millions upon millions of static and dynamic interconnections among blogs. These entities—ranging from e-commerce to the blogosphere, and many other large networks—do not have separate cyberspaces. They all dance simultaneously in an enormous, expanding interconnected network, with potentially every person in the world connected into it.

The virtual knowledge ecology is in there, too. Like the blogosphere, the virtual knowledge ecology is its own entity within the total network of relationships in cyberspace—though both interact with other bits and spheres that form the overall open Internet network.

Within any ecology nothing is completely isolated. To a small degree or in great quantity and complexity, each bit within an ecology is involved in interactions that form patterns. The idea of an ecology originated in life and environment sciences. Webster's dictionary defines an ecology as *the totality or pattern of relations between organisms and their environment.*[3]

Recently, network sciences have noticed that ecologies are networks.

The ecology of a pond is the network of the relationships among frogs, lily pads, mosquitoes, small and larger fish, birds, reeds, and the like, all participating in interrelated patterns of feeding, hiding, multiplying, and surviving. Within the network of the Internet, the virtual knowledge ecology is the interrelated patterns linking the bits of knowledge embedded as nodes. From those patterns, the structure of ideas is reflected into our minds as we explore the ecology and experience virtual learning.

Any bit that cannot connect is not a node in the network. If you take scissors and clip a piece away from a fishnet, the cut-off piece is no longer part of the network of knots and strings that forms the fishnet. You are left with two networks. The fishnet is an entire network. The piece that you cut off can no longer connect to participate in the patterns and relationships of the fishnet. The ecology of a pond is an entire network. The virtual knowledge ecology is an entire network. Networks of knowledge that do not connect to the open ecology are not part of it. This principle explains why what is called open content for learning commands the future of virtual learning. Virtual knowledge that is closed off into a private intranet or collection open only to paid subscribers is not part of the virtual knowledge ecology and is cut off from the future of global learning.

Open content is an idea discussed in many places in this book. The term *open content* is a shortened version of *open content for learning*. Both terms are used in online education circles to mean Internet content that is freely available online, without cost to the user. The use of *open* in the context of learning content resonates with computer jargon and tech talk about open: open systems with energy flow or closed system with no energy entering or leaving, open source, open software, interoperability, portability, and so forth. That sort of vocabulary can become dense in a discussion of online knowledge. Fortunately, sorting this out is unnecessary here because there is a stronger reason to use the word *open* than its trendiness in computer jargon.

Ideas themselves are open. Ideas are patterns that emerge from open connections. An idea like $2 + 2 = 4$ may seem complete by itself, but it is inherently connected to the idea of addition in general. Addition connects in many ways to other mathematical ideas. The idea of $2 + 2 = 4$ connects in many other ways. It connects to our apple idea when

It feels right and is perfectly natural to dump knowledge into a mind and then to expect ideas to emerge. Doing so is a key aspect of teaching and a fundamental activity of education as a whole. We are now learning the role of the network in the emergence of ideas. The mind is a network biologically, and its activity is a network of thoughts. It is fair to say—or at least suppose—that the ideas that come bubbling up in minds are emerging from a network of knowledge housed within the mind in which the ideas occur.

Can it be that exactly the same process is taking place with the Internet? It is clear that what is known by humankind has been dumped into the Internet. It is certain that the Internet is a network. Can it then be fair to observe that ideas come bubbling up in the Internet by emerging from a network in which knowledge is virtual (that is, simulated by computers)? I think exactly that is taking place.

The emergence of the virtual knowledge ecology and the opportunities it offers for education urgently demand our action. This is not a challenge to be left to presumed education experts. It is a global idea affecting us all, and it will cascade down through coming generations. It is very good news.

One path that could be taken is to revise forthrightly the institutions we have known as schools into the social and community centers a high percentage of them essentially are now. It could be that young generations will continue to connect with the virtual knowledge ecology for the most part when they are not at school, causing the schools we now know to fall into irrelevancy. Many of them already have, in terms of preparing students for advanced learning. What happens to the schools is not the same issue as engaging the virtual knowledge ecology. We should be concentrating on how to connect the new generations into the new virtual knowledge ecology.

One incident that led to my own commitment to getting the youngest generations connected occurred a few weeks after the United States troops arrived in Afghanistan in the fall of 2001. There was a newspaper article about the delivery of books, by way of donkeys, being made to school children in the Hindu Kush Mountains. I was provoked by the archaic delivery method—when the Internet was light years ahead of donkeys for connecting students with knowledge!

When ideas are open structurally, they pattern with each other. When

we have 2 apples in one place and 2 apples in another place. The 2 +
2 = 4 idea lets us know we have 4 apples by connecting the addition to
the apples. There would be no summary idea about the apples if the
ideas were not open to connection.

Ideas participate in patterns, giving rise to other ideas. One of the
most elegant patterns known is the syllogism, where the truth of two
ideas proves a third idea true. Famously, Aristotle tells us his syllogism:
Idea 1: Socrates is a man. Idea 2: All men are mortal. Therefore: Idea
3: Socrates is mortal. The syllogism is a pattern of deduction. Most idea
patterns are inductive, inducing ideas by pushing new connections. Although inductive patterning does not prove the new knowledge that it
spawns as conclusively as a syllogism does, inductive connections are
constantly expanding the frontier of what is known by humankind.

This is all pretty philosophical, but it is also stunningly practical. The
network that formed in cyberspace to become the Internet shows us
that closed off knowledge quickly becomes irrelevant. Putting it posi-
tively: Humankind has a new opportunity to interconnect everything it
knows, and we are doing just that. The open virtual knowledge content
network is an ecology of enlightenment that can be embraced by all of
humanity. Wow!

The necessity for learning content to be open in order to participate
in the virtual knowledge ecology is mentioned often in the pages ahead.
The reason that being open is necessary is not judgmental or idealistic.
The reason is the mechanics of networks. As explained with the fishnet,
to be part of a network, a node must connect into the network. In the
case of content for learning online, no connection is possible into the
larger network for a node of knowledge isolated by a password or located in a separate network, like the intranet of a university.

We are only beginning to appreciate the emergence of fresh new
ideas from the multiplicity of connections within the virtual knowledge
ecology. The more ideas that are added to the virtual knowledge in the
ecology, the more connections are available and the more virtual ideas
emerge. We see that when we dump lots of ideas into a network, dynamic patterns of meaning soon dance among the static nodes. The patterns are mirrored to us, so they begin dancing across the network of
our minds—tangoing, so to speak, with those in the virtual knowledge
ecology.

they get cut off, they cease enriching thought and knowledge. This happens in our minds and online. But, there is another way ideas should be open. Regrettably, ideas have, over human history, not connected very well with all individuals. Richly connecting into what is known by humankind has been routinely limited to the elite. The Internet will soon solve this inequity. How soon that will happen is up to us. The beginning is already well under way.

Human connectivity grows every day, in small and big steps. A big step was announced as I was writing this book, during the first months of 2005. A project led by MIT Media Lab founder Nicholas Negroponte and his wife, Elaine, is developing and will produce millions of $100 wireless laptops to distribute to students around the world. One day soon, computers from this project or another project like it will connect the virtual knowledge ecology for a child in the Hindu Kush. I predict the virtual knowledge ecology will be open to all kids everywhere in the near future, and that is a beautiful thing.

NOTES

1. *Webster's Third New International Dictionary*, Unabridged. Merriam-Webster, 2002. "Knowledge." Retrieved June 19, 2005, from http://unabridged .merriam-webster.com.
2. Ibid.
3. Ibid.

2

ATTITUDE

☀ 4 ATTITUDE OF AVOIDANCE

The virtual knowledge ecology is without a doubt the finest resource for human knowledge that has ever existed or even been imagined. It has been coming on the scene for several years. It is odd, if not blameworthy, that the central idea of what is known by humankind being freely accessible and cognitively emergent is not front and center on the education stage.

Instead, years ago the Internet education subject set the education world spewing issues, warnings, cautions, and confusion. The goal of the ideas in this *Attitude* section is to raise those matters and dispel them. At the least, the avoidance and objections of the education establishment are not reasons to evade exploring the virtual knowledge ecology.

The worst problem with all the avoidance verbiage is that it has confused the public about what the Internet can and will mean for learning. If you read through the following ideas, you will recognize them. You will have read and heard them from the education world from the early days of the Internet growth. It is time to ignore the blowing smoke and get down to understanding the virtual knowledge ecology. As we would tell the folks in Europe in 1500: Columbus did not sail to China, he discovered a new world.

It is frankly shocking that the establishment, to which we entrust our children to learn knowledge, routinely avoids talking about the virtual knowledge ecology. That must change.

5 CALL A KID TO FIX IT

A number of years ago, I was at a meeting where about twenty teachers in charge of Internet hookups at their schools were there to discuss their problems. After enthusiastic presentations from four of us on a panel representing different learning resources freely available on the Internet, the meeting drifted into a discussion of the troubles the teachers were having with technology. After several recited tales of breakdowns and confusion, a man stood up in the back of the room to proclaim that the best and perhaps only way to keep computers functioning in a school was to enlist a team of kids to do it. While the rest of the teachers listened and took notes, he spent several minutes describing how to put together and use a group of students to fix things.

The perception is widespread that kids know more about computers than adults, which somehow gets their elders off the hook for learning the skills. That is wrong and sets back progress. The truth about fixing computers in school is that things are a mess if and because the education establishment lets schools get by with adult ineptitude. Kids should not have to mentor adults.

When I was in grade school in the 1940s, the era of the great railroad trains was in full swing. My father was a train nut and so were my brothers. There was no family generational gap. My brothers relished Dad's railroad expertise and enthusiasm. Dad enjoyed sharing train experiences with his sons—and daughter.

Agewise being between my two brothers, I often found myself included in their railroad outings. I have a distinct memory of standing in railroad yards next to the wheels of a hissing steamed-up engine when I was so young the wheels were taller than I was. I have been inside a large roundhouse and seen an enormous steam engine turned around. I have been in several cabooses. When I was nine years old, I was in the cab of a steam switch engine as it worked the yards in Smithville, Texas. The cab of a coal-driven engine, which this one was, when the steam is up is not something you forget. To feed the boiler fire, a small metal door is swung open and the black fuel tossed through it with a shovel on to the flaming coals. The scene in the cab is deep black metal and hot red and orange fire. Being there is one of my favorite childhood memories. I had a very impressive father, with vast railroad knowledge, although his day job was orthopedic surgery.

The railroad obsession in my family was not about clinging to something from the past. It was cutting edge. My father kept up and kept ahead of innovation. Streamlining trains was new when he was in his twenties, and diesel engines came mainline when he was older than that. Innovation of many sorts was a central topic in family discussions. My mother was as much into innovation as Dad, and my little sister grew into the conversations almost as soon as she could talk. Decades later, we siblings continue the discourse and relish innovation. Though they are seldom cutting edge these days, I still love railroads and have taken the edgy Acela twice between Washington and New York City just for the fun of riding that train.

The adages "like father like son" and "like mother like daughter" capture expected behavior. Across the ages, there has been nothing at all unusual about kids patterning themselves and their interests after a parent. It is normal behavior that can be stabilizing for a family and its members.

What, then, happened with computers and the Internet? Why the standing joke that, if you have a computer problem, call a kid to help you? I certainly cannot imagine my father coming hat in hand to my brothers—much less to me—to ask for railroad information. Are kids today the innovation enthusiasts and all the rest of us old fogies? Did the generations of twentieth century lose their edge?

The true scenario is muddied up by the odd situation of the Internet and education. Why do kids know more about computers at school than the adults there do? Is it because the youngsters are the first generation of computer and Internet thinkers? Plainly, no.

The seminal pioneers of the Internet era are now fathers and grandfathers, not kids. One of the better-known older active Internet innovators is the inventor of the computer mouse, Doug Engelbart (1925–). Gordon Moore, chairman of Intel and giver of Moore's Law was born in 1929. Moore's Intel cofounder Andy Grove was born in 1936. The 2004 A.M. Turning Award, comparable in the computing field to the Nobel Prize, was given to Robert Kahn and Vinton Cerf. In 1973, they conferred for two days in a hotel conference room and emerged with the language by which networks communicate with each other. It is said that Kahn and Cerf, born in 1938 and 1943 respectively, made the Internet possible by coming up with the language.

Tim Berners-Lee, who invented the World Wide Web with its underlying rule of openness, was born in 1955, and continues to guide the web as head of the World Wide Web Consortium. Bill Gates and Steve Jobs were also born in 1955—a bumper crop year for the digital whiz kids of the 1970s.

In the 1990s, another set of geniuses emerged, including AOL's Steve Case, Jeff Bezos of Amazon.com, and Michael Dell, founder of Dell Computer, born in 1958, 1964, and 1965 respectively. It was not only a few leaders who were net-savvy by the 1990s, but thousands upon thousands of jobs were developed to create and service the industry. Millions of jobs in many, many enterprises, and more recently the Internet, utilize computers as an integral part of their work days and business.

A result of the movement of computers into the workplace is that, in millions of homes around the globe, fathers and mothers are digital role models for their households. It is silly to persist in assuming that children are introducing adults to the Internet and the computers that support it. The dearth of computer and Internet role models and mentors at school is inexcusable.

A reason the kids are so obviously in their own Internet world is that the education world in which they are expected to spend most of their time is Internet challenged. The kids are so far ahead in their understanding of the Internet from what they usually encounter at school that their increasing disconnect there is unavoidable and obvious. When they walk through the schoolhouse door, they enter the mid-twentieth-century world of my childhood, or even a school setting remarkably like that my father and his father experienced. In the sort of schools most children attend today, if there is a problem with computers that have been brought in from the outside world, it is no wonder they call a kid.

6 I DON'T UNDERSTAND THE INTERNET

For several years, claiming ignorance was a standard excuse for avoiding the Internet. In those early years of the Internet, when that was the thing to say, a lot of distrust developed from causes that had little to do with knowing enough about the Internet to use it. Searching for innocent things often turned up lewd pages. Computers crashed a lot, and the Internet came in very slowly through most kinds of connections. The dotcom bubble caused outsized expectations—and outsized disappointment. Meanwhile, the Internet was emerging into a huge and crucial part of twenty-first-century life and enterprise, in spite of these and other growing pains.

No one fully understands the Internet. It is too large, too complex, and too fast-changing to be grasped in more than large sketches. It is not hard, and usually fun and fascinating, to figure out the aspects of online activity that are useful to you.

The reason for engaging with the Internet is to take advantage of what it can do for you. I doubt I have to tell you that. It is important, though, for there to be a more general realization that it is not required to "understand the Internet" to use it. Continuing to cling to that excuse is like the stubborn folks who kept feeding hay to a horse and riding in a buggy because they did not understand the new-fangled engines. All they needed to learn was how to use the steering wheel, gas pedal, and brake. The point was to use a better means of transportation by switching to an automobile.

It is not necessary to know a lot about e-commerce to shop online. You can search for a job or employee with the greatest of ease by taking advantage of the easy-to-use yet very sophisticated software and operational techniques of online human resources enterprises. You do not need to know how the websites integrate purchases to buy a package that guarantees a seat on a flight, books your hotel, and arranges for a car service to pick you up at your door. There are dozens more thriving sectors of Internet operation, none of which you need to understand in any depth to benefit from what they can do for you. You can just jump in and drive.

It is interesting to watch—but not necessary to understand—how basic information is more and more taking up residence within the Internet. If you place your digital snapshots in an online service for sharing, you are using the Internet as a personal photo album that manages and displays your pictures online. Corporations, publishers, governments, and multiple other entities are trending toward doing the same sort of thing with their records and transactions as you do with your photos.

All that said, what is going on with the Internet in education? Disturbing digital rumbles are giving us fair warning that we all very much need to understand what is happening and why the Internet remains at arm's length from education. Our own kids are at stake, and the younger global generation's engagement of what is known by humankind is on the line.

☀ 7 THE INTERNET IS A BIG ENCYCLOPEDIA

It is easy to slip into the common misconception that looking up things on the Internet is like using a great big *Encyclopaedia Britannica*. Online resources, like the digital version of *Encyclopaedia Britannica*, continue to profit from that misconception by charging fees for their use. Using closed content, like the online *Britannica*, is very much like using its print version. It is a little better because a lot of the online *Britannica* articles are updated now and then and link out to related sources, but in other ways, the research experience is inferior to using open content. The deficits are explored in this Idea.

When in high school, my younger sister decided she might like to become a librarian. For practice, she cataloged all the books in our home. She came up with around three thousand volumes. My experience in grade school and high school had been that I seldom had to look outside our house to find books to do research for school reports. Growing up surrounded by books led to a habit (one that I have never shaken) of buying a lot of books. I love to look for ideas in books, read books, and live with books. I always have and still do use and treasure books. I am, in fact, right now writing one—and it is not a condemnation of books in any way.

Preparing school reports was something I enjoyed. The research was the best part for me—digging out ideas. My main source was almost always *Encyclopaedia Britannica*. We had two complete editions in our home. One was contemporary with me, published in the 1930s. This edition had big brown volumes that fit into the two shelves of the bookcase that came with the encyclopedia. The other set came from our

mother's childhood home and was published in 1911, a year after she
was born. The volumes of this much-respected *Britannica* edition had
soft leather, tan and gold imprinted covers and pages of fine, very thin
paper. The 1911 *Britannica* set occupied the bottom shelf of a bookcase
next to the living room fireplace. I spent many hours on the floor behind
a big easy chair next to the fireplace, flipping through volumes of the
old encyclopedia.

Sometimes, the older set was more useful than the newer one because it had articles that had been pushed out in later editions to make
space for more recent topics. I do not recall the subject of the report I
was doing that led me there, but I vividly remember several full-color
pages devoted to military uniforms in the older *Britannica*. By the time
I was doing that report, the world wars had transformed military dress
into camouflage. As a small child during World War II, I never saw soldiers dressed in anything but brown. There was no camouflage in the
old encyclopedia. There, I found pages and pages of the brilliantly colored European military uniforms of the nineteenth century.

Although Austin High in El Paso, Texas, where I was a student, was
an excellent high school by any standard, I seldom found myself doing
research in the library there. At home, there were plenty of books and,
the real bottom line was I usually could develop my topic using primarily the *Britannicas*. I recall one lengthy paper I did, probably in 1953,
on Stalin's purges, where the encyclopedias' histories of Russia and a
Life magazine article were my main sources.

By mid-twentieth-century standards, I had enjoyed outstanding research resources for a high school student. Such a concept as the open
content that forms the virtual knowledge ecology would have been in-
conceivable then.

College vastly increased the amount of research content available to
me as I entered Northwestern University in the fall of 1954, and I was
able to do my research in the stacks of Deering Library. The change,
however, was one of scale. Deering was like a great big encyclopedia in
that it was not open with instantaneous interactive connections to a
broader world—much less the whole world as we understand open content today!

Fifty years have passed since I wrote my report on Stalin's purges of the 1930s. When I entered "Stalin Purges 1930s" in Google recently, 22,400 sources were listed in .40 seconds.

If you have a home as my parents did fifty years ago, with four children growing up and going to school, you still have the option of offering your kids the *Encyclopaedia Britannica*. The basic print set starts at around $1400. You can also subscribe to use the basic set, along with other reference materials, online for $11.95 monthly or $69.95 annually (as of September 2005).

Today, parents who place the basic print edition in their home follow a grand tradition. But what they have done is to ask their kids to use a static resource in a dynamic world. That does not harm those portions of a student's research that have to do with information that seldom or never changes. It is unlikely that the year Columbus sailed the ocean blue will change, but even that could happen as historians and archaeologists ply their trades. Articles on subjects like genetics may well have been out-of-date before the ink was dry on the encyclopedia page rolling off the press.

Using a static printed encyclopedia is an obsolete way of researching any dynamic subject. It was very acceptable when I was a student because there was no other way available. I still have the zoology textbook from the course in which I studied the structure of cells in 1958. The book does not mention DNA, yet Watson and Crick had described the structure of DNA in 1953. Published in 1951, my textbook was still the standard for beginning zoology in 1958. That should be shocking today, yet obsolete textbooks are not a thing of the past in a lot of schools.

Since the Internet began to offer more and more subject matter, there has been an educational inertia about abandoning static research content. A large amount of content has been put online and then closed off from other content.

The online *Encyclopaedia Britannica* is an example of closed content for learning on the Internet. The articles in the printed editions are made available online to paid subscribers. *Britannica* teams strive to keep the articles up-to-date. The online *Britannica* offers tens of thousands of their own articles, as well as images, magazine articles, and website listings.

All of these form nodes in the encyclopedia's closed network. It is possible to travel the connections among the nodes. It is not possible for just anyone using the Internet to visit or link to these nodes from the outside. They are not part of the network of open Internet content for learning. They are not part of the virtual knowledge ecology.

If you are a protective parent who can afford the cost, would you not be doing the right thing for your children by paying for a subscription so that they can use the elite web of a few hundred thousand interconnected nuggets that comprise the online *Britannica*? Operators of quality closed content such as *Britannica* and many more, including many universities, promote their content as authoritative and easy to use, compared to the virtual knowledge ecology that is accessible and free on the open Internet.

But closed content is not part of the world we learn in and live in any more. Every kid knows it. Closed content is from Grandma's era. The real stuff is open content, but an awful lot of people do not know that yet. There are big differences, and there are several of them.

There is, of course, a moral high ground complaint that closed content causes a digital divide. Supposedly, for-pay knowledge is elitist and leaves out those students who cannot afford fees or tuition to attend universities whose learning content is not open on the Internet. For that issue to be valid, it must assume that somehow the closed content is superior to the open content. I do not think that is true now, and I am certain it will not be as the virtual knowledge ecology matures and everyone gets connected. Open content is refreshed often and tended by its authorities worldwide.

Here is an example that compares closed and open bird brain content sources: The February 1, 2005, online version of the *New York Times* "Science Times" reported that scientists have redrawn the anatomy of the bird brain. It turns out that birds are smarter than we thought. The *Times* referred to an article in the current *Nature Neuroscience Reviews*, which quoted the bird scientists as saying: "Nearly everything written in anatomy textbooks about the brains of birds is wrong."

My own immediate reaction was that even a bird brain could figure out what that means for public school textbooks: It could be as much as five years before they will be up-to-date about bird brain anatomy—that there is no longer any reason or excuse for spending school budgets on science textbooks.

I then proved to myself, and posted on my blog, that it is not hard to find the most up-to-date bird brain knowledge in open content at *no* cost to the schools. The *New York Times* article was going be open and free for a week, and then closed off, requiring a fee for access. The *Nature Neuroscience Review* online article only let you read a lead paragraph before having to subscribe to the journal (student rate $58 for a year).

But, the name of the lead scientist for the bird brain project, Erich D. Jarvis, was given in the *New York Times* article. Googling Jarvis led me to a flock of original sources, including Jarvis's own articles on bird brain anatomy. A couple of clicks from there and I arrived at Avian-Brain.org. This location in the virtual knowledge ecology has all the latest bird brain anatomy, continually updated by scientists who are studying it. A student can drop in on AvianBrain.org any time, at no cost, to look over the shoulders of the scientists doing the actual research that was reported in the *Times* and *Nature*.

I will argue throughout this book that closed content is steadily downgrading—and inevitably so, because it is isolated. Closed content atrophies and, as the Internet continues to grow and grow, closed content will atrophy more and more. Like a broken leg after weeks of confinement in a plaster cast, closed content loses its vigor and withers. I am convinced that no amount of expert editorial effort to update closed content and keep it attached to related links can maintain intellectual good health comparable to the vigorous authority of open content.

Open content that networks to form the virtual knowledge ecology is different because it consists of nuggets (nodes) that can be connected to limitless other nuggets from every sort of imaginable source. How can that be better than a single trustworthy source like an established encyclopedia or university? Open content is and remains more trustworthy because every nugget of open content is potentially vetted by everyone using the Internet. The nugget that is most liked—we can say approved of by open authority—can be identified mathematically by how many others link to it. That is how what you are looking for shows up at the top of the list you get in a Google search.

Nuggets of open content are selected by the combined trust of every authority using the Internet. Open patterns form among authorities on cells, cyclones, comets, and every other conceivable topic—some not so savory.

Instead of looking at the Internet as a big encyclopedia with many subject articles, it should be seen as a dynamic network of ideas relating to each other in cognitive context. It is the cross-referencing of an old-time encyclopedia come to unlimited life and connected massively to related interfaces on a global scale.

8 WHY ONLY OPEN CONTENT WILL ENDURE

We are conditioned to thinking that paying high tuition for enrollment in an academically superior school guarantees access to superior knowledge. The same conditioning makes us think of expensively printed books as delivering trustworthy knowledge interfaced in the highest quality writing, pictures, and charts.

The fact of the matter is that only open content will participate meaningfully in global learning once ubiquitous computing is in place. When virtually everyone on earth is using the Internet to learn what they once were expected to learn in school, open content will be the only Internet source.

A lot of content will remain closed on the Internet: company records, financial data, personal stuff, and so forth. But reading, writing, mathematics, history, literature, sciences, and the rest of what we knew as "school" knowledge will be manifested as open content interconnected into the virtual knowledge ecology.

The extent of the changeover can be compared to two other changeovers in transportation. When the automobile came along, the horse-drawn buggies disappeared from roads everywhere. When the airplane began to fly passengers, something different happened. Automobile and airplane transportation prospered in parallel. For learning content on the Internet, open content will take over as completely as the automobile wherever the Internet communication system connects.

The changeover will be total because open content is cognitively superior to closed in an entirely new way: It is interactive both with other knowledge assets and with its users. Its linking into and from other knowledge assets forms a cognitive pattern for its subject matter. That pattern can be explored by visitors as a means of learning and apprehended by them to teach them content. The interaction with visitors vets and augments open content.

It will not work out to have open and closed content in parallel because knowledge itself is connected and that connectivity is dynamic. Only open content will endure because closed pieces of content are excluded from the dynamics. In Idea 80, the resulting Grand Idea structure encompassing all networked subjects is explained. The premise is that what is known by humankind is a single interconnected web: algebra connects to trigonometry which connects to astronomy which connects to geology—effectively all ideas are interconnected. A closed off thought that fails to connect somewhere has no relevance. This is philosophical but, in a fascinating way, we can watch the already under way withering of closed content within the Internet.

Academic institutions that deny outside access to their knowledge assets, and learning companies and archives that limit access by charging money for knowledge, end up with inferior content. It seems odd that the highest quality knowledge would not be found in enterprises that make money from it, by generating profits to plow back into producing high quality assets. But it is not.

There is an inescapable reason why closed knowledge assets slip into the backwaters of global learning and grow stale. The reason has nothing to do with altruism, reflecting the good hearts of the open-content advocates. The reason is the network structure of the virtual knowledge ecology: Open content is accessible to all Internet visitors to evaluate and incorporate into their own activity by linking to it.

A knowledge asset closed and isolated in a single website may be an expensive animation of a scientific principle, an erudite essay by a field-leading professor, or a rights-protected journal article. Many of these kinds of assets exist in the closed sections of the Internet. The knowledge quality of what these assets contain may be absolutely first-rate.

Even the highest quality isolated assets are a cut below open content because they are isolated from the larger context of their subject. Although that isolation can be lessened by linking outward, incoming links are limited to paying customers. This is a severe cognitive limitation in our new learning world, which is based on dynamic as well as static connectivity.

In the new education within the virtual knowledge ecology, when a high school sophomore is preparing a report on the rotation of the moon around earth, he will do that in the form of a web page. He would want to include a link on his page to an animation of the rotation. Although he might be able, if he paid a subscription, to look at an excellent animation on a closed website, he could not insert it into his report because the report would be an open web page. The expensive animation is degraded by not being linkable and thus missing incoming connections to context.

The sophomore would probably not have that problem in the first place because he would have been unlikely to know about the expensive animation of the moon rotating around the earth. It would not have shown up in his Internet searches because the URL (Uniform Resource Locator) would have been closed to the public. Since it could not be linked to, the animation would appear far down on a search return list because the density of links determines the animation's search engine results placement. The vendor could advertise the animation on a search engine as an only recourse.

Still, our conditioning makes us suspect that the closed animation is superior because it cost money: If we could find it and link to it somehow, it would be the best animation out there. In Idea 42, the remarkable low cost of open content is described. In brief, cost is not what makes learning content superior.

The worst degradation of closed content is its isolation from the larger connectivity of ideas within the Internet. Conversely, interconnected open content is cognitively stimulating, authenticated by open access, and fun to explore.

9 CHILDREN NEED CULTURAL COMFORT

During the 2002–2003 school year, I taught logic and debate to seventh graders in New York City one afternoon a week at a small Christian school located on Park Avenue in Manhattan.

The sixth-grade teacher was a native of Africa who had grown up there, qualified as a teacher, and taught for a few years before emigrating to the United States. She is black and speaks excellent English with an accent that sounds British to me. Late in the school year, I organized a moot court competition among the seventh graders I had been teaching and asked if we could hold the finals in the sixth-grade classroom, with her students serving as judges and critics. She approved, and the event was scheduled.

On finals day, we seated the student judge, student bailiff (to maintain order), and student attorneys on a raised platform at the end of the classroom. As the sixth graders listened to the arguments and later gave their critiques, their teacher demanded (with a little help from the bailiff) and achieved that balance of enthusiasm, thought, and order that is the ideal setting for learning. She is a natural teacher and dedicated to her gift.

Over lunch one day, she gave me a pivotal insight into what is going on in education in many of the countries across the world that once were European colonies. She said it was a disappointment to her that her homeland was preserving and building colonial-type schools. Decades after its liberation, the assumption in her homeland was still that colonial school methods were how education was to be done. She worried and wondered that the traditions of her own people were not represented and that new ways of teaching were not being considered.

Colonial schooling was based on European traditions and, as such, was always an aberration across the empires. Since time immemorial, education substance has been local—based on geography and culture. At its best, a local education system would teach the kids what they needed to know to be useful and successful adults. In the awful tsunami of 2004, the Moken sea gypsies of the Surin Islands ran up their mountain to safety because their oldest people remembered learning long ago of danger signs they saw in the sea on the day the great waves hit.

Localized schools are institutions that prepare their students to belong to the local culture. As a graduate of El Paso, Texas, public schools Crockett and Austin, both named for founding heroes of the Texas Nation, a piece of me will always be Texan and I am proud of that. In the movie *Alamo*, the hero for whom my grade school is named, Davy Crockett—played in the movie by John Wayne—looks at the heroine hard and says: "There's right and there's wrong, you gotta do one or the other. You do one and you're living. You do the other and you're as dead as a beaver hat." (No footnote here, those are the words I remember and always will as part of my Texan conditioning.) I realize that in recent years the battle held at the Alamo has become a subject of controversy, and I am open to exploring the history. But my affection for Texas is not a matter of historical insight. It is an acculturation thing that became part of me long ago.

Acculturation is a tender, sensitive, and explosive subject. It is not what this book is about. It will help, though, to point out that acculturation is not identical with teaching children what they need to know to be useful and successful adults. Acculturation is certainly a part of being successful, which requires shared mores and fitting in. The sort of reverence I feel for Davy Crockett is a mutual bond with my old friends in El Paso and was helpful when I held staff jobs in Texas political campaigns in the 1960s. Davy is not something I have mentioned often— nor, frankly, admitted to readily—during the second half of my life, spent in New York City.

In most of what I have to say in the ideas collected in this book, my acculturation as an American is clear. Most of the specific references to schools in this book refer to locations in the United States. I write about what I know from my own experience. If you are reader—like the sixth-grade teacher I met—who knows schools in other countries, I hope you will apply examples from your own experience to the ideas I mention.

The huge shift under way for learning is that the virtual knowledge ecology is not geographical, it is global. It transcends localities and cultures and is available in common to students everywhere, along with anyone else who is interested. The emergence of the virtual knowledge ecology represents a titanic shift from localized learning to a common global knowledge resource.

Fantastic? Yes. Real? Absolutely. A good way to see how it works is to look at the open content rhetoric websites now available.

Along with teaching them the subjects of debate and logic, I introduced the seventh graders to the academic subject of rhetoric: the art of persuasion. Rhetoric is an example of pure knowledge that is not alterable by any culture. The color of mourning in the West is black; the color of mourning in Japan is white—reflecting cultural differences. The separation and sadness of mourning affect people of every culture. Rhetoric may be used differently in different cultures, but a metaphor is a metaphor in English, Japanese, Swahili, or Apache.

Rhetoric is a subject with origins in each of the earliest civilizations:

Egypt, Mesopotamia, India, and China. It flowered in the Golden Age of Greece and shone in the time of Confucius in China. It persists in theory and practice in many lines, through the march of eras and peoples. Rhetoric belongs to no culture and can be learned by twenty-first-century students from every culture. They can do it from common resources in the virtual knowledge ecology in websites including Forest of Rhetoric, Aristotle's Rhetoric, Rhetoric of Mencius, and Crow's Nest.

Section 4 of this book examines the vetting process that is inherent in the network environment of the virtual knowledge ecology. Fascinating factors are at work producing an entirely new organizational structure for what is known by humankind. The underlying mechanism is the connecting nodes of knowledge on the basis of their cognitive contact—on the basis of what they mean.

The "truths" that vary from culture to culture challenge and adjust the gears of the natural network, linking and making impossible a common resource for those sorts of truth. Students of the funeral business in the United States and in Japan need different web pages for learning appropriate dress and décor for their work. Texans and Mexicans teach the history of the battle at the Alamo with different sets of facts, both labeled "truths." But these confusions need not sidetrack understanding the virtual knowledge ecology. The vetting process explained in Idea 75 will resolve and refine content conflicts in a new way.

A metaphor is a metaphor, two plus two is always four, and an apple leaving a tree on its own always falls in a downward direction. Rhetoric, mathematics, physics, chemistry, geography, and geology work just fine on one website for all, so long as the language is translated and the illustrations are not culture-specific. Later Ideas will go into more detail on the workings of the virtual knowledge ecology as a common knowledge resource.

The larger observation, for now, is that a fundamental shift is in progress from local to global open knowledge content. The local school will soon not have the burden of providing and supporting access to rhetoric, mathematics, physics, and so forth. To study a particularized branch of physics, for example, it will no longer be necessary to move across some geography to attend the university where that branch is a specialty. As the open courseware movement unfolds, as described in Idea

54, more and more learning assets from specialized centers of higher learning will be accessible anywhere.

Knowledge is becoming available and free as open content in the virtual knowledge ecology. The virtual knowledge ecology is not located in a geographical place. It exists virtually, in open global cyberspace, and when the planet is effectively painted with Internet access, the virtual knowledge ecology will be in virtually every geographical location.

10 IS THERE A CONSPIRACY?

Does the education establishment avoid the Internet on purpose? Is there a conspiracy to keep the Internet out of education? Are there dens of pedagogues in academia who scheme to socially engineer our children—or were there in the past, explaining why education now has its woes? A lot of those who are upset with the failure of education believe such conspiracies are the root cause.

My answer is that I do not know, and I have not spent much effort wondering. My experience with conspiracies in general has been that they are not all they are cracked up to be. It is a lot easier to imagine from afar that plotters are at work cooking up schemes that cause things to happen than it is to actually cause things to happen.

My most upfront and personal experience with an alleged conspiracy of some note was as a staff member of the Committee to Re-Elect the President (CREEP) in 1972. The multifaceted conspiracy cooked up in the public's mind around Watergate was a doozy. Its genesis was a break-in at the Democratic offices in the Watergate building. A CREEP staff member, "Watergate co-conspirator" Gordon Liddy, eventually went to jail and later became a news radio guy without ever revealing what he knew. Very secret stuff!

Was there a Watergate plot to sneakily defeat the Democratic Presidential candidate? Was the cover-up orchestrated by John Mitchell and White House people (and probably President Nixon) a conspiracy? Did the press conspire to "get Nixon"? Was *Deep Throat* part of a larger conspiracy to harm the President? I was there and knew, at least slightly, all the players in the Nixon milieu.

My opinion is that the Watergate mess was about 1 percent conspiracy and 99 percent screw-up. It is astonishing to watch a lot of intelligent people who have gotten themselves some power proceed to do just about everything wrong. Such people are prone to responding to something not working well by either doing it more thoroughly or somehow managing to come up with something worse. A screw-up for them does not lead to rethinking policy so much as to goad them into going to greater effort to prove their policy is the right one—by doing it some more.

In the creation of a large-scale mess, hubris is a major factor, it seems to me, far more often than conspiracy. A person who is sure she is right and plunges ahead is likely to cause a great deal more harm than a person trying to plot with others in secret. Hubris just about always causes a mess, and secret planners just about always get caught. For whatever it is worth, the effect that watching Watergate up close had on me was to make me worry less about conspirators than about self-assured mistake-makers. It is also true that, when someone is screwing up big time, that person usually becomes defensive and secretive to the extreme.

As to the messes in education, looking for a reason by tracking down supposed conspirators probably does not justify the effort. If there were groups a century ago who plotted to socially engineer children by redesigning schools, their grandchildren have forgotten all about it. Perhaps I am guilty of hubris in my certainty about the value of the Internet for learning, but at least the conclusion is not inherited from earlier Internet generations because there are no such generations. Hopefully, my enthusiasm is fresh conviction for a new era.

It is usually a more fruitful effort to look for what may have gone wrong than who may have conspired to make it happen. In eleven Ideas later in this section, I criticize various ways in which the education establishment has responded negatively to the Internet. Following that series, Idea 22 describes the folly of considering education participation in the Internet only as technology.

In these critiques, I am not suggesting conspiracy. I doubt there is any now and do not know if there ever was—but I have no real way of knowing. I do think a lot of things are messed up and that hubris is a very real and present factor in compounding the malfunctioning. Figuring out how to fix things is something we all should be doing. I believe the virtual knowledge ecology will help in major ways.

💡 11 THE EDUCATION ESTABLISHMENT OGRE

The most wonderful people I have met over my lifetime are dedicated to education. Many work in schools, and many of them in awful schools. The following is not in any sense a criticism of them or of their thousands of counterparts across American and the world, in their devotion to children and learning. In fact, my comments throughout these ideas are the opposite: a tribute to them for trying to make things better, in often amazingly adverse circumstances.

The villain in this book is an ogre I have called the education establishment. Tales of traditional education woes cannot be told without an ogre character. Exactly who, though, is the ogre of education? Can the right princess—like the No Child Left Behind laws—kiss this ogre and transform him into a knight in shining armor or must he be slain? If it is option one, who is that princess? If it is option two, how do we identify this dreadful fellow and strike a stake through his heart?

Perhaps the ogre is actually a kindly character, like the animated movie star ogre Shrek. In that case, he would be doing a lot of the wrong things for the right reasons. He would have the lamest excuse of all for dumbing down our kids: He means well. His destructive ways would need correcting, just as those of an evil ogre would.

About eight years ago, I was in a small meeting with some executives of a Washington-based public relations firm that specialized in representing the education establishment. They worked for clients from the full spectrum of that establishment, not a certain sector or point of view. After a couple of hours of exploring ideas for how to get the education establishment's attention for some new things happening on the Internet, the executives began to be increasingly candid about how difficult it was to get any attention or action from the conglomeration of education entities. One of the public relation guys turned to me in the midst of these laments and said, "Do you know what we call the education establishment among ourselves?" I shook my head. He said, "The Blob."

So, we have an ogre named The Blob. Reform movements disappear into it. It offers no identifiable face to sit down with and talk. Though enormously wealthy and getting richer every year, it whines endlessly for money. The children it teaches slip a little or a lot nearly every year to learning less than the kids they follow. Wave after wave of fresh new teachers penetrate it briefly and are repelled. It hides in a collective cynicism that justifies jobs and profits, perpetuating the status quo. The Blob, shrugging, proclaims itself the professional expert and assures us there is no way to do any better.

The Blob is an unfortunate mix—in varying degrees, in many places—of many factors: bureaucratic entrenchment, vested interests, unwarranted tenure, misanthropy in the classroom, professional snobbery, liberal do-gooding, conservative stinginess, cynicism about other people's children, fear of kids, and quite a few other things. It is beyond the scope of this book to go on a wild blob chase and try to pin down and identify our villain. A lot of very good people have tried doing that and others are still trying—almost all with little luck. A lot of heroic people are caught up in The Blob, where they strive every day to educate children. But ours is a different and much more hopeful story of an entirely new phenomenon for learning that is flowering beyond the ogre's control.

I pause here to bring up the ogre because it is crucial to this book that you suspend listening to the education establishment as you read what I have to say. The Blob is very effective at blowing smoke. The ogre has programmed the public to react negatively to online learning. It is not easy to get beyond the concern and confusion The Blob causes.

Does The Blob really know more than you and I do about education? Does The Blob have any sort of real handle on the Digital Age we have entered? Is this ogre really better qualified than you are to judge your children and help them choose their path in life—and then to decide how they should be equipped for the twenty-first century? Should we really commit our kids by law to twelve years of confinement under The Blob?

The biggest threat The Blob has ever faced is the migration of education's most obvious commodity, knowledge, into the virtual knowledge ecology. The ideas that follow describe how the ogre has dealt with that threat thus far. As with most ogresque things, they are not pretty.

12 KNOWING THE BAD STUFF

Before looking at the response that the education establishment has had so far to the Internet, a pause should be helpful for some musings on the differences and similarities of the times children are experiencing today and those that we lived in as kids. I tell stories that are mine from over five decades ago. I hope you will bring some from the time of your own into the thinking. The issues and actions raised are very important to generations now young and those that will follow.

When I did my 1953 high school report on Stalin, described in Idea 41, I relied almost entirely on the information I could find in a 1930s *Encyclopaedia Britannica* and an in-depth article published in *Life* magazine the year I wrote the report. I did my research at the depth of the Cold War and the year of Joseph Stalin' death at the height of his power and control. I remember that the *Life* article was a detailed account of the purges of millions of Russians in the 1930s, plus a series of dark biographies of the dictator and his cronies who had perpetrated the atrocities.

I did not, nor was I expected to, take a look at Stalin's point of view in what I was writing. It was the McCarthy era, and anything pro-communist that filtered through from the other side of the Iron Curtain to a high school student in the United States was discounted as propaganda. My geopolitical views were formed in significant part by experiences such as writing my paper on Stalin. These days, because of the Internet, it is possible for students to take much richer global samplings as their geopolitical ideas develop in their minds.

The investigation of political affairs within the Internet is a messy business, but then political affairs themselves are messy. The Internet offers every sort of opinion on the historical events upon which geopolitics turns. I suppose if he could have done so in the 1950s, Stalin would have had websites justifying his genocides as required for the establishment of the glorious ideals of communism. I believe I would have profited from studying his arguments and gaining the insights they would have provided into how a dictator thinks and propagandizes.

I do not think a sixteen-year-old back then or now would fall naively for Stalin's justifications, especially if he or she had access to the views of everyone involved. If they could have done so in their day, I am sure there were people in Russian villages who would have told their stories by calling out on their cell phones or posting facts and images on blogs. Their silence when I was in high school was not because of lack of char-

acter or courage. They were isolated—connected in their own time and heard only as dim echoes over seven decades of distance.

We can, in fact, hear them better now because of the Internet than they could be heard in the 1930s. The following poem online, in "The History Guide," by Osip Mandelstam, is about Stalin. Titled *We Live, Not Feeling*, it was probably written in 1934. I found it in March 2005, on the Internet.

We live, not feeling the country beneath us,
Our speech inaudible ten steps away,
But where they're up to half a conversation—
They'll speak of the Kremlin mountain man.

His thick fingers are fat like worms,
And his words certain as pound weights.
His cockroach whiskers laugh,
And the tops of his boots glisten.

And all around his rabble of thick-skinned leaders,
He plays through services of half-people.
Some whistle, some meow, some snivel,
He alone merely caterwauls and prods.

Like horseshoes he forges decree after decree—
Some get it in the forehead, some in the brow,
some in the groin, and some in the eye.
Whatever the execution—it's a raspberry to him
And his Georgian chest is broad.

It is demeaning and shortsighted to rein in the research of youngsters—and it tap dances dangerously near to being a form of propagandizing them. As you read this, you may be agreeing in your mind about high school kids.

But what about the littler ones? Should they not be protected from the horrors that occur in their time until they are old enough to understand? My personal opinion is that the question is false: Children will certainly be aware of bad things, and our goal should be to help them assimilate what they encounter as reasonably as possible. But I do not have the psychological background to make a judgment on whether protected innocence is to be more valued.

The point is, they are going to know bad stuff whether we try to protect them or not. The little ones in Afghanistan are well aware that friends of theirs have missing hands because mines from a war remain buried and armed in their country. They may well be calmed as well as informed by learning everything there is to know about that war. The missing hands should not be an emotional trigger for a single point of view. The kids know the horror, but do they have access to the full truth—and from what worse horror could they possibly be protected by being shut off from the Internet?

Kids have a way of finding out the bad stuff, and I think they always have. My early grade school years were during the horrific climax of World War II. My father doctored returning amputees at an army hospital in Texas. Our third-grade class performed a play for the patients in which I had the star role of Tomboy Jo. I can still remember the lyrics of the theme song: *Tomboy Jo, I'd rather be a boy you know, I can jump and climb a tree as well as any boy you see.* I can also remember sitting on the stage under the piano (the imagined location of Jo's tree house) and looking out at the patients in the audience. I recall their army pajamas, wheelchairs, and crutches lying at their side and that there was at least one man who just had one leg. I knew full well the war was going on and that this was how these men were hurt.

In those grade school years, media information was scarce. The arrival of *Life* magazine was the major weekly look at what was happening in the world, along with a newsreel if we went to the movies on Saturday. We did not even have news radio (just a few newscasts over the day), much less constant cable television news. Limited as these sources were, I still knew that our soldiers were dying and being hurt. Radio conveyed a lot to my young ears. I can still remember—along with the lyrics to "Tomboy Jo"—the comfort of FDR's voice, Kate Smith's reassuring rendition of "God Bless America," and the frightening fascination of listening to a live radio rant by Hitler.

Today, the pervasive media makes hiding horror from little children more implausible than ever. The reaction in my Manhattan neighborhood that followed the attack on the World Trade Center included the very small kids. Our fire station on East 85th Street lost nine men in the

collapse of the towers. The station became a focal point for an out-
pouring of gifts, tokens, embraces, and tears in which hundreds of
neighbors took part for weeks.

Several times, I saw parents from the neighborhood accompanied by
little children standing in the station driveway talking with firemen. The
kids brought drawings and flowers. They would hand them to a fireman,
who would thank them and lean over to tell a little Tomboy Jo or Jack
that all the firemen were grateful for their gift and that things were okay.
More recently, there have been many reports of small children thinking
up projects and raising money for victims of the 2004 tsunami.

Preoccupation with the dreariness of the periodic horrors and trage-
dies that impact kids misses the wider excitement of their involvement
in the unfolding adventure of the times in which they live. There are
Mars rovers, animal rescues, archaeological discoveries, cures for diseases, new tools and technologies, and myriad ongoing events and discoveries. Much of the news that pours through the media is good news,
useful news filled with information valuable for children in the development of their minds.

Yet there remains in many classrooms the restricted and small-por-
tion serving of knowledge that was necessitated in earlier generations.
No self-respecting teenager should be asked to settle for writing a report on Stalin, or anything else, based on an encyclopedia and a single
magazine article. Doing so may assure the student scores well on a standardized test, but it does not prepare the student for the connected intellectual feast of the twenty-first century.

13 THE EDUCATION ESTABLISHMENT
ATTITUDES TOWARD THE INTERNET

So, why is the Internet not a powerhouse in education? A big part of
the answer to that question is the way the education establishment has
coped with the Internet. The next Ideas (14–23) review eleven facets
of the attitudes the education establishment has exhibited toward the
Internet.

The ideas that follow still dominate discussion in education circles when the Internet comes up. That is downright silly. The topics are very much dated; most of them belong back in the 1990s. None of them comes even close to focusing on how the Internet offers open content or the resulting virtual knowledge ecology. Many of them deflect attention from what is really going on with knowledge within the Internet. The access to knowledge content and the network behavior of that content—the major subjects of this book—are largely avoided.

These attitudes by the education establishment confuse and color public response. Perhaps you are sympathetic toward one or more of them. Most people are and, in doing so, they miss noticing the virtual knowledge ecology as it emerges to create the new Golden Age of learning.

You may want to just scan the following eleven Ideas, but it is worth looking at their subjects together here first as a group, to get an idea of just how thoroughly the education establishment has managed to avoid the virtual knowledge ecology.

THE ATTITUDES

Wire the Schools

The first response was to assume the Internet was a technology and to demand millions of dollars to wire the schools.

Technology Cannot Replace Human Teachers

Second, there was, and continues to be, a chorus of denouncement of technology itself, based on the position that technology has repeatedly failed in education because machines don't teach as well as human teachers do.

Books Are Better

Third, there was, and continues to be, a chorus clamoring to protect books as a better (than what?) medium for learning.

Ignore the Internet

Fourth, the Internet has, from its beginnings, been essentially ignored by many educators and schools—a fact that continues in a major way.

Reposition Present Education Techniques Online

Fifth, the old ways of education were repositioned online.

Control Internet Access to Protect Children

Sixth, the education establishment assumed control of Internet access on the basis that pedophiles lurk, pornography and gambling are out there, and kids will cheat.

Educators Must Choose What Students Use

Seventh, the education establishment took control of what Internet content students could use, assuming that kids cannot find the right materials, standards need to be met, curricula need to be followed, and children need grade-appropriate study materials

Education Must Retrieve Control of Open Content

Eighth, the education establishment strives to regain control of education materials that managed to become openly available online.

The Education Industry Creates Superior Content

Ninth, a tacit assumption is respected that materials created and produced for education—textbooks and the like—are superior to materials created outside of the education establishment and freely available as open content of the Internet.

Curriculum Standards Rule

Tenth, lockstep curricula and assessment continues to be based on testing and standards that ignore the connectivity among open content for learning.

Wire the Schools Not the Kids

Eleventh, K-12 students have been forced to use shared computers at school, in contrast to having personal computers of their own.

The following eleven Ideas are rejoinders to each of these responses. More important, the eleven Ideas show that much of what is being talked about in education circles is not relevant to the real world in which we now live.

14 ATTITUDE: WIRE THE SCHOOLS

The first response was to assume that the Internet was a technology and to demand millions of dollars to wire the schools. *Wired* was a very cool word in the beginning days of Internet emergence—undoubtedly reinforced in its coolness by the magazine of that name. *WIRED* magazine is still cool, primarily because it is about innovation and the future, and seldom about wires any more.

My favorite features in *WIRED* are the "Jargon Watch" and "Wired/Tired/Expired." Both savor the quick pace of our times by having fun with the latest jargon. In that spirit, we can say that, for education, wired is expired.

The crusade to "wire the schools" caught on in a big way a decade ago because it felt like the thing to do to move the kids into the future. About every decade in the twentieth century, a crusade came along to fix the schools. None of them has stemmed the decline of education effectiveness. The crusade to wire the schools gathered huge momentum and spent billions of dollars but did not markedly improve learning.

Wiring did not help education much because little of the wiring that was done ended up being used for learning. The relatively few classrooms that did get wired did not usually get mainstreamed into a school's academics and were prone to breakdown. A high percentage of schools that have been wired primarily use their computers to take attendance and keep records.

Wiring the schools also has failed because wiring to connect the Internet in the classroom setting has become essentially obsolete for learning—wireless works much better. At the college level, this reality has pushed campuses into the wireless age. What Internet availability there is in the K–12 setting remains mostly in the tired wired era.

15 ATTITUDE: TECHNOLOGY CANNOT REPLACE HUMAN TEACHERS

Second, there was, and continues to be, a chorus of denouncement of technology itself, based on the position that technology has repeatedly failed in education because machines don't teach as well as human teachers do. The assumed competition between a human teacher and the Internet, upon which this objection is based, is puzzling. If you will think back to your own favorite teacher—the one who taught you the most, or motivated you to learn, or simply believed in you—in what sense does that beloved teacher compete with your laptop? Would that teacher have been jealous of your textbook or the novel he assigned you as homework? Would he have not been pleased if you had learned something by independent research or from other teachers?

Probing the comparison a bit further, how would one of the not-so-good teachers in your memory compare to your laptop? Would even that teacher be threatened if you learned something online? The supposed threat of online learning to teachers makes no sense to me, at least when thinking about a school setting where human teachers are at work.

In the comparison between a human teacher and a nonhuman teacher, it is also true that there are times when a machine does a better job. When I was in high school, for example, my typing teacher was a human being in a classroom. The year was 1952, and the classroom where typing was taught looked a bit like a classroom today that is equipped with tables and computers. The difference was that instead of a computer, in front of each student was a large mechanical typewriter.

The typing teacher, a human woman, stood in front of the class and dictated drills, which were timed. There was a large chart at the front of the room that showed the placement of the letters on the keys of our typewriters. We were supposed to look only at the chart and not at our hands. The teacher dictated the drill, slowly in the early weeks and then faster as we became more proficient. As the drill text was read, we students banged away on the mechanical keys which lifted letter-bearing hammers that hit the inked ribbon and left impressions of letters on the paper behind the ribbon. When we reached the end of a line, a bell would ring inside our typewriter, and we would raise our right hand to push the lever that moved the roller with the paper to the right and up enough to begin a new line. At the end of the drill, we would roll the paper out of the typewriter by turning a knob on the side of the paper carriage. The teacher would once again dictate the words she had read before. We would mark our mistakes, calculate our accuracy in words per minute, sign our names to our papers, and turn them in for a grade.

A couple of years ago, I was in an elementary school in New Jersey during a typing class. Trust me, what the kids were doing there was an improvement over my typing instruction by a human teacher. Each student was sitting at a keyboard being tutored by a machine, a computer. The human teacher was working on a nontyping project with three of the children, while the other twenty or so students in the room were being taught to type by machines. To get an idea of how the kids were learning to type, doing a Google search for "learn to type free" will give you links to websites offering lessons that do not cost anything.

An important machine on the faculty of aviation academies is the flight simulator. I was in one once, watching a nephew of mine who was training to become a pilot. As I observed from behind him inside a large tin can on stilts, he sat at an exact replica of a pilot's position in a large aircraft. A landing scenario played, with visuals appearing in the mock windows of an actual airport at night, as he used the controls to simulate a landing. If he had done something severely wrong the program would have simulated a crash. Undoubtedly, the tin can would have shaken us fairly hard but no real harm would have been done, and he would have learned what not to do.

Wondering whether a human teacher is being replaced by a machine makes a little more sense if you are taking a course online and your human teacher is communicating with you by e-mail. The comparison is unavoidable between the distant tutor who seems to be mainly a name on the course e-mails and the favorite classroom teacher who once inspired and believed in you in person. At a distance, you cannot see her smile of approval and feel the encouragement in her voice—although broadband video may one day significantly personalize distance teaching.

The notion that a machine is a lesser teacher than a human because of the latter's personal human interaction turns out to be a two-way street. A typing tutor software program never tires of repeating the same exercise until the student gains competence—the same cannot always be said of human teachers.

Because a wonderful human teacher is one of the great experiences of learning, is there then no place for the Internet? Perhaps some are frightened by the prospect of a new world where *only* online teaching occurs? Certainly face-to-face, quality human discourse can be superior to relaying messages through a machine. But how much quality human discourse actually happens in today's world's classrooms? There should at least be a discussion as to whether very little learning in a live classroom or more learning at a distance is better—instead of no discussion because human teachers are wonderful when they are wonderful.

The logic disappears completely when the argument that humans are better teachers than machines is used to block the Internet from being used in schools. Are we to imagine thirty children sitting in rows learning from machines with no other humans present? Who has proposed that?

Not to be willing to consider using the Internet in education because teachers will be replaced by machines does not track with what is happening and could happen. When the Internet first loomed, no one really knew what it would become, and fear of replacing teachers with machines was part of the reaction of those who felt threatened. Now, we have a much better idea of what the Internet's role will be in learning. Dismissing it because it is a threat to teachers is an old and irrelevant thing to do. The role of the Internet has become the home of the virtual knowledge ecology into which all learners and teachers connect for knowledge.

Another complaint is heard from the education camp about the Internet and teachers. It goes something like this: Teachers should not have to be technology and multimedia experts. It is a fact of school life that the tech-savvy teachers with the digital bug are often the only ones who use the Internet in teaching. There are two misconceptions interacting here.

The first is that somehow, to use the Internet, a teacher must know how to install and maintain computers. In the business world, the computers are maintained by a tech staff, not the sales, executive, and clerical people. The education establishment is wasting money, not saving it, by failing to provide tech staff for computers. Expecting every teacher to be competent to keep a computer working is spreading training too thin and asking for poorly maintained computers.

Second, the same idea applies to the digital content teachers use to teach. For a teacher to be able to use exciting multimedia learning content, she should not have to build it. Multimedia content skills are getting more and more sophisticated and difficult to master. Yet, the complaint is heard that, for the most part, the teachers using multimedia are the ones who can build it. The underlying cause here is that schools tend to block off or ignore the rich and magnificent open content multimedia learning websites.

As will be clear from many of the discussions in this book on open content and the virtual knowledge ecology, the Internet does quite the opposite of requiring the teacher to be a technical or multimedia whiz. Instead, marvelous content is already available at no cost.

It is an odd, and at the least outdated, assumption that to use online content a teacher has to be able to fix a computer. It is equally strange to assume that to use virtual knowledge a teacher has to create it. Yet these sorts of discussions go on and on in education circles. The open content that forms the virtual knowledge ecology offers ready-to-use resources created by the finest technology, expert creative talents, and top knowledge authorities. What the teacher needs to know is how to get online and Google the subject she wants to teach.

A teacher should not be expected to build, for example, an Auschwitz multimedia presentation. It is doubtful a highly skilled teacher could come close to the excellence of the free open content tutorial built by PBS. That tutorial, "Auschwitz: Inside the Nazi State," is a thorough, expertly documented Flash study of the awful history of the tragic place. There are many more examples of outstanding open content in Ideas 52 and 53.

16 ATTITUDE: BOOKS ARE BETTER

Third, there was, and continues to be, a chorus clamoring to protect books as a better (than what?) medium for learning. A thirteen-year-old neighbor of mine who attends one of the better New York City public middle schools threw back her head and laughed when I mentioned textbooks. "Mine are always marked up, and pages are missing," she said with disgust. I had dropped by her family's apartment to work out details with her to look after my cats that weekend. When I got there, she was working at her computer. Clearly, she is not among those for whom books are the only place to be informed.

Once again, the discussion is mired in cloudy, complicated crosscurrents. Uncorrected Internet innuendo by Internet phobes and picked up by bibliophiles had a major impact. The cyber uninitiated very often name their preference for books as a reason they are not enthusiastic about an Internet role in education. Before returning to the textbook farce, let's look at how other kinds of books are faring in the Internet era.

To do that, we must not judge a book by its cover. The book's content is what determines the combination of Internet categories it falls into: archived on the Internet, simulated fully on the Internet, competes online with its counterpart in print, seldom read by humans except in print. A growing number of books are created on the Internet and might never be printed.

Already, a high percentage of all the books ever written are archived in cyberspace and virtually all will be there soon. With few exceptions, what is considered literature is openly online. Over the decade-plus that the Internet has been maturing, excellent websites for most notable authors have emerged as the work of experts on their lives and writing, like the rich cognitive concoction from the University of Virginia on Sam Clemens, *Mark Twain in His Times*.

This Clemens collection includes an e-text of *The Adventures of Huckleberry Finn*, complete with full text and original illustrations, yet it seems unlikely that a person who decided to read these adventures would do so sitting in front of a computer monitor. He is much more likely to read them in printed book format. Amazon.com is advertising a Penguin Classics version of Huck's adventures for $6.30 and used copies starting at $1.99 as I write these pages. The book is available to borrow at no cost from libraries. An enjoyable way to read Twain's delightful story is curled up with a book in an easy chair on a rainy afternoon, and that is what many people are still doing.

For several years, there has been an e-book movement striving to per-
suade the reading public to download book texts into handheld devices
and read books from the devices' screens. This effort has met with some
success and may be reaching a tipping point, where the idea will cascade
into popularity. The biggest market for e-books for a while was for "dirty
books," which could be downloaded anonymously, read off a handheld
screen instead of from a book with a printed cover, and deleted after
being read. Readers with less motivation have adjusted more slowly to
making downloaded e-books the standard reading format. Meanwhile,
the e-book device industry continues to work on making their products
more legible and responsive to human eyes, hands, and postures.

A niche trend in Japan to read downloaded books on tiny cell phone
screens belies the long-held belief that e-books required perfect ergo-
nomics to become popular. In the spring of 2005, the New York Public
Library announced a new eBooks and eAudio service. The cell phone
readers in Japan and the New York Public Library service may be signs
that the tipping point is near for reading downloaded books.

There are other uses for e-text versions of those books that are usually
read cover to cover in print. For example, if you were a student of literature and wanted to know how and where the writer Clemens used certain words and phrases, odds are you would use the searchable online
text of *The Adventures of Huckleberry Finn* and be grateful for the research advantages of digital text. If you were a teacher or speaker who
wanted to quote some of Huck Finn's colorful language, to find his
words, you would be more likely to use the online version of the text,
where the quotations could be found by text-search, than use a printed
copy of the book that you might have at home or could borrow from a
library.

The complete texts of the books and other writings of individual authors found online can be far better than a printed version simply by
being available and collected in one place. The website Tertullian.org,
for example, is a comprehensive collection of the writings of a lawyer
who converted to Christianity before 200 A.D. and wrote extensively on
the faith. In the past, it was unlikely that after nearly 2,000 years, all of
Tertullian's writings would be immediately accessible in one place, as
they now are at this website.

Quite a few books have been absorbed into cyberspace, virtually replacing their once indispensable print versions. During the years I worked in offices, I always had a dictionary, an *Information Please Almanac*, and an air travel guide on my desk. When I worked in politics, my desk books included a current copy of the *United States Congressional Directory*. In the latest years of my office life, I added a book of zip code listings. All of the books that I habitually referred to on my desk have now been absorbed by the Internet and simulated virtually as vastly more useful interactive references. What was once contained in the printed static references is now open content that is continually updated.

Other sorts of books absorbed into the Internet were born of the Internet, had a brief life in print, and then sank back into cyberspace. When notice first began to be taken that the net could be surfed, dozens and dozens of books appeared listing websites, giving them brief reviews and ranking them. These books gave the early Internet a big push. There were books on links for learning, links for kids, links for travel, and many other subjects. Individuals ventured for the first time onto the Internet, with one of those books in hand, typed in the address of one and then another of the websites reviewed in the book to surf the net. *Metalists* soon came along, listing clickable links for all kinds of subjects, and these were easier to use than the books. Search engines became more effective than the metalists had been. Both the metalists and search engines could stay up-to-date, while a printed book quickly became outdated by the fast-changing Internet. The book genre passed into oblivion.

Printed software manuals followed a similar trajectory, though their history goes back much further. Before the Internet emerged, the printed manual that came in the box with a software program's disks was crucial. Other than hiring an instructor or taking a class, a manual was the only way to learn how to use the software. An author specialty developed for writing the step-by-step procedures for using the features of a software program like Lotus or WordPerfect. Once the software was in use, a printed manual was the primary reference for the user. When the pool of software users became large enough to create a potential market of book buyers, competitive printed manuals appeared for popular software.

In 1991, I was learning desktop publishing by creating a forty-page education project book using Ventura software, which I was teaching myself by doing the project. I recall going to the McGraw-Hill bookstore in the lower level of the company's corporate tower on Sixth Avenue in New York to get a Ventura manual. There were three long shelves filled with manuals on how to use Ventura, which a salesman at the store told me was the most popular software subject at that time for manuals. The store had several sections filled with operational manuals for different software programs.

Quark appeared on my radar a couple of years later, when it was recommended to me by publisher friends for its cool new features. Quark quickly dominated the desktop publishing software field where Ventura had been king. Before long, I found myself learning Quark from the manual that came with the program disks and spending more time in the McGraw-Hill bookstore looking for Quark instruction books. As hard as it was to learn to trash books, software manuals were the first type of book I made the habit of throwing away. Once the new version of software is acquired, older version manuals are obsolete.

Today, core manuals for using software are no longer comprehensive and are nearly obsolete. Software programs can be purchased online and downloaded with no printed materials involved in the transaction. If you order the program CD, it will come in the mail with a brief printed manual or no manual at all. There are also both software company printed instruction books and competitive books from outside experts. The core instruction book from the software manufacturer, however, has morphed into an online help website with extensive, definitive, and continually updated explanations of every feature. For a large program like Quark, a comprehensive printed manual with the same information as the help website provides would be enormous and instantly out-of-date as it came off the press. Such a manual would be frustrating to use, because you would have to flip pages instead of clicking among interactive pages as a learner can do in online help pages.

One of the earliest and grandest technologies of the Industrial Age is printing. The printed novel you hold in your hand as you read is the work of five centuries of development. Its weight, shape, page color, text color, font design, and line spacing are mature arts. Combined, they place in your hands a close to ideal tool for visual consumption and bodily comfort as you read. It is superior in perhaps a couple of dozen ways—maybe more—to what you read on computer interfaces. You will get more comprehension and pleasure out of reading *The Adventures of Huckleberry Finn* in a printed book than you will reading the story from a computer. That fact is not a reason for being convinced that the Internet is bad for education. Nonetheless, the "I prefer books" attitude has held back progress in providing students with myriad advantages of using the Internet for learning.

A brand new book publishing method is budding and blossoming a bit within cyberspace: books published on the Internet that might never be published print. They, of course, are positioned to quickly morph into a printed avatar. If they are open content, anyone connected to the Internet can reproduce them on a printer connected to a computer.

There can be no reasonable sweeping argument as to whether books are better than computers because "better" depends on the content of a book and how a person is using that content. There is no logic in taking a stand that books are better because "I prefer books." Yes, my desk copy of *Information Please Almanac* was helpful, and I got very good at using it. But spending one minute at its avatar on the Internet infoplease.com should convince anyone that the Internet version is much better.

What then of school textbooks? More than $4 billion a year is spent in the United States alone every year on school textbooks. Why have textbooks not morphed as dictionaries, almanacs, and many other types of books have? Kids certainly do not sit down and read textbooks like someone would read *The Adventures of Huckleberry Finn*.

Obviously, the much-discussed Digital Divide seemed in the past to justify providing textbooks in schools where the students did not have Internet access. Is that the only justification? Once all students have access to the Internet—which is happening fast—will there be any reason not to put all the textbooks online?

Providing an online version of a textbook is incredibly inexpensive, compared to printing and delivering hard copies for the kids to use and share and wear out. It is technically very easy for one online fifth-grade textbook to be shared by every fifth grader in the world, and the virtual text that is shared will not suffer the wear and tear my middle school friend is so cynical about. Online textbooks can be updated in hours, not years. How many years will it be before every printed textbook that

American students are issued describes New Orleans as the site of a catastrophic human disaster instead of "The Big Easy"?

Pedagogical concerns are not a problem raised by the relocation of textbook material to the Internet, but are in fact much better solved online than in print. If there are four different theories for teaching fractions, there can be four different chapters to choose from in an online text. For every subject covered, an online textbook can have links to easier and more complex related topics, so the slower student does not get lost and the quicker student does not get bored.

There are a lot of other twenty-first-century textbook issues, not the least of which is their weight in backpacks, which is a genuine physical problem for many children. This is not the place to delve into these issues. We just note here that the wholesale, ongoing, very expensive school textbook habit needs to be extricated from the thoroughly confused discussion of whether books in general are preferable to the Internet for education.

Perhaps in the future there will be a recycle machine where you can feed a book you have read into one end and a new one selected from the Internet will come out of the other end. The machine would shred the old book, recycle the pulp into a paper roll, crank the roll through a printing process for the new book, cut, bind, and trim the new pages, then drop the book out of the machine into a tray. Trees would be saved and people could curl up with books for a good read in overstuffed chairs. The marvels of access and the interactive use of books online would be unaffected.

17 ATTITUDE: IGNORE THE INTERNET

Fourth, the Internet has from its beginning been essentially ignored by many educators and schools—a fact that continues in a major way. The summer before my senior year in high school, I attended the Northwestern University High School Speech Institute, which has been preparing kids for forensic speaking competition since 1931. The students who attend, known as "cherubs," are from the national cream of the competitive crop in debate and extemporaneous speech. The faculty are college debate coaches and speech professors and instructors.

The high school summer speech institutes held by several universities, including Northwestern, have very often been a pivotal factor in the learning experience of high school competitors who go on to win state and national tournaments. The virtual knowledge ecology is not competitive with learning experiences like the institutes. Discourse and the practice of competitive articulation are real-time, living experiences that are absolutely necessary for an individual to become educated. Nonetheless, a laptop with access to quotations and facts to be found within the virtual knowledge ecology is replacing the boxes of three-by-five index cards lugged around by debaters over the decades before the Internet emerged.

Debate was a major interest for me in high school. I did reasonably well, winning some tournaments with one or another partner. I was successful enough as a debater to get accepted as a cherub, though it helped that both my parents and my high school speech teacher were Northwestern alumni and that I added to the cherubs' geographical balance by being from the remote cowboy country of West Texas. The farthest I got in debate competition, though, was winning the West Texas regionals and then losing in an early round at the state championship. I had better luck as a coach several years later, when my boys' team won the state championship and the girls won regionals. In those days of *Ozzie and Harriett*, boys and girls competed separately.

The part I liked best about being a cherub—and I feel sure was the basis of my success as a coach—was my fascination with logic and argument. I remain convinced that teaching a teenager the basics of logic and turning him or her loose in a timed competition connects some important thinking circuits in young heads with great effectiveness. To my embarrassment, the summer I was at Northwestern, I won the Discussion Award and no rounds in debate. Discussion was consensus for which my debater's spirit had a lot of adolescent contempt. Nevertheless, I accepted the award and still have it on my shelf. It is a book by Northwestern professors James H. McBurney and Ernest J. Wrage titled *The Art of Good Speech*. Its pages are as instructive as ever. The speech art has changed little since Confucius, Aristotle, and others described rhetoric in ancient times.

I remember a couple of specific pieces of knowledge that I learned the summer I was at Northwestern. They are from the class on argu-

ATTITUDE   **5 7**

mentation. It was taught by a college debate coach named Max Cripe, whom I thought was the most adorable man I had ever seen. He had a teaching style that was on the flamboyant side, and fun to watch. In my award book, autographed to me by the five members of the summer faculty, he wrote, "Judy—It's been great—good luck, kid—Max Cripe." I remember my glow at reading those words from his pen.

Something I learned from Mr. Cripe—no first names for teachers in the fifties!—was what the strongest of all arguments is. It is an argument that is very much in play in the response of the education establishment to the Internet. It puts your adversary on the defensive and gives him a lot to do. It is the best of all excuses to ignore something. Mr. Cripe said, after a build up that got us cherubs very eager to know the deepest and strongest secret of argumentation, "The strongest of all arguments is 'So what?'"

So, what will happen if the Internet continues to be a nonfactor in most K–12 classes? If we seem to ignore the Internet, it is because there are more important things to worry about. Those sorts of shrugs are an effective way to bounce education talk away from the Internet and into laments of the problems in families, a reluctant admission of beliefs that there are kids who can't learn anyway, the need for more teacher pay and better conditions, and the decay of school buildings and other infrastructure.

In light of all those things, the Internet? So what? The strongest argument—the one Max Cripe taught me—has been used to avoid the Internet to extreme effectiveness by the education establishment.

18 ATTITUDE: REPOSITION PRESENT EDUCATION TECHNIQUES ONLINE

Fifth, the old ways of education were repositioned online. It always happens. When a new medium comes along, the first thing people do is attempt to reposition concepts and materials from the older medium into the new one.

A century after cars joined buggies in the streets, we still verbally measure automobile motor power as the number of horses it would take to pull the same load. For several years after animation was invented, the drawings that inhabited the fast-moving frames were essentially re-positioned from comic strips printed in newspapers. Walt Disney led the harnessing of the new animated medium's power of movement to create the enduring personalities of Mickey Mouse, Dopey, and Bambi. A lot of the material broadcast on early television was repositioned from movies and radio. Way back when the printing press came online, the first books were typeset from writing that for centuries had been copied by hand on to scrolls one at a time. It took a while to innovate newspapers, which capitalized on the new mass distribution power of the press.

In the mid-1990s, when the Internet began to emerge in a big way, the wire-the-schools response from education was accompanied by a repositioning of myriad lesson plans online. The response for placing content into the Internet from the education establishment was overwhelming to place process there instead. This is particularly odd because, earlier in the digital era, there had been some visionary innovation. Apple's Hypercard software was a tool for interactivity and hyper-connectivity, and there were teachers who saw and used these cognitive powers in the new digital medium before the Internet emerged. Macromedia's Authorware has been available for e-learning for years, but it has drifted into corporate network training delivery, more than into the venue of teaching school students.

The K–12 education industry did not follow the usual pattern of response to a new medium: reposition and then innovate. The repositioning of the knowledge content that education is supposed to convey was not done, at least not by educators. Repositioning the process of teaching, primarily lesson plans, was undertaken to some extent. But, for the most part, adoption of the new medium by the K–12 education establishment sputtered a bit and fizzled out.

As described in Ideas 27 and 53, higher education did reposition knowledge into the Internet, but not in a primary way. Individual instructors and some departments have made contributions of great value. The open courseware movement promises a major contribution from institutions of higher learning in the future—and that flow, pioneered at MIT, is gaining momentum.

While the education establishment fiddled and fizzled, something else happened. Totally unexpected is the fact that the positioning of academic knowledge resources is no longer under the control or influence of educators in general or local educators in particular. The ground has shifted so that those with power over education no longer have power over positioning knowledge. The Internet has usurped that role, and the creators of open content who are making and positioning primary knowledge are located outside of the education establishment. While the education powers-that-be have discussed what to do about the Internet, quite independently of the education policy makers, funders, and administrators, the virtual knowledge ecology is fast becoming the common global source for that knowledge. The new open content for learning is springing up from all sorts of sources, and its use is becoming global. Control is not institutional but is a function of the network itself.

The key change that has caused this to happen is the end of the limitation of geography. Rwanda has targeted 2017 as the year that all of its secondary schools will have wireless access. Mongolia has recently undertaken a program to ensure all its people are literate in English as a second language. The synergy of similar and related trends worldwide is erasing the geographical limitations of knowledge. Western countries, including the United States, are trending toward becoming latecomers to the virtual knowledge ecology because of establishment inertia.

Section 4 of this book describes the network mechanisms that vet open content knowledge websites and elevate the best ones to prominence. These mechanisms will drive the learning traffic from every part of the world to the few best websites for every kernel of knowledge students are seeking to learn. Those websites will be interlinked by the meaning of their subjects, again through natural networking mechanisms. From these networking mechanisms, the virtual knowledge ecology is already emerging and being used by learners in many countries.

Think what that could have meant if a subject network for tsunamis had emerged in the virtual knowledge ecology and had been linked into by students in virtually every country. It is impossible to imagine that, by 2017, high school students in Rwanda and Mongolia will be studying tsunamis from the sort of sophomore-level textbooks, printed in their regional languages, they use today. They will be studying their meteorology wirelessly in the virtual knowledge ecology's tsunami interlinked web pages. In this process, news of an impending tsunami would show up in that ecology very quickly because actual tsunami detection operations would be linked into the pages the students were visiting.

A threatening tsunami would probably not be on the top of the interest list for students in landlocked Rwanda and Mongolia, but the kids in Sri Lanka and Indonesia would study from the same tsunami web pages as their inland contemporaries and would spread the alarm quickly in their countries. The same web pages would be studied by students in Paris as well, where any young person knowing a vacationer in Thailand would quickly turn into a tsunami warning system herself, armed with a cell phone to reach friends in danger on the threatened beaches.

The main difference between the old medium of geographically based knowledge distribution and the new medium of the Internet is that, except for the knowledge in teachers' heads, knowledge will fully reposition itself within the virtual knowledge ecology and will only significantly be replicated across geography. Everyone will study from the same single virtual source. We have already reached the point where a student does not check a textbook or go to his school or local library to look something up. Instead, he goes online because what he is likely to find at a geographical location like a book or library is quickly becoming out of date.

Knowledge is repositioning itself, interlinking within a virtual network, where it organizes itself, and the best version of it emerges as the virtual knowledge ecology for common global use. It is impossible to reposition traditional, static sources of educational materials onto the Internet.

19 ATTITUDE: CONTROL INTERNET ACCESS TO PROTECT CHILDREN

Sixth, the education establishment assumed control of Internet access on the basis that pedophiles lurk, pornography and gambling are out there, and kids will cheat.

One Saturday in January 2005, I was a judge in the New York City public schools' citywide We the People competition, in which a panel of students respond to questions about the U.S. Constitution. When I came into the high school building in midtown Manhattan, one block from Lincoln Center, where the competition was held, I showed my driver's license to the policemen sitting behind the check-in desk inside the school's main entrance. While one of the officers wrote down my name and license number, the other one gave directions to a visiting teacher who was accompanying her students to the competition. He directed her to take her class to a different entrance because the kids had to be scanned by a metal detector before they could come into the school building.

Two months earlier, I had attended my fiftieth high school reunion in El Paso, Texas. On the Saturday morning of the reunion weekend, we were given a tour of our alma mater, Austin High School. In the main entrance hall, where there was no sign of a metal detector, we were proudly shown a glass-encased stuffed panther—Austin's mascot animal—and then taken on a tour of the new library and cafeteria. No one pointed out the depressions along the halls between the classroom doors. The lockers where we had kept our books had been inset into those depressions when we attended Austin. The lockers are gone now, because kids are not trusted any more to have their own private storage container. After the tour, we had a pep rally, with some actual cheers led by three classmates who had been cheerleaders in our day and who made us promise not to expect them to go down on their knees when they led the old yells. The curtain we had opened and closed for plays on the stage in the gym was replaced with a wall closing the stage, I suppose because students today are not trusted in the concealment of backstage.

There is a confused notion that I think contributes to not trusting kids today. Somehow, there is a sense that earlier generations were better behaved. In 1951, three years before I graduated from Austin High School, a toilet in the boys bathroom, about forty feet from my locker location at the time, was blown up one afternoon with a stick of dynamite. There was a study hall for detention, which was well populated throughout my high school years, and demerits were frequently distributed by the assistant principal. Cheating went on in classes, including by kids who copied other kids' homework.

What was different was the expectation directed at the students. You were expected not to do bad things and were punished if you got caught. I was not alone in my practice of never cheating. There were a lot of us who did not, and there was peer pressure to feel uncool about being prudish. But my worst thought about cheating was what my teachers and other students who trusted me would have thought if I had gotten caught. I was sure God would forgive me, and even my parents, but I would have felt terribly, terribly foolish if the entire school would have found out I cheated. No lockers and a walled-off stage are powerful symbols that students are "expected" to be thieves, addicts, and cheats. Nonetheless, I know many New York City public high school students who, distrusted or not, still do not cheat.

While we were waiting for the We the People rounds to get under way, I was chatting with another judge. She is a teacher in a private school, and we were discussing how her nine-year-old son looked around for things on the Internet. I mentioned that students in the New York City public schools (the world's largest school system) are blocked from using many websites. I said that was a particular problem because, if they found a permitted website that caught their interest, they were often blocked from following links on that website that led to related materials. She challenged me, finding what I said hard to believe.

A group of high school students who had volunteered to serve as timekeepers were walking by our table. I called out and asked them if they could openly use the Internet at school. They looked as surprised as my new judge friend had when I told her they could not. They confirmed what I had said.

One of the major lessons the education establishment pounds into the heads of children the moment they enter the school setting is: We do not trust you. The motivation that I am sure was my strongest deterrent to doing bad things is essentially gone. Students have no good name to protect. We have been spinning downward into less and less trust for decades.

I have no idea how we can return to a world where police scanners disappear from school doorways and lockers reappear in the halls. Perhaps we never will. Schools themselves may be replaced by less institutional locales. The laptop will almost certainly eliminate the need for onsite book storage and the spine-numbing backpacks that have replaced lockers.

One of the murkier aspects of the way the education establishment assumes the responsibility for controlling what children can and cannot do on the Internet is whether the motive is to protect the children or because the children are not trusted. Cited as justification for blocking students from Internet knowledge connectivity are supposedly rampant pornography, lurking pedophiles, and academic cheating. Those are three separate problems.

Pornography is a very big Internet business. It is a quick click or two away if you are looking for it. If you are doing almost anything else on the Internet, you almost never encounter it. This raises questions. Does the existence of the pornography justify not letting children use the open Internet? If it does, at what age should they be allowed into cyberspace? The censor's role changes here: For little children, protection is the purpose and, as the kids get older, it is a matter of trusting them to stay away from something.

A small child clicking through the Internet is highly unlikely to stumble on a pornographic web page. Letting someone in kindergarten click freely in the Seattle Zoo's multimedia section will give him all sorts of new things to think about, but not human sexuality. A lot of people vow that no child for whom they are responsible will ever be turned loose clicking a mouse on the Internet. With respect to young children, there are two reasons these people should reconsider. First, without supervision, young children are highly unlikely to get going at all within the Internet and, if they do, they will soon get bored. Second, if they did get lost, it would be unlikely to lead into pornographic web pages.

At whatever age it happens, the interest in sex a kid feels awakening within changes the parameters for what they should be doing on the Internet. My Victorian grandparents managed to keep my mother from knowing how babies were conceived until she joined a sorority after she had left home to attend college. I found out when I was in the second grade, in 1943, at an afternoon secret meeting of my girlfriends. I have a memory of girls passing the word around at school during the day that a few of us were going to gather in a grassy area by the street leading away from the school yard. I had no idea what the meeting was about. It turned out that someone had found a "rubber," and the girls were going to look at it. I do not remember the discussion, but recall getting the idea of how sex worked. Today, I Googled "how babies are made" and the top link was from BabyCenter.com. The details of the intercourse were extensive with illustrations of anatomy, but the page was not pornography. The meeting I attended in 1943 was more porno-graphic because we were fascinated by the rubber.

Realistically, in clicking around the Internet without supervision, grade school and middle school children are likely to encounter inap-propriate web pages. Do we teach, and trust them just to move on? Or, do we block them from exploring? Doing the latter holds them back from using the cognitive connectivity of the virtual knowledge ecol-ogy—and is becoming a more and more serious trade off. The type of kid who blew up the toilet at Austin High School is going to find the bad stuff on the Internet under any circumstances.

An early and justified fear for small children using the Internet is pe-dophiles. A great deal of progress has been made by law enforcement in stopping them from finding kids online, but the danger remains. A child's picture with name and identification should never be openly posted on the Internet.

A common way children get into trouble with odd people and situa-tions on the Internet is in chat rooms. There is no such hazard in the exploration of academic knowledge online. Kids must be trusted or su-pervised concerning wandering into chat rooms. At some point as they mature, they should be encouraged to explore knowledge on their own and freely.

We are midway through a transitional period from when children had no access to the Internet because it did not even exist to a day in which they will all have such access, no matter what we do about it. Cyber-space will become safer for children as open content better organizes itself into coherent networks, filtering for what you do want grows stronger, and the blocking of what you do not want more effective.

Yet, the day must not come when the power is given to anyone to censor the open Internet—and that means the pornography will re-main, pedophiles will roam until caught, and kids will be able to cheat. The restrictiveness of the education establishment will not succeed in protecting children, but it is succeeding in blocking them from the vir-tual knowledge ecology.

The third justification given for blocking students from openly explor-ing the Internet is that they will cheat either by wasting time playing games and the like or doing more overt cheating, such as buying canned written work to call their own. It is here that the control and trust factors become most painful.

The eight teams I helped to judge in the We the People competition had steeped themselves in knowledge of the U.S. Constitution without being trusted to use Internet freely at school. The timekeepers I asked about Internet blocking were volunteers who had given up their Saturday to help out with the competition. All of these students passed through a metal detector to reach the competition rooms. I was embarrassed to watch the kids reply to my question by saying they were not trusted—and do not think for a moment they do not feel demeaned by it. In my view, teaching them how to avoid harm as we are trusting them is the better way both to protect our children from harm and to give them the respect they deserve.

20 ATTITUDE: EDUCATORS MUST CHOOSE WHAT STUDENTS USE

Seventh, the education establishment took control of what Internet content students could use, assuming that kids cannot find the right materials, standards need to be met, curricula need to be followed, and children need grade-appropriate study materials.

For many decades—centuries, really—kids have been sent to school on the assumption that they would find and learn knowledge there. What happens when the freshest and most complete knowledge is not at school, but accessible on the Internet? The natural and immediate answer to that question from the educational establishment was that educators would decide what Internet materials the kids should use. Curriculum experts were made the judges of Internet content. Teachers were expected to learn how to find Internet content to direct to their students.

An early method for doing these new tasks reached a massive scale: creating online lesson plans into which specific web pages were inserted. This is, of course, a repositioning of pre-Internet classroom methodology into a new medium. It is a workable method and continues. The downside is that lesson plans with preselected Internet links do not take advantage of the new medium's connectivity outward from the selected links.

A good deal of confusion has gone on about how students might find the best—or at least acceptable—links to a subject on their own. A related puzzlement has been how students should cite the sources of the links that they use. Although this book is not the place to explore this, an interesting comparison could be made as to whether finding the right resources is easier for a student in the hardcopy world or online.

Clearly, it was far easier in the hardcopy world of my school years because there were so few places to look: classroom materials, an encyclopedia, nearby library, and that pretty much exhausted the choices for a K–12 student to do research. It was easier for a teacher to verify a student's research in those days.

We need to beware of the temptation to avoid Internet research because there are many places to look. Google and other search engines have greatly improved searching. As the virtual knowledge ecology matures, finding information through links of meaning will get easier and more elegant, as described in Idea 79.

As academic knowledge began to flow into the Internet in the middle 1990s, it also began to interlink by its meaning. The processes of interlinking are described in Section 4. One of the key parts of the interlinking picture was the way experts on a particular subject began to list their favorite links to material by other experts in their field. An expert's homepage became a node in a network about his subject, with links out to other nodes, which usually linked out farther and back and forth among themselves.

Hittite Homepage.com was an early favorite of mine. The experts on this web project used to have a comment introducing the website that said it represented the first time in four thousand years that everything about the Hittites could be found in one place. Hittite scholars have reorganized their interlinked online resources over the years. You can see how they are now arranged by doing a search for "Hittite."

Enormous amounts of effort and money have been spent attempting to shoehorn flexible Internet subject network assets into rigid curricula and standards to satisfy the establishment attitude that educators should tell students what to learn from what resource. The Internet is an ecology teeming with static and dynamic connections among nuggets of knowledge. Curricula and standards attempt to provide static lines of study and assessment. Attempts to coordinate the virtual knowledge ecology and the rigors of pedagogy have been discouraging to those who have tried.

Grade-appropriate material is even harder to bring into focus. Things children need to learn are not set loose into the Internet by grade level. There are static websites with age-targeted materials, but open content is seldom designed, for example, for the fifth grade or sophomores.

Rather than looking at learning materials as grade appropriate, it is possible to view academic subjects as beginning with simple ideas and building toward more complex ones. Learning cell biology, for example, includes a sequence from cell, to nucleus, to mitosis, to genes, to DNA. This sort of relationship is a natural one for the Internet to interface. Because the different steps in complexity relate to each other in a network interface, they will naturally link among themselves. A network with interlinking of that sort is a pedagogical marvel. Students who are ahead can keep moving without getting bored. Students who are not up to speed can linger wherever they need to until they are ready to move on or catch up. Everybody can check out what leads to what.

It seems futile and very confusing for educators to assume selective control over the Internet content students use. The teacher is a guide, to be sure. But the control over how something like the structure of a cell is organized is ultimately up to the cell.

21 ATTITUDE: EDUCATION MUST RETRIEVE CONTROL OF OPEN CONTENT

Eighth, the education establishment strives to regain control of education materials that managed to become openly available online.

Soon after the 2004 tsunami wreaked tragedy across the coasts of the Indian Ocean, a classroom resources company announced the availability on its website of Internet resources on the tsunami. Probably several resource companies whose customers are schools offered competing packages. No one could use the packages without purchasing a subscription to the companies' services.

The company I looked at boasted a map of the devastation, links to profiles of twelve affected countries, selected articles, and "more." Perhaps the map and the profiles offered were closed content, created or purchased and firewalled by the company. The articles were almost certainly owned or leased by the company and only available through paid subscription. It is likely, but not certain, that some of the material was linked to open content that could be found by searching the Internet. It is almost certain that many of the closed materials in the packages linked out to open content.

Other paid services for sale by the company offering the tsunami links include matching of links on the Internet to the curricula standards of the states. There are a lot of states and a lot of standards. This is very big business. It is the sale of selective control to open content used in classrooms by company education specialists. Internet management activities of this sort may be well intentioned, motivated by profit, a reflection of the laziness of teachers, or simply the habit of mind that educators control knowledge and serve it in pieces to students. What the reasons are really do not matter. The methods have never worked very well and will soon be washed away by the virtual knowledge ecology.

Already, a subject like the tsunami can be much better understood and much more can be learned about it by exploring it in the freshness and interconnectivity of open content. You will know why this is so—far more directly than I can describe here—if you will take a few minutes to look at the links a search engine gives you when you enter the word *tsunami*.

The top link in Google, which appeared when I searched for *tsunami* in March 2005, was open content from the Department of Earth and Space Sciences at the University of Washington. An introductory note on the web page explained that, because of intense interest in tsunamis, they recommend a group of "offsite" websites they had listed on the page for their visitors to use while they are were in the process of reorganizing their own popular tsunami website. For good measure, an illustration was placed to the right of the link list depicting the difference between regular waves that are seen on the shoreline and the more dangerous tsunamis.

The links suggested on the page had been selected by a university department specializing in the subject covered, not by an education company staff. The five listed websites were jammed with superior explanations, illustrations, and data. The links' sources were U.S. government specialists at USGS and NOAA, the Pacific Tsunami Museum, the tsunami research group at the University of Southern California, and at Carleton College. The last link, from Carleton College, contained a group of animations for recent, historical, and hypothetical tsunamis. The five links listed on the page comprised a comprehensive resource for the subject. All of the resources suggested by the University of Washington were free and open and updated constantly by top scientists in the field.

One map, country descriptions, and articles pale in comparison and suffer from relying on less expert layers of management. Someone at the for-profit company has to be paid to monitor the list to be sure it does not grow stale. In a quickly moving topic like tsunamis, that is no easy task. In contrast, ongoing updating is a dynamic natural function in open Internet content. The fact that the link discussed here appeared as number one on the Google search means it was linked to by most other comparable websites—its gatekeeper is the collective users of the Internet.

The tsunami content for sale by education companies is content under the control of the education establishment in two ways. The purchasing school is getting content strictly passed through an education gatekeeper. Someone has looked at the tsunami map and approved it. Second, a lot of online content that is paid for by schools is owned and controlled by the company that charges for it. A company like Encyclopaedia Britannica creates its content and charges for its use. ProQuest, a major supplier of paid content to schools, owns thousands of periodicals that it has converted into digital files and for which it sells subscriptions to school libraries and other outlets where students can use them.

Intuitively, it is tempting to think that controlled resources offered by education specialists are superior to what is freely open online. That has never been true, and the contrast is deepening and widening. The open content superiority is caused by the network structure, which allows top experts in academic fields to keep open content up-to-date, rich, compelling—and connected to related top-flight materials. The tsunami experts, not the education experts, are offering the finest online learning content.

Another reason closed content degrades is that it cannot be linked to from outside the password or firewall that seals it off. As pointed out in several places in this book, the spontaneous grouping of related sites like the University of Washington scientists posted for tsunamis cannot include a link from closed content, such as a *Britannica* article or something in a periodical owned by ProQuest. Intuitively, that sounds like the closed content would be missed, downgrading the open content network of related links.

In practice, that is not what happens in the ever more massive and ever more dynamic Internet. A locked away article—say something written on Indian Ocean tsunamis in the summer of 2004 six months before the big waves hit land the following December—becomes essentially obsolete in 2005 and thereafter. Its owner, in its closed-content status, has to send in an editor to bring it up-to-date or the article's value deteriorates into quaint, historical, outmoded science.

22 ATTITUDE: THE EDUCATION INDUSTRY CREATES SUPERIOR CONTENT

Ninth, a tacit assumption is respected that materials created and produced for education—textbooks and the like—are superior to materials for learning created outside of the education establishment and freely available as open content on the Internet.

From the beginning of Internet emergence, the education establishment has viewed what students might learn from materials online as supplemental to their school learning. The assumption has been that the education industry creates materials that are produced and evaluated by educators and therefore superior to what is online.

The discussion in Idea 21 of tsunami learning materials describes the authority and freshness of Internet open content for the subject of tsunamis. It seems impossible that anything in textbooks or other for-school learning materials could compete in providing knowledge about tsunamis to a student who researches the subject on the Internet. As rich, expert, simple, and complex tsunami open content continues to be posted and updated online by the scientists at the universities of Washington and Southern California, at the USGS, and NOAA, along with tsunami experts around the world, it becomes odd at best to claim there is better tsunami material in textbooks. The very expensive textbook resource does not come close to competing with the free open-content resource. As the ideas in Section 3 describe, tsunamis are one sample from essentially all useful knowledge subjects now interfaced freely online.

Nevertheless, the products of education experts continue to flow into the schools. A multibillion dollar education materials industry is based on the assumption that things to be learned need to be recast by education experts into materials designed for learning—primarily textbooks. The process has two steps. First, educators formulate knowledge into learning materials, which, in the second step, are then distributed to states, districts, schools, and students in print and other old media. Obviously, the second step of distribution can be achieved by the Internet. The one real argument for distributing textbooks that remains is that not all students are able yet to use the Internet. That will change, hopefully soon.

But what about the education experts who author the materials? In Idea 23, the perceived need to prepare materials for education standards is discussed. In addition to the standards push, a lot of the recasting-by-education-experts argument has to do with grade-appropriate learning materials. The fifth-grade math book is written differently and contains simpler math than the eighth-grade math book. Authoring is a large specialty in the education industry, where expertise is plied to design age-appropriate learning materials. There is no reason age-appropriate materials cannot be placed online, and sometimes they are. But a deeper flaw in the grade-appropriate knowledge dole is now made plain by the Internet.

The network environment has a major advantage over age-appropriate learning materials distributed in books. Fifth graders using the fifth-grade math book are expected to learn its content and then wait until the next year to move on to new content in their sixth-grade textbook. For students who fail to learn parts of the content in the fifth grade, catching up the next year becomes a burden. Just as painfully, the student who easily masters all the fifth-grade content must wait a year—or two or three years—to connect to the mathematics that follow naturally in cognitive context. For the quick learners, continuity and context in learning are lost by waiting to learn what comes next until the sixth, seventh, or eighth grade. The slow learners lose continuity and context, too, because they are disconnected from knowledge they did not master in previous grades and become lost in the ideas that build on the missing base.

Network structure reveals the root of these difficulties. Chopping a subject into natural sequence really is not what is going on in the making of artificial grade steps for knowledge because, for most subjects, there is no inherent sequence. Most knowledge is more of a network than a sequence. In math, you are still using fourth-grade arithmetic as part of the trigonometry you learn in college. The date of the landing of Columbus in the Americas is just as relevant to fourth-grade history as it is to a graduate seminar on Spanish settlement. In the subjects called *advanced*, the network of ideas has become more complex than what is termed *elementary*, but all the nodes are there.

When different nodes of the network are scattered among grades, the relationships among the nodes—which are a significant aspect of their meaning—are not there. These obstacles are overcome in the virtual knowledge ecology, where the network of a knowledge subject can be explored with mouse clicks as a student connects ideas in her mind. She can connect Columbus to the Americas in the fourth grade, and in any grade explore the connections that enrich that first small pattern of her own discovery: history. Her own network of ideas grows more complex by linking more nodes into what she knows.

The education industry justifies its very expensive recasting of knowledge by arguing that education experts are required to present knowledge by grade level. Yet, grade level appropriateness is a contrived way of organizing learning material, in contrast to the internal network of meaning of the knowledge itself that is mirrored by embedding it into a digital network. Grade-level printed materials are not interconnected or interactive; they cut off links to simpler and more advanced ideas, thus limiting both slow and fast learners. The surprise of the network mirroring of knowledge in the open Internet is that it allows a learner to enter subject material at his or her own level and progress through knowledge both to review simpler concepts and move on to higher ideas.

Textbooks aimed at specific grade levels have no way of linking into earlier or more advanced knowledge for their topic, causing yet another demotion of learning. Textbook authors face a justifiable concern that not all children in specific grades will understand challenging material, so they have tended to include no more than the average common denominator. The result is that the content is dumbed down.

The network mechanism of the virtual knowledge ecology has no such concern. For example, the California Turtle and Tortoise website links to pages of its own, and it links beyond to provide a comprehensive network of turtle and tortoise knowledge for every level and branch of interest. This cognitive connectivity is beyond the scope of any older medium, least of all print.

Another confusion about who should be creating educational content can be cleared up considerably by focusing on the distinction between curriculum and content. A natural teacher or a trained educator will fit the definition of a pedagogue—a word whose root in Greek means *lead a child to knowledge*. Although the word *curriculum* has many meanings, it is helpful here to define it as a tool of leading and not as content—the content of a curriculum, then, is knowledge.

Textbooks are traditionally curricula with embedded content. Since the Internet came along as a competitive content location, and now a superior one, textbooks have become bigger, more elaborate, and more expensive by adding more and more illustrations, features, and elaborations of knowledge. This trend has allowed textbooks to hang on to their curriculum role, but it has not kept them up as the superior knowledge source. This expensive—and for children backbreaking—trend continues with no real end in sight. If the attitude that the education industry creates superior content was correct in the past, that has now changed. The virtual knowledge ecology is superior.

23 ATTITUDE: CURRICULUM STANDARDS RULE

Tenth, lockstep curricula and assessment continues to be based on testing and standards that ignore the connectivity among open content for learning.

Starting in the 1990s, when the Internet began to emerge, the assessment movement also emerged with parallel gusto. Specific areas of knowledge, listed by grades and subjects, have become the basis of tests that students must pass to move through the grades. The assessment rendered by the testing not only judges the kids, but the schools are judged by it as well.

The premise for the standards and testing is that it makes sure schools teach and children learn. This is not the place to look into whether either teaching or learning is enhanced by the testing. What concerns us here is that the virtual knowledge ecology is enhancing learning by integrating the way two camps of educators advocate teaching and learning be conducted. Static standards are increasingly at odds with the new dynamic venue of knowledge that has brought the two camps together.

A division of opinion among educators simmered, and sometimes boiled, in the last decades of the twentieth century. One side held that all children should acquire a certain and common pool of knowledge. The other side argued for exploratory and discovery learning. Without anyone planning it or anyone expecting it, the Internet has now given us a marvelous synthesis of the two in the virtual knowledge ecology.

Meanwhile, the two emergent education trends—the migration of knowledge onto the Internet and the standards assessment in schools— have meshed only to a very small degree by the insertion of some Internet links into standards-teaching curricula here and there. The measure of what gets inserted is whether it relates to a subject standard on a test the students will take in a particular grade.

In Illinois, late elementary school students prepare for their science tests by learning how to answer this standard question: 12.A.2b Categorize features as either inherited or learned (e.g., flower color or eye color is inherited; language is learned). Not until late high school in Illinois do students prepare to respond to this standard test question: 12.A.5b Analyze the transmission of genetic traits, diseases, and defects.

GlaxoSmithKline (GSK) has a website with richly interlinked resources designed to help interested visitors in "Understanding Genetics." Included is a "Just For Kids" section. Even early elementary school students could start learning something about genetics in these pages, and there is more to be learned about genetics in the GSK website than most students learn in high school and probably college as well.

Embedding a page from the GSK website into a curriculum to fit a single standard does introduce students to the website. But the motive is absent to learn more than just the question the standard asks. Interestingly, the GSK website offers a "Test Your Knowledge" page that in effect tests broadly what could be learned from working with the knowledge presented by the website. That is a different matter than using their extensive network of genetic knowledge to answer one specific question. Once again, the GSK materials offer an elementary student connections to move ahead if she is curious and a high school student to go back and get what she did not understand when she was younger.

Embedding links into curricula fails to taking advantage of the virtual knowledge ecology because students have no incentive to follow their curiosity into a knowledge-rich network like the GSK website. The urgency of looming standards tests keeps the focus on classroom drill, as teachers and students narrow their focus to bits instead of making connections.

Would students be learning significantly more if they were using the time now spent learning how to answer questions on standards tests, instead interacting with the virtual knowledge ecology? I think so.

24 ATTITUDE: WIRE THE SCHOOLS, NOT THE KIDS

Eleventh, K–12 students have been forced to share computers at school, in contrast to having personal computers of their own. It is completely understandable that, in 1996, when the Wire the Schools crusade began to take off in earnest, there was no real expectation of school kids being issued individual computers as they had been issued textbooks for over a century. Schools were pictured as having an Internet wire coming in, like the electrical cables did. Internet access would be distributed through the school in a like manner to electricity. The focus was on wiring and donating the computers of that day (or those businesses were replacing) to the schools. Focus was not on wires to connect individual students to computers. In fact, a single computer in every classroom was then a lofty goal.

In those days, the Internet generally came in over telephone wires and a computer's Internet modem could be plugged into the jack and, if things went well, the Internet appeared on the computer's monitor screen. Gradually, classrooms began to have a single computer with Internet access, or a few. The term *computer lab* came to mean rows of tables with a computer attached to the table in front of each chair. I visited a grade school in 1999 that had a computer lab in which there was a computer for each seat, with its monitor recessed under a flat glass tabletop so that the computers did not block the teacher's view of the students. But the individual computers in labs were not used by only one student. Classes rotated during the day and week through the computer lab, with a different child using the computer in each class session.

If the education establishment had heartily embraced computers—as the law and business establishments did—things would have been done differently. In law firms, businesses, and many other fields, the desktop computer was a personal computer. If it was shared, individuals had personal sectors protected by their own passwords. A person's computer quickly became his tool for many tasks. He used it to do his job, as his filing cabinet, for e-mail, and, before long, it became an extension of its owner's memory.

Not so for students when they are at school. For the tasks their parents do on a computer at work, kids at school remain, even today, primarily in the pencil and paper world and continue to carry their extended memory scribbled in notebooks and their files on their backs. Perhaps this is part of the reason they have taken to sending text messages on their cell phones.

It seems odd that the kids got such short shrift. There was endless talk about the millions of dollars needed to wire the schools, and then billions were raised and spent. But no crusade developed to supply students with personal computers. The habit continues of businesses and corporations donating their old computers to schools when they upgrade their employees' machines. Hand-me-down technology is a handicap to taking advantage of the virtual knowledge ecology.

As early as the mid-1990s, laptops worked well. In the mid-1990s, to receive the Internet, laptops had to be plugged into a jack, which would have been needed at each student's desk to accommodate them. That cost would have amounted to equipping each desk with a telephone jack, following a procedure that had become standard in offices, where connecting a computer to the Internet on each desk had become routine.

The frequent objection is heard when laptops for students are suggested that the kids would lose and break them. One of the few isolated attempts to one-to-one students and computers was made in September 2002 by giving every seventh grader in Maine a laptop. The kids did not destroy their machines. Known as the Maine Learning Technology Initiative, the project continues and has had key successes. The Maine initiative was the rare vision of then Maine Governor Angus King and did not come from within the education establishment.

Generally speaking, over the past decade, while fathers and mothers have been issued personal computers at work and laptops to take on the road, their children continued at school to sharpen their pencils and lug their books. Now and then, they spend a class hour using a wired computer fastened to a table—or more recently issued, a wireless laptop from a rolling cart.

Meanwhile, the virtual knowledge ecology has been weaving the open content network from which students of the future—and today's computer-equipped kids—will learn in common. The attitude of the K–12 education establishment has shown little indication of softening in moving to equipping kids instead of schools.

It looks, however, certain now that students will acquire personal Internet access in other ways. Many have already. The kids will, it seems, rarely be wired at school—they will instead be wireless wherever they are. They are already far down that road in college.

25 THE RESPONSE OF THE AMERICAN PUBLIC

The first enthusiasm for the Internet as a wonderful new factor for education did not last in the public mind. For a while, the Wire the Schools crusade had major momentum, but that faded. There has been little public push to get students online at school thereafter. The main response to Internet use by kids has become apprehension.

The eleven Ideas (14–24) in this section describing the attitudes of the education establishment explain a lot. The reactions from education were in the main suspicious or down right negative. For the public to sustain enthusiasm for the Internet in education, it would have had to do so with little help from educators, or more probably, in spite of the vibes radiating from the education establishment.

The Internet has also raised parental suspicion by engaging the kids in ways that have nothing to do with learning and which parents often question or do not understand. The chat rooms that attract children appear to waste time and have proven possibly dangerous. Parents were alarmed to know that a child surfing the open Internet could happen upon hard-core sex images or be tempted by gambling websites and other unseemly distractions. Video games seem to turn kids who might have been on the baseball team into couch potatoes. The tech-heads who have gone into geekdom have disappeared into a world that barely existed in Mom and Dad's day.

It is at least worth wondering what would have happened if education had embraced the Internet, as was done by almost every other sector of American enterprise and society. If the same amount that was spent on textbooks had been spent instead on supplying each student with a laptop and equipping each school desk with a plug-in jack for the Internet, much would have been different. There is little reason to doubt that, for fiscal or infrastructure reasons, K–12 could have embraced the Internet because this is pretty much what really is happening at the college level, although slowly.

In an imagined world in which education embraces the Internet, a lot more attention would have been focused on creating and organizing online learning materials and switching over to using them. A more concentrated online organizational effort by the education establishment would have made more progress in sidelining pornography, gambling, and the like from the knowledge resources students use. The grade levels in schools would have become less rigid, as subject organization would have become more prominent than the rigid lockstep standards. Students would have relied more on distant tutors, including nonhuman ones. There would be other changes. Schools would be different and could potentially morph into something little like the schools of the nondigital past.

Whether intentional or not on the part of the education establishment, education has not changed much during the decade plus of the Internet era—protected in significant part by the public's sentimentality about schooling. I feel it too, and understand why it is so powerful. I cherish my school memories and my classmates, with whom I am still in touch more than fifty years after we were in school together.

The notion of schools makes it very hard to bring about change. We all have powerful feelings about the school experience—good or bad—so that we find it nearly impossible to jump beyond those feelings to imagine radical changes or even no schools at all. How do you respond when I tell you that we might need to start all over on figuring out what our kids do all day as they are growing up? How much alarm takes over your thinking when I tell you that schools might go out of existence? How powerful is your sense that you do not want to deny your children what you cherish about school? How quickly do arguments come to your mind that induce you to dismiss me as plain wrong, so that you are no longer hearing what I am saying? When that happens, you have joined the ranks of the defenders of the education establishment.

If there actually is something far better that we could offer our children, why does it alarm us so much even to consider slaying the real culprit of dumbing down and delinquency: the schools? I think the answer is very simple: Our association is so powerful between childhood memories and schools that we cannot imagine a childhood without schools. We need to get over it.

26 THE KIDS' ATTITUDE

Anyone under the age of ten today was born into the Internet era. Adults who were children in the 1980s and 1990s watched the computer morph from nerd toy into a magnificent tool of communication and commerce. Young people have now for three decades witnessed an exhilarating global innovation and its initial impact.

That is quite a contrast to my own decades as a youngster, when the global scene rolled by from the Great Depression, through World War II, and into the Cold War. I grew up to possess deep and strong beliefs in the individual and that the key to global progress is the end of tyranny. The coming down of the Berlin Wall and subsequent emergence of significant freedom and development in many parts of the world have been joyfully confirming to me. I am left with a powerful sense of the possibilities for the progress of civilization and individual human achievement. As the kids would say, I find that very, very cool.

Certainly, what I think about many things has always been affected by what I knew as a kid. That is true of everyone. It is true of today's kids. Those of us who did not grow up with computers need to keep in mind that somewhere around half the population did. Those of us who make education policy regarding the Internet need to realize that kids today cannot remember a time without the Internet. Even children isolated in remote parts of the world will know, once they possess the Internet, that it belongs to their time. Computers, digital communication, and the Internet will never be a new concept that needs to be introduced to anyone born in the twenty-first century.

Recently, I visited one of my nephews and his wife and their two daughters. The girls were eight and five in 2005. When their dad was out running some errands, the eight-year-old picked up her mom's cell phone, punched a couple of keys, held the phone to her face, and asked her dad to buy some balloons for a party we were having that evening.

In the living room, I later spotted a plastic toy that looked like a laptop. It did not connect to anything or do anything when you punched the keys. The five-year-old explained that the batteries were dead. The device was some sort of game for learning words by punching a keyboard. These days children are learning to type as they learn to talk!

These grandnieces of mine do not use the Internet much, if at all, because their parents are dissuaded by several of the reasons mentioned in this section of ideas. It is clear, though, that when their girls do interact with the Internet, they will embrace the familiar. The eight-year-old already communicates effortlessly by mobile wireless connections. The five-year-old is interfacing with interactive language drills by punching keys.

When these girls do a high school research paper in a history class, it will be ridiculous to give them a printed magazine and expect them to pull encyclopedia volumes off a bookshelf. I feel quite sure that, in less than a decade, when I visit this family each girl will have an inexpensive wireless connecting device where she will do all of her research using the Internet.

Already, graduate students and college kids look to the Internet as the primary location of the knowledge they seek to acquire. That way of accessing knowledge creeps inexorably from three directions into becoming universal. First, the use of the Internet is moving downward from graduate and college students to high school and middle school youngsters and into use by littler children. The time is very close (or here) when a five-year-old's plastic toy that teaches letters is streaming its content from the Internet. A second movement is the spread of the Internet into global populations. A major undertaking mentioned in Idea 3 is to get millions of $100 laptops to students in developing countries.

The third creeping certainty toward ubiquitous student computing is that kids get older every year. I was amazed by the first computer I owned back in 1983, and absolutely blown away the first time I saw the Internet in 1996. My grandnieces are completely blasé about the Internet and will be even more so by the time they get to high school. The biggest contrast, I believe, between the attitude of kids to that of older generations toward the Internet is that the kids accept it as a given reality. They understand it as where you go to learn something. Their attitude toward school is seriously soured when they are not allowed to use the medium of knowledge that belongs to their time.

27 THE COLLEGE LEVEL CLEARER COURSE

Several years ago, a friend of mine who was on the board of a college described the effect the Internet was having on the board meetings he attended. He said that the board was always given an agenda of matters for discussion at the meeting. Items would be taken up one-by-one in the order in which they were listed until it came time to discuss the Internet's role at the college. No matter where the Internet was on the list, he said, as soon as it was on the table for discussion, the meeting would break down and nobody would talk about anything else until they adjourned.

There are numerous important and interesting issues vis-à-vis the Internet and college-level learning. In the area that is the subject of this book, content for learning, content in digital form and more recently content delivered by the Internet, has inexorably flowed into the academy and been increasingly created there.

Having a personal computer became a habit for college students as the Internet burgeoned. In the early 1990s, forward-looking instructors began to put their syllabi and some of its content online. In 1994, the University of Texas Web began publishing a collection of college instructors' online content in the WorldLectureHall.com, which remains an important open content website and is described in Idea 53. By the late 1990s, CDs were replacing textbooks in medical schools, and medical CD content was trickling online. More and more scholarly papers were placed online and interconnected.

Virtually every college and university has now established an intranet and moved administrative and knowledge-related content behind its firewall. Sometimes, portions of the intranet content have been placed as open content on the Internet. In April 2001, the Massachusetts Institute of Technology announced its commitment to place openly online the materials created by their faculty for the courses they teach. The MIT Open CourseWare project had placed the materials from 900 of its courses online by September 2004 and was aiming in early 2005 to have virtually all of MIT's courseware online by 2008. Many other colleges and universities contribute to the open content that is forming the virtual knowledge ecology, and their sources and forms are highlighted in Idea 53.

A major story with many aspects to it can be told about the changes caused by the Internet for libraries, including college libraries. For the purpose of this book, the key point is that the primary location of human knowledge has become the Internet. Increasingly, the most up-to-date and complete version of a particular piece of knowledge is located on the Internet. In part, brick and mortar libraries have become places people go, including college students, to use a computer to access the Internet. When students have their own computers, they no longer need to wait in line for a library computer, or perhaps go to the library at all. Often, the type of research once done in college libraries is done in a dorm room—or on the rapidly multiplying wireless campuses under a tree in a campus quad or meadow. Books are not obsolete, but they are no longer the only tool of research—or in some fields, the main tool they once were. Academic libraries have taken a leadership role in digitizing books. A splendid example is the University of Virginia Electronic Text Center. Among the center's eclectic open content, free to the public, are the works of 136 American fiction authors who wrote between

1789 and 1875, a *Dictionary of the History of Ideas*, 300 Tang poems in Chinese, and Osip Mandelstam's *Tristia* in Russian.

As the Internet emerged, an obvious matter for colleges to take into consideration was whether to use the Internet to deliver education outside of the traditional classroom—a process that has acquired these three main names: online education, distance learning, and asynchronous learning. Institutions of higher learning were compelled, simply by the new opportunity the Internet gave them to do so, to decide to what extent, if any, they would participate in delivering learning via the Internet. Idea 29 delves further into the distant learning subject.

The Internet had established a major presence in higher education before things began to become unwired, and higher education has moved a long way into the wireless era. Intel sponsors an annual listing of the 100 Most Unwired College Campuses. Nearly all U.S. college campuses have taken some steps toward going wireless, and the momentum is growing. Students on wireless campuses are able to use the Internet without plugging their computers into a jack at the end of a wire. There are all sorts of advantages.

For colleges, wireless is cheaper and more doable than wiring. Venerable old ivy-covered structures that once seemed impossible to wire can now provide the Internet to students by sporting a few small transmitters. The inflexibility and discomfort of computers attached to tables is fading. The intellectual change is even sweeter. Students and faculty have the many advantages of their own personal access to the Internet in a device that is also their center for research, writing, and storing information.

It is an odd and unfortunate quirk of educational reality that wireless personal computing is not the accepted practice of students before they come to college. In high schools and lower grades, there has not been a similar momentum toward the Internet. That needs to change.

28 THE EXTRA-EDUCATION LITTLE-NOTICED MORPH

As talk, turmoil, and the far-from-complete embrace of the Internet have now muddled along for years within kindergarten through university education establishments, the attitude of the extra-education enterprises has been to accept and advance digital, interactive instruction. They have demonstrated the pedagogical powers of the Internet and become highly reliant upon them.

Although the community of licensed tutors, testing coaches, corporate trainers, and their kind can be looked down upon by educators as suspicious extraterrestrials, the enterprises they ply move a lot of knowledge into people's heads. The extra-educational corps have to succeed in moving knowledge or they lose their jobs, making them very tough critics of pedagogical methodology.

A visit to Macromedia.com's Showcase>Authorware will give you a sampling of leading-edge interactive courses. When I stopped by there recently, the Showcase included a description of digitized courses American Airlines uses to refresh the training of pilots, flight attendants, maintenance crews, engineering staff, and their reservations and airport customer service people. Another example in the Showcase was Crown Cork & Seal, the world's largest maker of consumer goods packaging products. The company reported saving $500,000 a year by replacing instructor-led classes with self-paced courses on the web.

The vast majority of extra-educational online activity is hidden in portions of the Internet that are firewalled within intranets or are proprietary. Understandably, American does not want flight attendants from other airlines picking up pointers from its courses, and Crown Cork & Seal wants to protect the competitive ways of doing things it teaches its employees.

There is certainly nothing surprising or wrong about charging money to take courses in the extra-educational world. Business is business, as they say. Competitive profits also drive competition to improve the product—in this case, to do a better job of teaching. Whether a professional or tradesman signs up for a course online or offline, the course is a business expense. Perhaps one day apprenticing will become more popular and younger people will get a financial break in using course materials of this sort.

There are times when open online courses offer an advantage, such as in teaching customers and potential customers to use products. A window on that sort of extra-education venue is open on the Sun Microsystems Online Courses page. The online tutorials that the page lists can be entered with a click or two so that developers who have Sun products can learn how to use them. The tutorials are open content and, as such, part of the virtual knowledge ecology. There is no reason a twelve-year-old—anywhere in the world—cannot learn what the Sun courses have to teach by working through them on her own. There is no reason to think that is not happening as you read this idea.

A rapidly unfolding new aspect of extra-education is online conferencing. As broadband gets broader, and videoing simpler, training gets a lot easier than it once was to conduct online in real time. It will get easier still, and probably become a major factor in corporate and professional training and related fields.

For the purposes of this book, the vigor of the extra-educational online movement proves a key point: Online learning works. It is not some zany pipe dream of anti-educationists. Let there be no confusion about the efficacy of learning online because it is producing results all the time.

29 DISTANT LEARNING IS MANY THINGS

Back in the 1960s, when I was starting out in the working world, a very popular way to learn new material was by taking correspondence courses. My own venture into learning from a distant school was completing three Famous Artists School courses on drawing and painting. They were absolutely wonderful and succeeded in giving me a solid grounding in the visual arts.

Putting in the mail your check and completed sign-up forms for a Famous Artists course led to a wait of a couple of weeks before the beautiful big books that were the basis of the lessons arrived by parcel post. As I remember them, there were three books for a course—giant loose-leaf ring binders with thick hard covers, in each of the three primary colors, yellow, red, and blue.

The pages of the books were filled with instructional sketches and completed drawings and paintings by the famous artists who were part of the school. The artists were really famous people like Norman Rockwell, Stevan Dohanos, Robert Fawcett, and Ben Stahl.

As a student, you worked your way through the lessons in the books.

When you completed a lesson, you would do an assignment it presented and mail that to the school. In a week or two, the lesson would come back in the mail with comments and an overlay sketch with suggestions from someone at the school.

Although it was not e-learning (electronic), this was distance learning for sure. The Famous Artists courses I took also were asynchronous learning, fitting another term used for courses delivered over the Internet. In asynchronous learning, the student works at times not synchronized with the instruction. Is the electronic difference the only one between the distance learning I experienced and its twenty-first-century avatar? In a general way, at least, it is possible to think of most distant learning today as essentially the correspondence courses of the past repositioned on the Internet. The predigital age courses delivered content and tutoring through lesson comments.

As a matter of fact, the Famous Artists School is very much alive and well, as its website illustrates. Looking through how the courses are conducted today, I could see almost no difference from the procedures I followed. The major change seems to be that the school now has a handsome website by which it can market its courses.

The Famous Artist School was acquired in 1981 by Cortina Learning International—an even earlier pioneer of distance learning. It was founded in 1882 by Professor Rafael Diaz de la Cortina, who enlisted Thomas Edison to develop cylinders to record his language-teaching method for delivery to distant students.

Now there is a new and booming online learning industry. Its participants range from large, entirely online universities to small websites offering courses to be paid for by parents of homeschoolers and kids falling behind at school. Many universities and colleges offer some or many courses online. There are online public schools, usually serving students who are disabled or living in remote locations. Recently, these schools are experiencing strong enrollments from youngsters with jobs or other reasons for not wanting to attend a regular school. There are all sorts of online courses outside of the education mainstream.

In this introductory set of ideas about attitudes, it is key to clarify that conducting online learning is not an aspect of the virtual knowledge ecology. The virtual knowledge ecology is open content potentially usable in nearly every learning format. In conducting online learning, the virtual knowledge ecology's content may or may not be used. It is possible to study from a book and refer to illustrations in the virtual knowledge ecology. Conversely, you can study online and refer to knowledge found in a book.

There is a deep pitfall of confusion here that can easily be tumbled into during a discussion of education. The process of learning and the knowledge acquired are not the same thing. Pedagogy is the action of leading a child to knowledge. What the child drinks into her head is something separate. She could also stumble onto it without being led. There is very interesting work being done in digital pedagogy—the methodology of delivering knowledge at a distance or from software. Digital pedagogy is, however, not the virtual knowledge ecology. Like other pedagogy, the digital kind can, but does not necessarily have to, use knowledge content from the virtual knowledge ecology.

The emergence of the virtual knowledge ecology to which millions and soon billions of individuals are connected will cause us to look at the role of pedagogy in new ways. It may be quite possible to learn from the virtual knowledge ecology with no pedagogy around anywhere. Perhaps the best way to learn is when knowledge itself is compelling. A painful example of that is a child touching a stove to learn it is hot. The hand is burned and the lesson learned directly between subject and student.

The marvelous works of Rockwell, Dohanos, Fawcett, and Stahl that graced the big notebooks of the Famous Artists School radiated beauty and artistic insight from the printed page. My sense is that the genius of the Famous Artists School has always emanated from these drawings.

The virtual knowledge ecology consists of the ideas that radiate from content—and that emerge dynamically from the awesome new network facility for interlinking those ideas by their meaning. I was living in El Paso, Texas, when I studied from the Famous Artists notebooks. Although there is a wonderful small museum in El Paso, my opportunities multiplied for viewing and comparing the artistic ideas taught in my courses when I moved to New York City, into an apartment three blocks from the Metropolitan Museum of Art.

The pedagogues have a lot of work to do to focus distant learning effectively in the computer age. The emergence of the virtual knowledge ecology is a separate phenomenon. Already, visiting the virtual knowledge ecology is a lot like passing through the grand pillars of the Met to be swallowed into a sumptuous ecology of artistic ideas. As surely as touching a stove teaches heat, standing in the Temple of Dendur on view at the museum requires no pedagogy to sense the ceremonial grandeur of ancient Egypt.

30 RESPONSES OF VARIOUS COUNTRIES

A fascinating story can be written, perhaps ten years from now, of how the Internet was embraced by different countries across the world as the primary source for learning what is known by humankind. Perhaps the theme of that overall story would be to explore how various countries were the same and how they were different—or tried to be different. It is too early to tell the story because we are only in the prelude. My conviction is that they will all embrace it fully because there will be no other sensible choice.

The global importance and irreversibility of the relocation of what is known by humankind into the open Internet is comparable to the discovery by Europe of the Americas in the fifteenth century. There was never a way that the Americas were going to be undiscovered. The Internet is not going away. The point was reached some time in the late 1990s that—short of global catastrophe on the level of nuclear holocaust or collision with a major meteor—a very great deal of knowledge will be accessible from most places on the planet. The same knowledge will be accessible in all of those places. When that has happened, the Bible could be read in any of those places and so could the Koran and so could the teachings of Hinduism and so could the teachings of atheists. But access to different points of view is not the subject of this book.

The virtual knowledge ecology is not the collections of faith or speculation or opinion or points of view. It is the collection of the knowledge all humankind has acquired: how to grow grain, the theorems of geometry, the number of continents, the way cells work, and other useful knowledge. The virtual knowledge ecology content is the same for all people in all countries.

Countries, like schools, are finding that the stuff of knowledge that the virtual knowledge ecology offers is no longer coming or interfaced from within themselves. It is available to their people from beyond their sphere and control—unless the Internet is censored, as has happened in many schools and some countries.

Up to now, most of the virtual knowledge ecology's content is linking out from Western countries. As the story unfolds further, that is changing and will continue to do so. The future best website for Mesopotamian agriculture might well be based in Iraq, with remote participation by archaeologists and historians in other places. A student in Korea studying Ur will go to the virtual knowledge ecology to find the Iraq-based material and follow the links to the associated experts based there and elsewhere.

Inevitably, the creation of nodes of knowledge that join the virtual knowledge ecology network occurs from the inside outward, essentially one node at a time. It is false to think of countries creating content networks appropriate for themselves within the open Internet. Within the open Internet, their students will simply use the best link from wherever it originates.

What countries can do to participate is to stimulate the contribution of their particular knowledge to the virtual knowledge ecology. The Seychelles, for example, are rare granite islands that remain from the separation of massive Gondwanaland into several continents, leaving flora and fauna on the Seychelles that have fascinating ties to distant continents. Knowledge of this part of the earth's history can be shared from the islands directly through a website. Their small islands, where sea birds nest, are ideal to locate a nesting cam so that the entire world can observe the family life of these birds from far and wide.

There are, of course, culturally sensitive issues in what children learn as they grow up. These issues should not be confused with what is known. It deprives a country's kids of basic knowledge to make them wait to use the Internet until geometric theorem tutorials are decorated with local illustrations. I know saying that suggests that I either do not know that cultures are different or that I am insensitive. I would simply answer with my conviction that, like acquiring literacy, connecting people to the Internet will lead to new skills and to understanding basic subjects like geometry, even if they never understand the decorations. I think kids are smart enough to learn to learn from pure knowledge and that, when they are doing that, the decorations that pamper culture distract from the geometry. You may disagree.

To get an idea of whether culturally sensitive illustrations are deemed crucial in the commercial online world visit Nokia's China pages. Although the text is in Chinese characters, almost all of the illustrations of people and phones are non-Asian images. Over a quarter of the people in China now have cell phones, making the market there huge. If the Nokia marketers thought cultural matches were meaningful, they would use them. Other corporations have used generic illustrations without pictures of people, making their multiple-language versions of web pages culturally neutral. Corporations with multinational websites have pioneered the duplication of content for different countries and are useful places to get ideas and check sensitivities for educators working to duplicate knowledge web pages for the same markets.

It is wrongheaded to apply cultural sensitivity up front to the useful knowledge all of humankind shares. The geometry website that goes to the top of the search engines because the most people use it will do so because it is about geometry and not mired in culture. What is known about geology, physics, and even history should not be culturally sensitive because that sensitivity screens out understanding and skews the cognitive processes. I say even history because different countries teach a same historical period by providing often different perspectives and emphasis. As Ideas 70 through 74 describe, the network laws of the virtual knowledge ecology cause an objective vetting of these differences.

The constructive attitude of countries toward the virtual knowledge ecology is to participate in connecting its people and in adding its own useful knowledge to that ecology—to a new global learning venue that belongs to each human being on earth.

31 THE ACCURATE ATTITUDE ABOUT TECHNOLOGY

Much obfuscation is caused by calling almost everything that is happening regarding education and the Internet "technology." It is a habit left over from the awe we all first felt when computers came along: "What an awesome technology," we said. Education has not developed much of a technology-free Internet vocabulary.

What we are in the habit of calling education technology is a bunch of things that mostly can be divided into education hardware technology and education software technology. Both kinds of education technology are a part of information technology. The virtual knowledge ecology that is the subject of this book is neither hardware nor software technology. The only, albeit primary, role of technology in the virtual knowledge ecology is that computers simulate knowledge virtually, thus freeing it to form an ecology of meaning. We would not have that without the technology, but the result is not the technology. If you fly from Chicago to Miami in an airplane, your trip to the Florida sun is not the airplane, fuel, or pilots. The trip is the content of the aviation.

The virtual knowledge ecology consists not of hardware and software but rather the content of hardware and software. The content is not any kind of education technology—it just lives inside the technology where it has a life of its own. There is nothing mystical about that. The content of a textbook is not the textbook either.

Information technology contains, processes, and sometimes creates information in general. Education technology, too, contains, processes, and sometimes creates the information students learn for whatever they are being educated about. Information is not technology. The virtual knowledge ecology is information and therefore not technology. If that sounds tedious it is because these distinctions need to be repeated until they become understood.

The technology hardware used for education is mostly the same technology as banks, hospitals, publishers, and so forth use: servers, wires, and the rest. Much of the software technology used in education is the same as commercial software as well. Some software technology is developed specifically for learning, and that software can correctly be called education technology. Some of the true education technology is digital pedagogy: It leads students to knowledge.

Computer hardware provides a platform, and software makes things happen on that platform. Both are needed for there to be information content but in no sense is that content technology. (Sorry, but I felt like saying it again.)

Content is the substance of the virtual knowledge ecology, which is the subject of this book. How content behaves in the virtual knowledge ecology is not fundamentally controlled or affected by hardware or software. Computer technology creates the virtual place where the knowledge collects, but the meaning of the open content in this ecology causes dynamic ideas to form. Sounds amazing? Yes, it is awesome!

You do not need to know much about technology of any kind to fully understand and use the virtual knowledge ecology. In fact thinking about the Internet's role in learning as technology is a sidetrack down which education has lost its way. Teachers complain that they do not want to master the Internet technology. People who work in libraries have had technology stuck into their titles. There is a general misconception, described in Idea 5, that children and geeks control computers. Technology is a turn-off.

As far as the ideas in this book are concerned, all you need to know about hardware technology is how to turn on a computer, operate its mouse, and open the Internet. That is about it. Driving a car works the same way. The technical knowledge required for that begins with how the door handle and seat adjustments work. You then need to be able to fasten your seatbelt and put your key into the ignition. You have to know how the pedals on the floorboard function, that turning the key starts the motor, and how to use the shift stick. If it rains, operational knowledge of the windshield wipers is crucial and, if the sun goes down, mastery of the headlights is required. The rest is visual and body coordination and software in your head—not automotive technology.

After you have learned to drive a car, the rest of your relationship with the vehicle is only seldom technical. The machine needs gas periodically. Sometimes it breaks down and needs to be worked on by a mechanic. Your technical relationship with your computer can be no more complicated than with your car. You can, if you wish, be like my brothers were as teenagers, when they spent much of their waking lives hanging over a fender rebuilding their car engines. But that technology relationship with your laptop or PC is no more necessary than it is with your sedan or SUV.

Nevertheless, in the education world, discussions of the Internet continue to be about "technology." Technology conferences are held. Technology specialists are trained and hired. The role of technology in education is debated. Most harmful, teachers believe they will never "get" whatever it is about technology they are going to have to know.

The technology misnomer alone is a major obstacle to seeing the virtual world of content that the technology has simulated. Certainly, schools need hardware technology staff to install and repair computers. But these personnel are like mechanics for automobiles. The role of the Internet in education is not about the hardware technology of the machines. It is about information content that inhabits the technology.

The big stage where the future of global learning is playing out is the relationship between the already enormous Internet and the portion of content within it consisting of what is known by humankind. The Internet has become the go-to place to learn.

Schools often use their hardware more like a bank, hospital, or publisher does than apply it very much to education. Schools usually have closed intranets that keep administrative records private and communicate with teachers, students, and parents. These intranets are not part of the open content that is the subject of this book and that forms the virtual knowledge ecology from which the new world of learning is emerging.

Technology is a false word to use when talking about how the Internet impacts learning—false in both basic meaning and the actual use of the technology that educators are supposed to be talking about. Using the word technology obfuscates what is really happening, and that is not a beautiful thing.

The following are some thoughts on how the term education technology got going down the wrong road. As described in Idea 14, when the Internet began to emerge in a major way, the main response from the school world executed a loudly touted, very expensive movement for wiring schools. Wiring schools was definitely technology: installing cables and computers. Education technology came to mean installing wires and computers—and soon the meaning of the word slipped over to the activities of teachers and librarians turning the computers on and extracting information.

No one could have anticipated, in the mid-1990s, when the Wire the Schools crusade took hold, that everything it accomplished in terms of hardware would be obsolete soon after the turn of the century. Now that wireless technology is proving to be better than wired for delivering the learning content of the Internet, wireless installations are already up and running in more than half of all college campuses in the United States, and momentum is strong toward ubiquitous campus access.

In contrast to what had been done at colleges by late 2004, less than one thousand of the more than 25,000 high schools in the United States had even begun to use a wireless platform. The wireless access to the Internet in lower grades was negligible. Money was still being thrown at the technology line in school budgets, much of it going to closed for-profit library software and subscriptions. Some of the education technology money was being spent to purchase regular laptops for students, which is discussed in Idea 96. Significant amounts of educational technology money is also spent on administrative procedures, which may or may not be helping children learn. The wiring that has been placed in schools has proven in many cases to be used primarily in recording attendance, filing reports, etc.

Education technology has pretty much come to mean the use of computers in schools. The ruckus over school "technology" has rumbled on, pretty much obscuring the reality that the learning is about content. By labeling almost anything that has to do with learning related to the Internet as technology, critics find false justification for hurling these and other accusations:

- Computers are machines, and humans are better teachers.
- Other school technologies like classroom films and slide shows did not create a revolution and neither will computers—which is just another technology.
- Technology is too fleeting, creating "flickering minds" as one book says.
- The low usage of computer labs proves technology is inappropriate in education.

As debates and laments about education technology have droned on for years, something dazzlingly important was going on for learning completely outside the technology setting: The virtual knowledge ecology was forming.

The emergence of the virtual knowledge ecology cannot be credited to any technology that was in place in schools. In fact, the education establishment lifted no finger to build it and has almost completely ignored or opposed using the new ecology of knowledge every step of the way.

The Internet is one network on top of another network. The first one, which is technology, is composed of computers scattered across the world, connected to each other by wires, glass, and beams. The network that sits on top of the first one is virtual, consisting of information that comes to life dynamically when the computers send signals to each other. The virtual knowledge ecology is that portion of the information that is the content of what is known by humankind: science, humanities, and the like.

The virtual knowledge ecology is an absolutely free resource for education that is far better than any previous kind of learning resource and getting more wonderful all the time. The free aspect has challenged the ingenuity of several kinds of profiteers, who have created closed Internet content and sold it back to the schools.

The future of global learning, then, is being transformed by technology (the computers, wires, glass, and beams) that has nothing to do with the schools in particular or education in general. The technology that creates the virtual knowledge ecology that now holds the world's primary content for learning is the technology underlying the Internet itself. It is the same technology that supports e-commerce, the blogosphere, pornography, and all other information content of the Internet. Garden-variety computers—specific to education in no way—interface that content, and wires and wireless computers deliver it.

It is not at all necessary to know about the technology that underlies the virtual knowledge ecology as background for the ideas in this book. If you are interested, though, the rest of this Idea is a quick recap of some of the things going on under the Internet hood.

The technology that operates the Internet actually only does one thing: It connects anything in it to anything else it contains. For that to happen, everything that is going to connect has to be reduced to very small parts. You, for example, might want to send an image of a cricket you are studying over the Internet.

To get the necessary smallness, all of the content in the Internet universe is digital. Digital means represented by numbers. The Internet uses binary numbers, allowing only two digits: zero or one. Nothing moves as content within the Internet except zeroes and ones. To send the cricket image, it must first be reduced into a string of zeroes and ones before it is turned loose in the Internet. When a computer somewhere receives the string of zeroes and ones, it will use them to tell its graphic program how to display a picture of your cricket on its monitor screen.

Anything that enters the Internet has been converted into zeros and ones—text, images, sound, whatever. The efficiency of that is huge. In the analog world that we have been used to, text travels around in books, images are portable in scrapbooks, and sound needs to wiggle itself out of speakers. All of the digital stuff just mixes together as it zooms around the Internet on wires, glass, and beams that are able to do just one thing: allow zeroes and ones to move through them at the speed of light. It is not necessary to know how the conversions are done to appreciate what they accomplish. But, if you are interested in knowing more, there is an excellent basic explanation of the subject in HowStuffWorks.com at the "Bits and Bytes" article.

It is not too hard to think of a string of zeroes and ones zooming like a comet through wires and glass and beams. But strings like that are not allowed in the Internet, only packets. Before it gets loose in the wires, glass, and beams, the string of zeroes and ones that represents your cricket is broken into many short segments called *packets*. Each packet has an identifying *header* (of zeroes and ones, of course), which includes the address of where the cricket image is supposed to go. Packets are tiny, made up of usually 1,000 or 1,500 *bytes*. Each byte is 8 *bits* (8 zeroes and ones in a sequence that stands for a number, letter, color, or something else). Everything travels the Internet as a packet of 8,000 to 12,000 zeroes and ones. When your computer receives incoming packets, it decodes the sequence of the zeroes and ones and interfaces them as text, images, or sound.

The packets do not travel together. As soon as they are sent into the Internet, they go their separate ways. Each one looks for the least crowded and fastest path to the address where it is supposed to end up. If someone in Boise clicks on a web page to get your cricket image and the page is on a server in Tampa, one packet that is a piece of cricket might bounce off a satellite through Hong Kong, then Sydney, and a couple of times in Europe. Another packet could go through Baltimore and San Francisco. When all the packets reach the requesting computer in Boise, they reassemble themselves and display your cricket.

There is only one way I can get it into my head that even more complex paths than I have sketched are being taken simultaneously by packets representing everything moving on the Internet. I sort of understand it when I am told my brain is much more complex and always much busier sending messages than the Internet. As I type this, my neurons are firing axons instructing my fingers. Axons can only fire or not fire. The information my brain processes is digital: fire or not fire, zero or one.

Just as your cricket must be reduced to packets to enter the Internet universe, anything that has a location in that universe must have a URL—*Uniform Resource Locator*. The magic here is in the uniform aspect. A URL is a number and nothing more than that. All URLs are equal. The playing field is absolutely level. Amazon.com and your blog or website URL are equals. Every page on every website has its own URL. Within a website, all URLs for each separate page are equal to each other and to their homepage and to my homepage and to Amazon.com's homepage. A major magic of the Internet universe is in the uniformity of its resource locator numbers.

Uniformity means anything can be connected to anything else. It is a structure of liberty and equality. Communication occurs among equals. Bigger things are built by connecting smaller things. This can get philosophical, but that will sidetrack us from the theme of the ideas collected in this book. Uniformity is a structural environment where openness causes unlimited connections. Perhaps it is oversimplifying to say that learning and thinking are matters of making connections. What you need to know about technology as background for this book is that the Internet is an open universe containing connective technology.

I have gone into some detail in sketching how the Internet works because the smallness—the little bitty pieces—is the basis of the incredible value of open content. Idea 69 titled "Minimalization" will explain why.

32 CAN PEDAGOGY BE WHAT IT TEACHES?

A resolute hubris that we must overcome as we try to understand the Internet's potential role for education is the blithe assumption of educators that putting their equipment online is the same thing as embedding what is known by humankind into the Internet. There are huge and crucial differences between the equipment and the content it claims to convey.

Examples of pre-Internet educator equipment massively repositioned online are lesson plans, curricula, standards, courses, and syllabi. Examples of equipment native to the digital ecology and used for educating are learning objects, distance learning courses and tutors, and—more recently—platforms structured as the user-contributive wikis and individual-author blogs. Examples of knowledge are arithmetic, history, biology, and the like.

Educators do a lot of knowledge embedding into their equipment and use the end result as teaching tools and organization. They did that throughout the twentieth century so routinely and relied on the resulting apparatus so systematically that there is now a common impression that knowledge is part of the pedagogy. That impression is false. One does not learn the lesson, one learns the arithmetic, history, or biology the lesson presents. One does not learn the blog, one learns the knowledge content of the posts.

As knowledge began to show up on the Internet, the distinction began to reappear between the conveyance and its contents—between the pedagogy and the knowledge. To look at an example: In cooperation with NASA, on June 16, 1995, two astrophysicists began to post online the Astronomy Picture of the Day (APOD). The scientists, Robert J. Nemiroff and Jerry T. Bonnell, have continued their daily posting for over ten years. Except for the day-to-day structural aspect, the daily pictures are almost pure scientific information and insight. Undoubtedly, the images have been included in many lesson plans over the years, but the images are not lesson plans.

The APOD website is definitely educational. It is almost impossible to drop by without learning something. The quality of the information is first rate and backed by the authority of its two astrophysicists and its NASA web host. Conversely, APOD is not meant for or dependent on education. It is simply knowledge.

The Theban Mapping Project is a direct presentation of knowledge from the location where that knowledge literally is being dug up. It is not designed for or targeted toward students other than in the sense that any of us who are interested in the ancient Egyptian Valley of the

Kings are students of the subject. Nonetheless, the website includes an interactive timeline of ancient Egyptian history that would be terrific, nearly pure knowledge to use in teaching and learning for elementary school through college. The knowledge on this website beckons pedagogy to come to it. Sticking pieces of the website into a lesson plan or curriculum seems odd and clumsy.

It is possible to quibble and take the position that anything that presents knowledge is a form of pedagogy. You could say that the timeline form of presentation of the history of Egypt was a form of pedagogy. I would reply that the facts presented on that timeline were knowledge. Facts such as that Rameses II was in power just over 1,200 years ago and that his mummy was found in 1881 and is now in the Egyptian Museum in Cairo, are bits of knowledge.

The distinction I am getting at is at the root of the word *pedagogy*. The etymology begins at the root word's meaning *agent* or *escort*, the idea being that a pedagogue is the agent who escorts a student to knowledge. That agent or escort can be a human teacher. The equipment the teacher uses can also be pedagogical, serving as an agent escorting a student to knowledge.

A textbook, course, curriculum, and lesson plan are all pedagogical equipment—tools that are kinds of agents that escort students to knowledge. Before the Internet came along, just about the only way most students were escorted to knowledge was through the agency of teachers and their pedagogical tools. The teacher and the tools he used predetermined to what knowledge they were escorted and in what order.

When I taught world history to three classes of high school freshmen in 1960–61, the first thing I did on the first day of class was to write a list of ten major events on the blackboard in scrambled chronological order. The events were something like: the fall of Rome, the discovery of the Americas, World War II, the building of the great Egyptian pyramids, Napoleon's conquest of Europe, the Golden Age of Greece, the beginning of agriculture, the American Revolution, the conquests of Genghis Khan, the Korean War.

Of the nearly one hundred students in my classes, only one was able to arrange the events in the order in which they occurred. The kids had almost no knowledge of world history. Two semesters later, the only knowledge that would be added for each of them would be whatever they learned from my efforts to escort them to knowledge through lectures plus a few looks into their history-impoverished textbooks. Their progress toward the knowledge of history depended on my success as a pedagogue and their responses as learners.

The next section of Ideas will describe how online access has become the freshest, most complete, and most authoritative knowledge that exists. Thousands of sources like the APOD and the Theban Mapping Project await students. Repositioning the sort of pedagogy I practiced forty-five years ago would be embarrassingly inadequate. Nevertheless, a very great deal of such pedagogy has been repositioned onto the Internet.

Two large challenges are presented by the fact that what is known by humankind is now openly interfaced on the Internet. The first challenge is what to do about all the non–Internet-based knowledge the education establishment is used to creating and using. Why should there be astronomy images in textbooks when the APOD is freely available online? Why describe the Valley of the Kings in printed resource materials when it is so elegantly interfaced online? Why have textbooks and libraries at all?

As discussed in Idea 22, the education establishment will argue that kids "don't get it" unless they are given grade-level materials. That reasoning is very seriously called into question by legion websites like APOD and the Theban Project. The pedagogy in play with a human teacher sitting alongside a student and looking together at either website has two age thresholds. First, the child has to be old enough to understand anything at all. Surely age two is too young, but is age five, or seven? Another threshold comes along when the teacher may no longer be needed, unless she can supply knowledge additional to what the website is serving up on its own. With the slotted grade-appropriate materials school kids are used to, there comes a point when many of them know everything the materials offer and their time is wasted by looking at the materials further. Boredom sets in, something that will not happen in the virtual presence of the astrophysicists of APOD and Egyptologist of the Theban Project.

The second challenge to established education from the migration of the best knowledge to the Internet is to figure out what to do to make pedagogy work when the knowledge is online. If that is where the knowledge is, how are students escorted there? What justification is left for any nonhuman agent still to be anywhere except on the Internet? Why have a static Egyptian history timeline printed on paper when a magnificent interactive one is available freely online? When does the human teacher ever need to use the old-time knowledge embedded in a lesson plan instead of a digital learning object? Making pedagogy work online must include swinging attention to the Internet-native tools that are natural agents for escorting students to virtual knowledge.

We will return to some of these challenges in Section 6, at the close of this book. For now, it is important to keep in mind that the so-called learning materials that abound online are often primarily pedagogical equipment that was originally conceived to have knowledge embedded in it and not to be used alongside the open knowledge content of the Internet. Even when the resources used in pre-Internet formats are online, the impulse is still very strong for teachers, curriculum writers, and textbook publishers to think of any knowledge they pull in from the Internet as supplementary, as they continue to represent a lot of knowledge in older ways. They thus downgrade their definitional role as pedagogues, as agents to escort their students to knowledge.

If you think that sounds abstract, I hope you will take a minute to look at an astronomy image printed in a book, then look at today's Astronomy Image of the Day online—and then, think again. Making the comparison ignites a whole new approach to what pedagogy may become as the Internet matures and the virtual knowledge ecology emerges more fully.

The ideas in the *Aggregation* section describe how the organization of knowledge changes spontaneously when it is embedded into the Internet. It interlinks on the basis of its meaning—its cognitive content. Cognitive bits of content link to each other in patterns of meaning and form networks.

Both the APOD and the Theban Project websites are networks. The APOD's homepage has a new image every day with text below it linking to related information. When you reach the homepage, you are at a node of the APOD network. When you click a blue, highlighted piece of text, you move to another node, where you will find links to still further nodes.

The Theban Project is more obviously a network structure. On the homepage, navigation bars across the top and bottom offer nodes to enter. Two major associated networks, structured around atlases for the Valley of the Kings and the Theban Necropolis, are featured and two others, "What's New" and "Articles" are offered below the atlases.

There are aspects of the Theban Project website architecture that are pedagogical. The featuring of the two atlases immediately conveys that there are two main areas of knowledge the website interfaces. Entering either of the atlases becomes a highly interactive learning adventure within a multidimensional network.

The underlying pedagogy has to do with the network structure. There is no doubt that the atlases at the Theban Project are networks you experience interactively as you visit nodes and learn their content. The blockbuster pedagogical innovation is that, because ideas are networks, the online network pattern of the atlases seems to be reflecting ideas with which you are directly interfacing as you use the website. This is all virtual but I think very real. It is simple, but powerful, that looking at the homepage display of two atlases tells you there are two networks of knowledge in here. Clicking through one of the atlases, moving as you do there from tomb-to-tomb, mirrors into your mind the geography of the ancient valley.

Can pedagogy be the same thing as what it teaches? The new cognitive networks forming the virtual knowledge ecology seem to be showing that, yes, it can be, at least in a virtual mirror. The reason this could be so is a jumping-off point to a much larger vision. That reason is the fact that human thought and the Internet are structured the same way. They are both networks. An idea is a pattern. A website is a pattern. Idea patterns link to each other to form larger networks of ideas. Websites link to each other to form larger networks within the Internet.

In Idea 80, I take this line of thinking to my conclusion: that the virtual knowledge ecology is becoming one unified, universally accessible reflection of what is known by humankind. Like the blogosphere, this network exists within the Internet. This network is the Grand Idea that belongs to us all. Future education will be devised and executed to take advantage of the grand idea now forming in the virtual knowledge ecology. You will have already been there if you took a look at the APOD and Theban Mapping Project.

33 THE "IT'S ONLY ACCESS" MENTAL BLOCK

The next section of ideas is about access to knowledge on the Internet. Describing this access is a necessary prelude to explaining the greater innovations that it ignited.

The dawning of the new global Golden Age of learning is delayed because people tend to think access is all there is to the Internet's role in learning. Some of the smartest people there are—smart about other things—have frozen their thinking about Internet knowledge at the access stage. If you are afflicted with it, your mental block goes something like this:

> I tell you there are awesome learning assets available on the Internet.
> *You say that you, of course, know that.*
> I begin to lose you the first time when I say that the assets are better than their counterparts in old media.
> *You are thinking of the Internet as one of several places to go to find pretty much the same knowledge: books, libraries, and so forth.*
> I point out that the latest version is usually on the Internet.
> *You soften a little.*
> Then, I tell you that there are great new values to knowledge on the Internet that can only be found on there.
> *You ask me what those could be.*
> I say dynamic knowledge aggregation spawns new ideas and that knowledge emerges spontaneously from the virtual knowledge ecology.
> *Your eyes have glazed over.*

We will get to the spawning of knowledge part in the *Aggregation* section ideas. For now, as you read ideas in the section on *Access*, please remember that what they relate—wonderful as it is—is only the necessary foundation to a much more exciting virtual knowledge ecology emerging from the open content found online.

③

ACCESS

💡 34 THE GREAT CONTENT CASCADE ONTO THE INTERNET

The long and the short of access is that, beginning around 1995, what is known by humankind began cascading onto the Internet and it has not shown signs of ever stopping. By the end of the century, the Internet had become the primary location for knowledge and had begun to spawn knowledge within itself that exists nowhere else.

Many sorts of knowledge cascaded into the Internet. One of the most significant kinds to do so—for its impact on the future of humanity— was the useful knowledge for which education has been the traditional steward and transmitter to new generations. The realization that education is no longer the primary locus of that sort of knowledge, or its primary transmitter, has raised pivotal questions about what education should do about the change and whether education will even exist as a independent institution in the future.

Before any sense can be made of these changes, the story of the cascade itself needs to be told, which I have done in a general way in this section. As Idea 35 relates, I have been closely watching the cascade for a decade. Few, if any, other observers of the cascade of academic knowledge into cyberspace are more qualified than I am as a general observer. The observations in this section are all my own eyewitness accounts.

This section of Ideas tracks the cascade into the Internet of the knowledge of which education has traditionally been the custodian and dispenser. It is a spectacular story of one of the most fundamental changes in human history.

🔅 35 THE AUTHOR'S VANTAGE POINT

Since the summer of 1996, when I saw the Internet for the first time, the primary productive goal of my life has been harnessing the new online medium to improve and spread learning. It may be that I have looked at more web pages with learning content than anyone on earth. Here is how that happened.

After teaching high school for one year in the early 1960s, I quit in frustration. I had experienced the workings of a school, and my conclusion was that I either had to devote the rest of my life to trying to help fix things, or walk away. I took the coward's route and walked.

In 1968, I was hired by Thomas W. Evans, for whom I worked thereafter as his Wall Street law firm secretary until 1992. Evans was prominent in political affairs, as one of Richard Nixon's law partners. He initially hired me out of Texas to work on Nixon's national campaign staff.

During the more than two decades I worked for him, Evans was a national leader in private-sector efforts to improve education. He wrote two books about schools. He was education chairperson of President Reagan's Private Sector Initiatives group and, in that capacity, founded and led for six years a White House–sponsored national and international Symposium on Partnerships in Education. He was invited to be on the Board of Trustees of Teachers College Columbia University and served there for several years as chairman.

As Evans's secretary, to some degree I was in on all of these activities and at the least had a terrific vantage point for observing them. I played a major role in a MENTOR program that Evans founded and headed in the New York City public schools. He dubbed me coordinator, and the management of MENTOR was out of my desk at the law firm from 1982–91. MENTOR paired law firms with high schools—eventually climbing to forty-five pairings in New York and the replication of the program in twenty states. I did most of the direct work with the people in charge on both sides of the pairings. I visited many schools and got to know teachers, principals, and chancellors. A lot of these people became heroes to me, but I was once again appalled by what was not happening for learning in schools.

In 1992, I left my job with Evans as he transitioned from partner to counsel for his law firm. I thought about what to do next and made my decision after reading Lewis J. Perlman's 1992 bestselling book *School's Out.*[1] Perlman said computers were going to cause the education system to implode, and I decided to help. I cashed in my pension and bought top-of-the-line computer hardware and software. After four fairly abortive years, I had learned a lot about operating computers, but the education scene had pretty much passed me by. That was the period when the Internet was gearing up to begin its major emergence. By 1995, I had developed a small desktop multimedia business and was producing brochures, booklets, and illustrations for print.

In the summer of 1996, I got a mailing from the Art Directors Club of New York inviting me, though I was not a member, to register for a luncheon. I accepted, paid a small fee, and attended. One part of the program was a projection of the live Internet onto one of those old-fashioned home movie screens that stood on a tripod. What I could see on the screen, between the heads of the many people at the crowded luncheon, was very ugly text. The connection was intermittent. My life, though, was changed.

I wondered if the Internet could be a better way for students to engage knowledge than the faltering attempts of schools to deliver it to them. I began to do a lot of reading and research. Everything I found fueled my enthusiasm. In August, a few weeks after the luncheon, I began writing an article on my new favorite subject with the intent to submit it to *WIRED* magazine. That article is published for the first time in this book as Appendix 1. *WIRED* did not respond when I submitted the article that fall, and again when I resubmitted it the following winter.

Called "The Cyberschool Cascade," the article describes some events in the early migration of knowledge into the Internet. I have some pride in the fact that much of what I said there has happened. My enthusiasm for the Internet has only increased over the years since I first wrote about the cascade.

By the fall of 1996, I was hooked up to the Internet at my multimedia studio and had begun very primitive projects for websites. I attended a small Internet expo; there were no big ones yet. There was a session by Monsterboard.com where I learned how to look for work online. One December day, I was looking at the Monsterboard and found a part-time writing job posted for JUMBO!.com. I replied. Dick Firestone responded by e-mail that he did not need me, but I kept his e-mail. A few weeks later, I wrote him about a piece of business I could not handle that had come my way to see if he wanted me to refer it to his shop. He responded that he did not, but said "You are my favorite writer." That was nice to get, but we had had no other contact than two e-mails.

On a day in early March, my phone rang. It was Dick Firestone, who yelled, "Get down here. We need you." I took the subway to 34th Street, found the JUMBO!.com operation in a small building on 33rd Street in the shadow of the Empire State Building. Dick hired me to write instructions "a grandmother can understand" for downloading files from the Internet. I had not the slightest idea how to do the downloads and was old enough to be a grandmother. Dick thought I was perfect for the job.

For about a month, I hung out at JUMBO! writing download instructions over and over—told each time by Dick to do a new revision. To this day, zipping and unzipping downloaded software unsettles me. What I did begin to learn was the inside workings of the Internet and websites. For all the chaos that was to ensue from my early entry into the Internet to my exit at the bubble burst, there was never a moment I did not feel like I had found nirvana. This was home and heaven at the same time.

You may be wondering what had happened to my vow to do improve education using computers. The chance to fulfill it, frankly, fell right into my lap. I have my own deeply held theological thoughts on why it happened—and you may think of it as fate or luck. In any event, I got a perfect assignment for what I had hoped to be able to do.

About a month after I first rushed down to 33rd Street, Dick called me into his office. I sat down and looked at him across his desk. He said, "I want you to create a homework channel for JUMBO!, and you will be in charge as senior editor." I am quite sure I had never mentioned my interest in education to Dick. Since that April day in 1997, I have devoted my primary energy to interfacing knowledge within the Internet for students to use to learn. There was huge satisfaction and strength in doing something in which I believed and to which I was and am still committed. My enjoyment of my Internet nirvana has been icing on the cake. I am sure that enjoyment is rooted in the aura of innovation that excited my childhood home, as I described in Idea 5.

The ideas that follow in this section are based on what I started watching as soon as I walked out of Dick's office and have continued to watch ever since. These days, I am hunting out and posting superior links to knowledge in my "Subject Sampler" on my GoldenSwamp.com website. I started doing that exact same thing at JUMBO!.com in April 1997.

Dick told me on the first day to start by making an index, and I asked him what he meant. He said to list all the subjects taught in school, like math, chemistry, and so forth. The homework channel would then have links to all the web pages I could find for each of the subjects. That was a natural for JUMBO!.com, which was a website made up of channels of the kinds of files that could be downloaded for free from the Internet. There were channels for clipart, fonts, games, screensavers, sounds— and many more sorts of digital files. Why not math, chemistry, and so forth? I am sure I got a lot of clarity from beginning to participate in online education from the perspective of channels by school subject, applying JUMBO!'s method of channels for various kinds of files.

Throughout the remainder of 1997, and continuously until May 2001, I directed the knowledge-collecting project Dick assigned to me that day in his office. By the fall of 1997, the homework channel was getting a lot of hits. Dick decided even more traffic could be stimulated by creating an e-mail newsletter. I got one of his calls one afternoon saying he wanted me to write a weekly Top 5 newsletter, reviewing five subject links. From September 1997 until May 2001, I wrote the newsletter, which was increased about halfway along to the Top 8. I had to find, evaluate, pick, and describe five (then eight) really excellent learning links every week. Doing the newsletter forced me to focus on creative and excellent work being done in building open-content learning web pages. In the rest of this *Access* section, I describe a lot of what I saw in the process over those years.

I began to get some staff help in early 1998, and by the summer of 2000, about twenty graduate students and two Ph.D.s had worked for me, mostly part time, finding, evaluating, and organizing links in their knowledge-subject specialties. By that time we had created interlinked packets of 35,000 study subjects incorporating 150,000 open content links to study subjects. The interlinking we did caused surprising things to happen, which I later realized were glimpses of the virtual knowledge ecology. Describing those here is getting ahead of the cascade story, which had to take place before the virtual knowledge ecology could emerge. My early sightings of virtual knowledge ecology behavior at HomeworkCentral.com are described in Idea 59.

The name of what started as a JUMBO!.com homework channel changed: HomeworkHeaven.com, NoSweat.com, and settled finally on HomeworkCentral.com. Eventually, HomeworkCentral.com got bigger than JUMBO!.com, which was then sold to Jupitermedia, leaving the once homework channel as a website and business unto itself. Soon after it became independent of JUMBO!, the new HomeworkCentral.com company was purchased by BigChalk.com and integrated into a new website by that name. BigChalk.com was folded into ProQuest in 2003. In June 2004, ProQuest took HomeworkCentral.com offline. About eight months after it went online in early 2000, BigChalk.com began to jettison the management of the companies it had aggregated. My exit came in May 2001. It had been, as Dick Firestone predicted it would be when things began to take off in the early days, quite a ride!

In the ensuing years, I have continued to watch, learn about, and write about online knowledge. The description of the cascade that follows is my eyewitness account. I will never know if I really have looked at more web pages with learning content than anyone on earth. That does not matter. What does matter is what I saw.

36 HEWLETT FOUNDATION INITIATIVE

In the fall of 2004, I received an invitation to a meeting at the William and Flora Hewlett Foundation in Menlo Park, California, in the heart of Silicon Valley. When I arrived, I found myself in the beating heart of the open content for learning movement. It was both a thrill and an honor to mingle with the founders, pioneers, and edge-cutters of what I would argue is now a key impetus for global learning.

Grants have been made by the Hewlett Foundation for significant open content initiatives, whose representatives attended the meeting and reported on their programs. The foundation's website at Hewlett.org has details. The rest of the two-day meeting was devoted to the exchange of ideas by this truly remarkable gathering of creative innovators. Participating was, for me, a rocket sled ride into the future of a phenomenon that I had been focusing on for nearly a decade. It was also affirmation that the cascade of content I had been so hands-on in assisting was only the first stage of a bigger change. The people at Hewlett were fully at work on the next phase: shaping open digital content into new forms.

The meeting had a character similar to the small Internet expo I had attended eight years earlier. Great big ideas had been born, and the people who were present at the creation were in attendance. I learned a great deal from them and was both awed and heartened by their vision and accomplishments.

In a nutshell, they are leading the opening of the knowledge content of the academic world into the open Internet, where students across the planet can use it freely. There is more about who they are and exactly what they are doing in Idea 55. From my perspective, I was grateful for a firsthand look at a great new stage of the cascade of what is known by humankind into the virtual knowledge ecology.

37 TECHNOLOGY WAS THE FIRST NECESSARY STEP FOR ACCESS

The awful text quality and repeated disconnects that marred the Internet when I first saw it in the summer of 1996 were offset at that time by the excitement of seeing a brand new baby medium barely out of the womb. Like an infant animal, including us humans, not only cognitive improvements were needed. Like a living baby, the physical development was a lengthy and complicated process.

The Internet had to learn to crawl before it could walk. Soon, it was toddling and growing like a weed. Coordination improved, and it fell down less frequently. The Internet was physically a robust adolescent by the turn of the century and has continued to mature in dependability and the acquisition of skills.

The Internet's cognitive development is, remarkably, a similar parallel to the maturation of an animal's physical and mental growth. It is also true that, like the mind, the Internet will be capable of learning long after it physically matures.

The Internet is not through developing physically, including both in size and technical sophistication. Around 15 percent of the world's population was using the Internet in 2004. My bet would be 90 percent will be within another decade. Broadband has improved, but will get far better still. Devices for interfacing the Internet are becoming more diverse and able to do more. As Idea 57 discusses, mobile, ubiquitous computing is on the horizon.

The physical development, which is usually lumped under the word technology, was a necessary first step for the Internet. Technology is, however, separate from content. What you think about takes place in your physical brain, but it is not your physical brain. Yes, possibly synaptic changes are necessary for you to know that $2 + 2 = 4$—but whether or not your brain changes, or you even have a brain, $2 + 2$ will always equal 4.

The virtual knowledge ecology consists of stuff like $2 + 2 = 4$ that is the open content of the Internet. The physical things that make up the Internet are absolutely necessary for the virtual knowledge ecology and its open content to be available there. But $2 + 2 = 4$ is knowledge content that can be found in other media, including books and your brain. For the past decade, knowledge like $2 + 2 = 4$ has been cascading on to the Internet. The following Ideas tell that story. The following section, *Aggregation*, explains how the cascade ignited the explosion causing the virtual knowledge ecology. But next, we must begin with the cascade because that is where the story starts.

38 WHAT KNOWLEDGE IS

The word *knowledge* is a real troublemaker in Internet lingo. The old word knowledge has been applied to so many types of online information that its pre-Internet meanings for learning are badly diluted.

On a deeper level, there have always been profound questions about the meaning of knowledge. Epistemology is a venerable branch of philosophy devoted to those questions. There are also pedagogical battles over the meaning of knowledge. For the purposes of this book, common sense is going to be more useful than philosophy.

One of the basic purposes of education is for students to gain knowledge. The virtual knowledge ecology is formed by content openly available and consisting of the kind of knowledge an education aims to impart and students aim to acquire. In this book, the knowledge that is herein called open content is the kind of knowledge that education is meant to impart and those seeking education hope to acquire.

Academic knowledge is a term often used to mean the sort of knowledge involved in education. But academy relates to school, so that academic knowledge has built right into the term the implication of having to learn it at school. The Internet has now become the primary location of the knowledge once controlled by the education establishment—by the academy. It is useful to look a bit deeper into the independence of knowledge from the academy.

The word *knowledge* has a traditional meaning that tends to get lost in the Information Age. The knowledge content that is the subject of these ideas is useful knowledge, which is that traditional meaning. But what it that? Sorting out what useful knowledge is, and thus identifying the content we are talking about, takes some doing.

Knowledge management was coined as a phrase in the Internet world as something different from information management. In referring to it in the Information Age, the word knowledge means a special sort of information. Often, it is the assets of an organization, such as a corporation, including what is in the organization's records and what its people know and know how to do.

Perhaps there was some confusion as to the meaning of the word *knowledge* as far back as the seventeenth century. Benjamin Franklin and other early luminaries of the American Philosophical Society did not simply say their interest was knowledge. They called it *useful knowledge* and said that they pursued equally: "all philosophical Experiments that let Light into the Nature of Things, tend to increase the Power of Man over Matter, and multiply the Conveniencies or Pleasures of Life." To become learned was to acquire such useful knowledge.

In the seventeenth century, useful knowledge that came under the definition of philosophical included sciences, humanities, arts, technologies, and the contemplation that is still called philosophy in our time.

All of the sorts of knowledge meant by the word *philosophical* in Ben Franklin's time were included in what he meant by *useful knowledge*.

The phrase *academic knowledge* has become a way of designating the sort of subjects that Franklin's crowd thought of as philosophy. As mentioned above, that does not work very well, especially any more, because it defines knowledge by what schools (academies) teach. By all means, schools should be teaching things that "let Light into the Nature of Things, tend to increase the Power of Man over Matter and multiply the Conveniencies or Pleasures of Life." But the education establishment does not define or own these intellectual bailiwicks—no one does. We each have every right to learn them on our own during school years and throughout our lives.

The Internet has become the primary location of all the kinds of knowledge mentioned above and many other sorts of knowledge and information. What is referred to in these ideas as open content is the same stuff the American Philosophical Society called useful knowledge. It is what is discussed in Idea 2 as what is known by humankind. That stuff is the knowledge content of the virtual knowledge ecology, as it is called in this book.

Content is an old word, too. It is burdened with the confusion of having two completely different meanings that depend on its context. When I was contentmaster at HomeworkCentral.com, I put a sign over the entrance to our department: *We Are Content*. In the Internet world, content is derived from the idea of what the Internet contains, and that can be a lot of different stuff. For our purpose, content is written, visual, sound, design, concept, and other cognitive stuff accessible from the Internet. The definition includes the new knowledge that emerges from the dynamic behavior of the content within the network ecology of the virtual knowledge ecology.

39 KNOWLEDGE MOVED

The major and tacit reason for education has been to deliver knowledge. Whether or not it has been successful in that delivery in the past does not matter anymore. The new question is how can education be expected to deliver something it no longer possesses? Knowledge has moved onto the Internet.

Established education no longer controls the primary substance of what its students are supposed to be learning. That substance has been liberated from geography. Knowledge now flows in the limitless Internet, where it is mixed, enriched, and evolves freely as the virtual knowledge ecology.

In the latter years of the twentieth century, knowledge picked up and moved out of books, libraries, laboratories, archives, and every other traditional knowledge nook and cranny into the digital medium. As the Internet emerged in the late 1990s, the digital knowledge repositories began to interconnect online. The most complete, fresh, and authentic knowledge now emerges dynamically from open content within the Internet—a process that is quickly expanding with the swelling Internet. The knowledge continues to refine itself and to grow in further levels of detail.

The assumption that the knowledge students are expected to learn during the years they are in school is available both at school and on the Internet is false. What the schools now offer is very much less knowledge, knowledge less connected to related information and often knowledge that is stale. This increasingly serious defect in schooling is new and worsening. It is irreversible. It is a final nail in the coffin of education as we knew it in the twentieth century. Education operations had always been developed around the location of knowledge. In the American Old West, a schoolteacher was picked and an often one-room building with a bell on top was built by the townspeople. The teacher would ring the bell to gather the children of the town around her (sometimes him). The knowledge the children came to the school to learn was located in the teacher's head and in usually a few books and wall pictures in the building with the bell on top.

A church I once belonged to has a long history in New York City. In the middle of the nineteenth century, the women of the church formed Sunday schools for the immigrant children who worked during the week in factories. On Sundays, the children came to the church's schools to learn English, reading, writing, and arithmetic. They came because the women had that knowledge to teach them these basics—along, I feel sure, with some lessons from the Good Book.

Even private tutors worked on the same principle. They contained knowledge in their heads and supplied students, or directed them, to books where knowledge was to be found.

Through centuries and cultures, the idea of schools as places of education and learning has assumed those who attend will find knowledge there. That principle includes, of course, colleges and universities. It also includes libraries. Great libraries have been the mark of great cities. Public libraries have been taken to neighborhoods to distribute knowledge geographically.

The great content cascade described in the following section is the story of the movement of knowledge out of geographic locations to a virtual place for which geography will become irrelevant. Knowledge accessed from the Internet can be accessed from any geographic location to which the Internet is transmitted. It can be accessed by anyone located where the Internet is transmitted, if the person has a receiving device. When the entire planet is painted with access and each person on earth has a device, geography will cease to be relevant at all to Internet access.

Universal access is a stunning concept, and one that is becoming a reality, as what is being called ubiquitous computing. It is important, though, to get past the idea that the Internet is just a new location to access knowledge. That it is, but access is only a first step toward something better.

40 WHY KNOWLEDGE ACCESSED IN THE VIRTUAL KNOWLEDGE ECOLOGY IS SUPERIOR

Knowledge moved and, for learning, that has turned out to be a very good thing. Content for human learning that you access online retains all the good qualities it has when you find it in print, film/video, broadcast media, and elsewhere—plus the online content is superior in several ways.

An example of where the online advantages are obvious is the Nature Genome Gateway at Nature.com. Although most of Nature.com's articles are inaccessible without a paid subscription, the Genome Gateway is offered by the journal to the public at no cost. The Gateway is wonderful open content for learning.

Online knowledge is superior to print and film/video because it can be updated swiftly and continuously. This quick updating is obviously crucial for a field like genetics, which changes almost every day. Other academic fields, though, can no longer excuse a sloppy attitude toward keeping what students use current. The events of 9/11 sent a chill of obsolescence through every textbook on modern history, culture, and political science. The tsunami of 2004 did the same for many earth science subjects. The time is overdue to abandon textbooks, if only for their pervasive obsolescence in an era when we can finally do something about that.

The same is true for the quality of the authority where students go to learn knowledge. Nature.com's Genome Gateway is created, monitored, and used by top experts in the knowledge of website interfaces. The U.S. Library of Congress offers eclectic access to original documents from American history and literature. The British Library has a feature called "Treasures in Full," with free digital editions of Shakespeare, Chaucer, and much more. Museums, laboratories, professors—experts in the full range of human knowledge—are directly interfacing what they know online. This form and degree of authority for what students can use to learn make secondary authority outmoded.

Online knowledge is superior to older interfaces because the interface itself is cognitively more forceful. A web page can integrated several media into presenting and explaining an idea. Text, images, video, and sound are all available. Although some compelling beginning work has been rolled out, integrating multimedia to express concepts of science, history, and other fields, as the saying goes *we ain't seen nothing yet*. As the march toward greater broadband and ubiquitous computing continues, digital multimedia expression interface will increasingly outshine the dreary print pages of education's past.

A fourth and fabulous superiority of online knowledge for learning is interactivity. A student can tell a web page to do something and get a response. A web page can ask a student to do something and react to a response. The web page is hardly as smart as Socrates, but there is a cognitive exchange. As with multimedia, the possibilities for learning what interactivity holds are just beginning to emerge.

In Idea 78, we will return to the subject of the superiority of online knowledge to add into the mix the quantum superiority of networked knowledge. The four superior qualities discussed above apply simply to accessing one web page—one node of what is almost always a large relevant network. As discussed in the *Aggregation* section, the network takes learning into an entirely new venue.

You may be musing now that the ideal medium for acquiring knowledge is from a living, expert human teacher. I certainly agree that is true. To have walked and talked with Socrates in the sunshine of Golden Age Greece would have been the best of all possible ways to learn ideas. Just as I can, you are probably able to recall moments in your own learning experiences when a living person was teaching you, and the unsurpassable experience of interchange from mind-to-mind occurred. I would argue, however, that when Socrates is not around, the virtual knowledge ecology is the next best thing.

41 OPEN CONTENT ONLY IS ACCESSED FROM THE VIRTUAL KNOWLEDGE ECOLOGY

Open is an old word that now designates one of the most fundamental new Internet issues and trends. There is a great deal of discussion of open source, open access, open network, and the like. The virtual knowledge ecology is comprised of open content for learning. Open is used in all of these phrases in the same sense it is used for a tennis or golf tournament: Anybody can participate, as discussed in Idea 3.

As the term is used for content on the Internet, open applies to one of only two states. Either content is open or it is not open. Being a little bit open does not work. Degrees and costs of getting into content that is not open are irrelevant. The reason this is so is mechanical. Only nodes of free and accessible content can link to and from other nodes in the virtual knowledge ecology. It is the linking that counts most when it comes to knowledge.

It has become increasingly clear, as knowledge content for learning has become accessible on the Internet, that only open content participates in networking that counts. Content must be open for it to be able to network with related content, thereby enriching and refining all of the knowledge involved. Content that is open experiences peer review and can be enriched by the wiki effect, where experts edit and augment it. Open content's most important cognitive aspect is that it is free to participate in dynamic networks. Content that is not open is externally static. These mechanics will be further elaborated in other Ideas.

There remain many virtual knowledge content web pages locked away and distributed only for pay. Some are on educational institution websites for the exclusive use of faculty and tuition-paying students and individuals. Others are owned by large and small for-profit enterprises that sell content to schools and individuals. Another large amount of knowledge content is available for pay from online periodicals. There are other closed-off repositories of several kinds.

Nevertheless, the open content that is forming the virtual knowledge ecology is comprehensive for K–12 through undergraduate studies. As I have watched the open content knowledge coming online now for nearly a decade, it has steadily and consistently become generally complete and then increasingly rich to increasingly deeper levels of detail.

I believe the proprietary knowledge folks (who sell knowledge) lost their battle to dominate online content for learning several years ago. In Idea 7, I mention the limitations of the closed online content of *Encyclopaedia Britannica* and describe finding superior content to that published in a *Nature* journal article. The justification for shutting off content for those examples, and for most closed content on the Internet, is for the hosts to be able to pay for producing the content. There would be nothing untoward about that, if it actually made the content superior.

The reason the future of knowledge content is an open one is not about money. It is about content quality. Content that is closed off loses cognitive value because it is isolated. The network structure of the Internet has radically added cognitive value to knowledge assets by connecting them to each other, and that cannot happen unless they are open. When they connect openly, the whole becomes more than the sum of the parts. When content is left out of the network, it does not participate in the dynamic whole. Instead, it withers, goes stale, and becomes irrelevant.

The *Life* magazine article on Stalin I used in high school in 1953 is not readily available for linking into the dynamic network a student would make in 2005 to study the subject. ProQuest offers its subscribers issues of *Life* as far back as the 1980s and perhaps further. I am not sure, because without a subscription I could not look through the content of a site like ProQuest. The search engine spiders have the same problem I did, so they do not report content that is closed away in proprietary websites. If the *Life* article that I used in 1953 on Stalin's purges is available only in closed content, the spiders cannot find it, and it does not show up when someone uses a search engine to do Internet research.

Several ads returned on a Google search I made for *Life* magazine offered old issues as far back as the 1950s for sale in hardcopy. To link to the article I studied back then into research I might do on the purges now, I would have to figure out the date of the *Life* issue where the article appeared, probably from a library service. I would then have to get my hands on a printed version of that issue and scan the pages displaying the article. I could then put the scans of those pages on to my website.

I might bother to dig up the old article because I remember it, but a high school student researching Stalin's purges today would neither find it nor know it existed. There are plenty of excellent open content sources for the purges. Two of the best ones, which I quickly found with a search engine, are from The History Guide and the Library of Congress.

My recollection of the *Life* article is that it contained excellent and detailed accounts of the purges and their perpetrators. I suppose if it were available to link into a dynamic network researching the purges today, it would add nuances from the 1950s that would be interesting. The article could still participate and contribute as open content. The factual material it contains would not be missing because other more recent open content does a thorough job of presenting the history.

The open content that is readily findable easily duplicates content that is closed off, and the open content is dynamically linked to newer material and refreshed by its authors and users. Closed content, meanwhile, is diminished in its isolation.

42 WHY OPEN CONTENT IS A BARGAIN

Can content gold be coined for free? Yes. Somewhere in this section, you might expect to find the history of great amounts of money being raised and spent to move content online and to create magnificent websites for learning. The economics of open content for learning are quite the opposite. Costs are infinitesimal, especially when measured against usage and coverage.

The trick to understanding the economics of websites for learning is to forget the economics of textbooks. All of these textbook publishing factors are gone: printing thousands of books, selling them to hundreds of schools, shipping them for broad geographical distribution, and expecting to replace them when they wear out. The sections of knowledge content that would be collected into a textbook can be instead made into websites. Publishing a textbook costs thousands of dollars. Creating a website using the same content as the textbook is cheap, virtually free, or generates an income by attracting visitors to related profitable web pages.

The table of elements is an example of a small piece of the content found in every basic chemistry textbook that appeared online in the early 1990s as open content. A table of elements digitized is better than anything that can be printed in a book or on a wall chart to learn the subject because the digital version is an interactive table. A student can click on oxygen or cadmium or rhenium to open a page with details for the element.

Three such tables occupy the top spots in the major search results today. One is maintained by Los Alamos Laboratory, the second began several years ago as an eighth-grade science project, and the third is hosted by the University of Sheffield in England and has been online since 1993.

The cost of the Los Alamos table was once absorbed by the Los Alamos budget. The table's cost now is close to nil since it has not been changed much, if at all, since 2003 and is displayed on the laboratory's website. The former science project guy is now accepting a few ads to help with the small cost, which he underwrites personally, to keep the site online. The university table has links to a bookstore, which probably means money is being made offsetting any website costs by selling books to visitors who find the store by using the table. Hundreds of thousands of people have studied chemistry using these web pages. The maintenance cost is negligible and the cognitive gains significant.

As she states in a letter to her users posted on Luminarium.org, the website is a labor of love by Anniina Jokinen. An early jewel of open content, begun in 1996, Luminarium has been entered to study medieval seventeenth-century English literature by multiple thousands of students. No one has paid to use it and Ms. Jokinen states that it makes no profit. The site connects to Luminarium Poster Store operated in affiliation with AllPosters.com. Hopefully, profits from sales of the handsome posters help to underwrite the costs of maintaining the website. Those cost are very small for an established web collection displaying a subject as stable as literature from a distant time.

An Internet project coordination entity called Learner.org, funded by the Annenberg Foundation, has built and operates many outstanding units of open content for learning. One of their big ones is Journey North, through which monarch butterflies, hummingbirds, tulip gardens, and other spring migrations are tracked online. The project provides sharing and tracking of observations by K–12 students across North America. Begun in 1995, the project's scope and participation have increased annually. Underwritten philanthropically, Journey North costs the education sector nothing.

There is a lot of variety in the economics of different websites that qualify for the virtual knowledge ecology by their excellence in learning content. The big picture to keep in mind is that every one of the examples is free to use—is open content.

The purpose of taking a brief economic side trip here is to point out that focusing on where the money is coming from does not give us a focus at all. The future of learning has moved to the Internet, where knowledge is not going to cost much. That shift is downright surreal compared to the over $4 billion the United States alone spends annually on textbooks.

In fact, the burst of the Internet bubble a few years back was caused in part by trying to spend too much money on education online content. Big studios with overpaid staffs did not produce any online content more compelling than the beautiful work like the popular tables of elements, Luminarium, or Journey North. Museums produce elaborate websites using their own funds and placing superb open content online that has the authoritative commentary of their curators. The companies that spent big dollars to create content for sale could not make their products either as authoritative or handsome as the work of the museums. No one has figured out how to get users to pay for expensive learning websites when the open content is at least as good and often better.

One key to why websites offering knowledge are not hard to develop is the knowledge itself is the value of the website. It is the chemical elements that make the online tables interesting, the poetry of Chaucer that leaves the Luminarium visitor enriched, and the migrating Monarchs who inform the children.

Another fundamental reason the cost of open content can be negligible is that it is inherently cheap to create and maintain in ratio to its use. Even if an overpriced studio managed to charge $50,000 to build a website, that comes to only $1 per student after 50,000 students visit it, and a penny a kid after 500,000. Websites containing many kinds of content—like the structure of the solar system or how fractions work—often do not change much or at all over long periods of time, extending their value and making them cheaper still.

There is an open content alchemy, converting old media versions of knowledge into golden open content for essentially no cost. There will never again be an expensive and powerful content-producing industry. Diverse and scattered experts who know their fields best will generate open content—as they have been doing now for a decade. When all students are connected to the Internet, they will each be able to learn from the top authorities in the field they are studying, and to do so for free. That is a breathtaking bargain.

43 LITERACY AND LANGUAGE

Obviously, a person must know how to read in order to acquire more than a minimal education. Ubiquitous computing will, I think, cause universal literacy. There is no question here whether the chicken or the egg comes first. Getting someone up to speed using a mobile computer that accesses the Internet and making that machine their own will allow and cause that person to learn to read.

Waiting to give someone Internet access until he can read is backward. Interacting with the Internet through his own computer both motivates him to read and gives him material to master. He can learn to read what he wants and needs to read, yet have no limit to the resources for advancing his skills and knowledge. He is connected and the resources are interconnected. This is a huge contrast to struggling in a literacy class, often with limited reading materials and a teacher whose own literacy is limited.

There is a WI-FI project in five remote villages in Nepal that has allowed farmers to communicate with each other between villages that are unconnected by roads. Their laptops connect them to the Internet to obtain weather and crop information. It is a fair assumption that using the computers motivates farmers to learn to read what they need to know. And they get something much more. They and their families now have the full range of human knowledge at their fingertips.

Common sense tells us that at least some, and probably many, of the villagers are improving their reading skills by using their laptops. The villages are also planning to use their Internet access as the base for distance learning. Literacy has become for them not an isolated project but an integrated aspect of their commerce, society, and education.

The volume and quality of reading material suddenly available to the Nepal villagers is a huge change. Before they had the Internet, perhaps a newspaper now and then would arrive in a village. What else would a literate person have to read? Probably not much. The villages are separated from each other by a two or more days' walk. Getting to a library or bookstore would be a very rare event for one of these people.

There are neighborhoods even in the most developed cities around the world where quality reading material is almost as scarce and unattainable. In any environment, having a computer with Internet access provides reading material ranging from the daily news, to stories of every kind, to science, technology, and virtually everything else a person might want to read. (Yes, the slimy stuff too.) The reader can pick what interests him and choose material at his own reading level. The Internet is an unlimited resource for reading practice.

Internet interfaces can also be created that assist people in learning to read. An example is Starfall.com, a free public service with learning and practice tutorials that help teach children to read. The incentive both to learn to read and to provide open content that teaches people to read will multiply as more individuals go online.

Literacy and learning require materials to read in a language the reader can understand. For everyone to be able to use the emerging global knowledge commons that is forming the virtual knowledge ecology, one of two things has to happen. First, everybody needs to learn a single language, and all the content of the commons has to be in that language. Perhaps many think that language will be English. Looking now toward Asia's emergence, perhaps Mandarin and Hindi are in the running. The other possibility is that the content has to be interfaced with the ability of the reader to see it in his or her own language.

Nepal languages provide an example of the challenges multiple languages raise for a knowledge commons. Nepali, an Indo-European language, and Bhasa, a language of the Sino-Tibetan group, are both spoken in Nepal, with Nepali the official language. Published in Kathmandu, the *Nepali Times* has online versions in English and in Nepali. A visitor can toggle between the two versions by clicking an icon in the masthead. On my computer, I cannot see anything but the pictures in the Nepali version, accompanied by strings of question marks substituted for the Nepali text. If I downloaded and installed the Nepali font, the question marks would be replaced by the language's script, repeating in Nepali the material I can read in the English version.

The *Nepali Times* homepage links to BBCNapali.com, which provides world news in the Nepali language. The BBC publishes an online section of world news in forty-three languages.

A farmer or student in the isolated Nepal villages can use the village WI-FI connections to read the *Nepali Times* and the BBC news in English or Nepali or both. If the villagers know only the Bhasa language, the news pages would provide no more than reading practice if they were attempting to learn English or Nepali.

There are several trends toward making Internet knowledge accessible by conforming what language people know to the content they study. We have been looking at one of them: cloning a website in more than one language. The Louvre Museum in Paris, for example, offers its gorgeous website in Français, English, Español, and Japanese. It is a much smaller task to translate an existing website than it is to build one from scratch. For an elaborate site like the Louvre's, clones in different languages make a lot of sense.

Neuroscience for Kids has been a pace-setting website for learning since 1996. It is the work of Eric H. Chudler of the University of Washington. As is his admirable habit, Dr. Chudler gives us a look at the future by having portions of the website available in Spanish, Slovene, Chinese, Portuguese, Italian, Korean, and Turkish.

Cloaked though it is in advertising, HowStuffWorks.com is one of the most broadly useful knowledge websites online. It contains many explanations of practical mechanics, electronics, and the like that would be very helpful to people like the farmers of the remote Nepal villages. For the farmers to use HowStuffWorks.com, either the site must be translated into Nepali or the farmers need to learn English. My guess is that when most of the people in Nepal have Internet access, many sites like HowStuffWorks.com will be translated into Nepali and many other languages.

With around six thousand languages existing on our planet, it seems highly unlikely that every website will be translated into every language. It also seems highly unlikely that, when most of the people around the world are connected to the Internet, they will settle for not being able to use it because they cannot read what it says. Demand will be a big factor in determining which sites are translated into which languages. Clearly, the BBC already thinks there is sufficient demand for news in forty-three languages.

Even as recently as when I was in college in the 1950s, when books were printed in English, if they included a quotation from something written in French, the quotation was usually not translated. The reader was expected to know French. Latin phrases also often appeared without translation. Steadily since that time, English has become the language of science, technology, and other fields.

English has also dominated the Internet early on for the logical reason that the Internet first expanded mainly in English-speaking countries. Today, with the explosive expansion of industry in Asia and communications everywhere, language dominance may be up for grabs. It will be fascinating to watch what happens.

A major factor that has only begun to impact the language facility for reading Internet content is software translators now moving down the development pipe. The day is not far off when the text of HowStuffWorks.com can be fed into one end of a computer and come out the other end in Napali or Bhasa. This new translation power may leave individuals with the choice of remaining fluent in only one language. It is hard to know what will happen a decade from now.

A final point about the Internet and languages is a wonderful piece of serendipity. The Internet came along at just the right time as a possible way to stem the global trend toward the extinction of many dialects and languages. Penetration of once isolated areas of the planet, broadcast media, and rapid transportation had, for more than a century, been eliminating the usefulness of once geographically isolated languages. Today, these languages are beginning to be recorded virtually on the Internet. Efforts are under way to preserve disappearing languages, although it is going to take a lot more work in many locales.

44 THE CONTAINER IS NOT THE CONTENT

I confess I could never figure out what Marshall McLuhan meant by "the medium is the message." Experts on McLuhan say he did not mean that the message should be ignored; he did not mean that the conveyance that delivers that content is either the same thing or equally of value. The radio over which I heard Hitler's voice in 1943 was not the message of his ranting. The plasma screen and the broadcast signal are not the Super Bowl the crowd is watching in the sports bar; the screen and the signal are oblivious to the fact that the Patriots are winning.

It is equally true that the web page and the digital image are not the message you see when you look at Leonardo da Vinci's "Madonna and Child (Madonna Litta)" on the website of the Hermitage in St. Petersburg, Russia. The content is the painting. Splitting hairs is not useful here. The actual painting is, of course, in St. Petersburg, not on your monitor screen. However, a lot of knowledge about that painting is interfaced and thereby accessible to you on your screen. You can access further knowledge by reading the text below the image.

The monumental confusion in the field of Internet learning rests on the habit of educators of making little distinction between the medium and the message. Lesson plans, courses, and learning objects are often referred to as learning content. These items are definitely content themselves that is contained on web pages. But instead of being knowledge, they are a sort of content that contains knowledge.

This may seem like I am splitting hairs, but calling containers open content for learning has been a severe detriment to the blossoming of online learning from within education . The problem is that it has been tempting to reposition predigital containers like lesson plans online and then look around for knowledge to stick into the container's slots. Online knowledge is text, images, sound, animation, and other interfaces that convey and express cognitive meaning. Knowledge expands online by connecting related bits, as the *Aggregation* section explains. Lesson plans are teaching equipment that can include knowledge bits inserted and sequenced into the procedures. Mixing the two approaches squelches the online knowledge and emaciates the lesson plan.

The ideas described next are about different ways that knowledge is contained and pointed to so it can be accessed. As the word *container* implies, they hold content like the voice of Hitler, the Super Bowl, and da Vinci's painting. It is by interfacing through these containers that a student, or any of us, comes in contact with the knowledge.

I belabor the point somewhat because the education establishment has been quick to say that online education content is not effective in conveying knowledge to students. I am convinced that much of the ineffectiveness lies in the media that education has used and not in the knowledge to be found. In evaluating the Internet as an education source, the distinction between the medium and the message (the knowledge) must be made.

45 DIRECT, INDIVIDUAL ACCESS

The Mars rovers named *Spirit* and *Opportunity* are space heroes of 2004–2005. They have an extensive website called Mars Exploration Rover Mission, created and maintained by the Jet Propulsion Laboratory (JPL) at the California Institute of Technology and hosted at NASA.gov.

The Rovers Mission website as a whole and many of its parts are all and each examples of a very common type of online knowledge that is created for a general audience outside of the education establishment. The relationship of the Rovers Mission website to education is actually the reverse of education establishment control: the JPL has prepared education materials to offer to schools and students.

The core of the Rovers Mission website is knowledge about the rovers for the general public. There are mini-internal networks with detailed information on the rovers' mission, science, technology, and people, plus a multimedia section with images and video. Ongoing news is provided and there is a "Flight Director's Updates" box with a link to the latest report and earlier postings backward into the history of the mission.

The first of the four kinds of access described in this brief series of ideas is the web page itself, when that web page is a container of knowledge that is designed for education only secondarily or not at all. There is a wide, deep, and rich spectrum of knowledge that is maintained on the Internet for its own sake. All it takes is a little experience in finding it. You can easily figure out how to reach the knowledge directly and on you own. A great deal of the knowledge you will find has nothing to do with the education establishment and schools.

WebMd.com—discussed more in Idea 53—and similar websites provide comprehensive information on diseases. Weather websites provide current weather conditions, satellite images, and records for hundreds of cities around the world. The USGS covers earth science in depth, and NASA covers the sweep of space sciences. Museums have poured the arts online, offering great beauty manifested in magnificent digital images and accompanied by expert commentary. History has become a standard website section for countries, localities, sciences, businesses, and many other sectors of society. Great and lesser authors have outstanding website tributes to their work accompanied by comprehensive archives, prepared and hosted online by coteries of their admirers and scholars. Information on the workings of governments, legislation, and the courts is available at the source. See, for example, the Library of Congress website called Thomas.

These and similar web locations for much of what was once thought of as academic knowledge are very often no longer housed in academies (schools). However, a very great deal of first-rate knowledge is based at university and college websites, but when that knowledge is open content, as much of it is, its use is not controlled by those academies.

The kind of websites mentioned above are designed and organized along the connections of the ideas within the knowledge itself—not on some progression over time that has been figured out as a classroom or curriculum sequence. The goal in how they are authored is to facilitate the individual visitor in finding and exploring the knowledge for herself.

The author of a WebMD web page for a disease struggled to create a page where a visitor can get the knowledge on her own. He tried to think of other ideas that his content would bring to her mind or would help her understand the disease, and then he connected to those with interactive links. The web authors at USGS, NASA, museums, literature websites, and government pages all take that same approach. A great deal of the most creative and effective learning material is put online by noneducators and aimed directly at the individual visitor to the website.

46 SEARCH ENGINES AS ACCESS

When I am looking for open content knowledge, I think of using a search engine as a place to start—a place to find an entry point that will lead me into an open network of the particular knowledge I am seeking. Getting to the knowledge I am looking for is a two-step process when I use a search engine.

As an example, using the most popular search engine Google, for my first step I entered the words *elephant anatomy* in the search box and pressed Return on my keyboard. In 0.26 seconds, Google displayed a list of about 144,000 web pages. The order of the pages was established by the vaunted Google algorithm—its confidential formula for calculating which website the most people looking for elephant anatomy have used or linked to it in the past.

In step two, I clicked on the link at the top of the list. That took me to the anatomy page of a website titled Elephant Information Repository. The center of the page had a large photograph of the profile of an elephant, with clickable labels for: brain, ears, tusks, teeth, trunk, feet, skin, hair, and internal system. Below the interactive photograph was this invitation: *The Elephant Anatomy: A detailed resource for learning about a part of the elephant. Don't be shy, click on "Harry" the elephant and explore.*

A navigation bar across the bottom of the page underneath a long, small silhouette of a herd of elephants included a link to the website's "Link Page." That page offers eight categories of elephant links, along with this text invitation: *Please click on one of the categories provided to browse the hundreds of links to elephant and other related sites around the world!*

The interlinking offered to the visitor by the Elephant Information Repository makes step two very different from step one. The search engine offered a list of websites that contained the two words *elephant* and *anatomy*. I put those words into quotation marks like this *"elephant anatomy,"* thus limiting the search to finding only that exact phrase, instead of instances where the two words appeared near each other, and searched again. That time Google only found about 5,230 web pages and the Elephant Information Repository appeared as the second, not the first, link on the Google list.

In step two, as a visitor to the Repository, I am in an environment created by humans who know a lot about elephants. My confidence is heightened by knowing Google put it on the top of its list, because humans who are looking for elephant information choose to look at and link to the Repository most often. All of that suggests that the anatomy information is going to be trustworthy. It means something else that summarizes the stunning new research and learning power of the Internet: The links list that the Repository offers is chosen by people who know about elephants.

A search engine is a sort of secondary knowledge container that tells its user that the links it contains might be what he is looking for. Search engine listings are picked from the chaos of the Internet by software spiders who can only see text and identify words. The order of the search engine results are determined by a mathematical algorithm, which ranks web pages by how often they are used, which is a secondary way of harnessing the visitors' choices. Interconnections among web pages that contain open content for learning are made directly as the choices of experts in the area of knowledge they interface.

If you visit the Repository, you will see that it has a strong bias toward elephant conservation. As a teacher or student, it is important to recognize bias. Certainly, a search engine spider has no idea whether a web page that has the words *elephant* and *anatomy* on it is slanted toward a certain point of view. The search engine ranking is helpful in eliminating unreasonable bias. A web page biased toward slaughtering elephants for their tusks would be very unlikely to show up at the top of a Google search return list because few people would have used the web page, and the algorithm would give it a low listing rank.

The way the Internet is maturing, subjects are becoming more and more represented in cyberspace as interlinked networks. The initial concept of one comprehensive website, with a homepage on top and subsidiary detail pages for the topic of the site has been fuzzy from the beginning. Today, homepages are more of a structural and internal device than they are part of the user's interfacing with knowledge content. Any web page can seem like a homepage to a visitor who has found what she is looking for.

In using a search engine to access a knowledge subject, it is a good idea to open a few of the top links on the list that a search returns. The Internet is not organized. The list of web pages returned by a search engine has no organization except the underlying usage algorithm. The websites on the list are disorganized in terms of their content. This clutter of search engine listings has been made worse by paid placement by advertisers, artificially inserting paid-for links at the top and sides of the page. The advertising has an upside by underwriting the marvels of search engine technology and service. The downside of clutter needs to be understood by scholars as a necessity in my view. Advertising gave us the news and entertainment content of print and broadcast. In a free market, advertising is a means for the public to protest bias. Print news journals that are ad-free tend to be underwritten by partisans and express their underwriters' point of view. In any open medium, the ads have to be sufficiently unobtrusive to allow the content to be seen and heard. That principle operates on the Internet, including search engines, as it does in any public medium.

Research and learning in the new cyber world are, at this point, a matter of reaching with a text search into an enormous mass of disorganized information and then selecting from the web pages that the search engine lists. I believe there is a pivotal improvement here for learning. From an encyclopedia or textbook, a student gets a piece of knowledge that has been precooked by an author who has devised and followed a recipe of organization for the knowledge she is reporting. That precooked knowledge is served up in the isolation of the print in which it is published.

Raw knowledge from the Internet is scattered about as network nodes, placed there by various sources who interlink their stuff here and

there. The profound new difference is that those links are very often
formed by reflecting and extending the meaning of the knowledge itself.
Two clicks into the links listing on the Repository of elephant-related
web pages led me to PBS's marvelous Elephants of Africa site and from
there I clicked into its host section on PBS where its *Nature* TV shows
have been preserved as websites.

A search engine provides access nodes for entering a subject network
in which you can move along following meaning from node to node in
an open environment of unlimited knowledge.

47 REPOSITIONED OLD KINDS OF ACCESS

In Idea 32, I argued that there is confusion caused by thinking of pedagogy as the same thing as what it teaches: That, just because there is a
lot of education stuff online, it must mean that learning is happening.
From its earliest stages of emergence, the Internet has abounded with
repositioned education materials such as lesson plans, curricula, standards, courses, and syllabi. These things are not the knowledge they are
designed to convey.

Neither is this pre-Internet pedagogical equipment automatically
useful for accessing knowledge in its new digital network location. Many
of the repositioned pre-Internet educational methods have been re-
tooled to incorporate online knowledge. Examples of forward-looking
lessons plans created for the Internet can be found in PBS's *Nature* collection, like the elephant lesson plan for grades three through five called
"Kalahari Explorations."

But does retooling pre-Internet education equipment and methods
preserve a flawed past and fail to take advantage of the migration of
what is known into cyberspace? In what is a provocative change, the
Internet has separated the knowledge that education is supposed to
teach from pedagogical scheduling and techniques where it has been
characteristically embedded for many decades.

As far back as 1961, when I taught in a public school, the freshman-
level world history textbook the State of Texas gave me to use with the
students contained a very limited amount of historical knowledge. What
was there was all I was supposed to teach. The book was organized

around social issues and what historical facts there were had not been sequenced in chronological order.

The methodology of teaching in a new era, when the cognitive substance to be taught is to be found in cyberspace, requires some rethinking. The world history textbook I was given was 90 percent social studies curriculum and 10 percent history. The history of times like the Golden Age in Greece and the global discoveries of the fourteenth and fifteenth centuries—fact-packed periods whose impact echoed down the centuries that followed them—showed up now and then as cultural events. The historical fact count for those towering subjects was very small.

In a textbook like I used back then, the connection among the facts it contained was the particular social studies and cultural viewpoint that formed the organizational basis of the textbook. Any lesson plan is basically like that. There is the theme for the classroom work for the day or week. The theme provides a sequence for the facts to be learned as the lesson is taught.

Repositioning a lesson plan like that onto a web page becomes a series of links to knowledge separated by explanations and activities. It is structured linearly over time. In a classroom, a teacher needs the structure of time over which to roll out ideas. But the lesson plan mounted in a web page misses the chance to relate the knowledge in the natural network structure a web page offers.

There is no sequence at all in the elephant anatomy website described in the previous Idea. The visitor looks at a profile of an elephant and she can choose to click on brain, ears, tusks, teeth, trunk, feet, skin, hair, and internal system. A linear container for knowledge like a lesson plan is usually awkward on a web page. Repositioning from old media to new media almost always seems to be like that.

48 OPEN CONTENT FOR LEARNING THAT IS NOT PART OF THE VIRTUAL KNOWLEDGE ECOLOGY

A lot of different kinds of items that can be called open content for learning have poured into the Internet. There are lesson plans, assignment sheets, courses, books, lectures, tests, and tutorials. The virtual knowledge ecology consists of open content that is part of what is known by humankind. A lesson plan is not something you learn, nor is a test. A course contains some things that are part of human knowledge, but the scheduling and presentation are not part of what is presented. A book can be mostly knowledge or contain some knowledge.

There is no philosophical or doctrinal reason for insisting that the virtual knowledge ecology be thought of as only open content for learning that is human knowledge itself. The necessity to do that is mechanical: human knowledge is a network, and the more pure that network is kept of noncognitive stuff like assignment lists and tests, the more purely the knowledge can interconnect on the basis of its meaning.

For the same network mechanical reason, this is also why knowledge content is most usefully placed on the Internet as open (it must be in order to connect) and minimalized, so its smallest bits are available for linking in a subject network. With both conditions met, a bit of knowledge about a hummingbird nest, having its own URL, will link within the virtual knowledge ecology into hummingbird species information, backyard garden planning, and bird migration websites. Further, the hummingbird nest bit is available to be linked into other types of open learning content outside the virtual knowledge ecology, such as lesson plans, courses, and tutorials.

49 CONTENT THAT CASCADES INTO THE VIRTUAL KNOWLEDGE ECOLOGY BECOMES GLOBAL

The geography and ecology of the Gobi Desert are exactly the same whether you study them in Utah, Uganda, or Ulaanbaatar. In Mecca, Mandalay, and Moscow, the length of a side of a triangle is always going to be less than the sum of the lengths of the other two sides of that triangle. The outcomes of the Battle of Hastings and the Battle of Granicus will remain the same no matter when or where they are studied.

Throughout these pages, I have referred to the knowledge content of the virtual knowledge ecology as what is known by humankind. As we make plans and decisions for the education of new generations, we should begin by being clear and pure about building upon a base of knowledge that is true. This is a very simple and powerful principle, and it is the intellectual keystone of human liberty. That liberty is protected in a new way in cyberspace: Because the Internet is inherently global, its open portions will be purged of untruths as superior information rises to the top of search engine results.

Since the scattering of humanity across our planet eons ago, people located in different parts of the world have grown up learning different knowledge. The range of that knowledge has been from fairly similar stuff in mathematics, technology, and basic sciences to quite different versions of history, literature, and philosophy—not to mention religion. The Internet not only gives us an opportunity to change this diversity of knowing. The Internet is causing that to happen, whether we like it or not.

The virtual knowledge ecology is forming inexorably on its own. Geographers and ecologists around the planet use and share the same virtual knowledge resources. Mathematics and other sciences are following that pattern. History, literature, and philosophy are doing the same thing at the senior scholar level. The history and original literature of all religions is globally available as it never has been before because it is online. In the main, school children around the world are not yet using the shared sources, but that is changing and will change much more.

I fully understand that pedagogy has strong cultural characteristics. This book, however, is not about pedagogy. The virtual knowledge ecology is what is known by humankind, and it is knowledge that our entire species holds to be correct and useful. That sort of knowledge should not present real problems to any pedagogy. Geometry, geography, and genetics are useful knowledge for every culture. Over time, subjects like history, which are now at variance in the schools in different cultures, will be refined within the global virtual knowledge ecology.

One of the most interesting realities I learned from spending four years heading a team that gleaned the Internet for useful knowledge was how few subjects there actually are. We reached a point at HomeworkCentral.com when the graduate student specialists who did the subject gathering felt the job was done. The total number of subjects was less than 35,000. Of course, just about all of those could be broken down into greater and greater levels of detail, but the possible subjects the team rounded up for study through four years of college topped out at around 35,000. But as explained below, the number was really about half of 35,000 because the subjects often appeared two or more times in the new network method we created.

A look at the Dewey Decimal System for categorizing human knowledge will give you a sense of the limited number of subjects of any size. The Dewey system is a hierarchy with these ten main subject trees: computers, information, and generalities; philosophy and psychology; religion; social sciences; language; natural sciences and math; technology (applied sciences), the arts and recreation; literature and rhetoric; and geography and history. Each of these major trees spreads to ten subcategories, which in turn can be divided again into ten, and their parts can do the same until there are no more slivers of topics.

In the Dewey Decimal System, the number of topics multiplies at each new branching. There are ten topics at first and then 100, and then 1,000 and then 10,000, and then 100,000, and then 1,000,000. An example from the system goes like this:

500 natural sciences and math
520 astronomy and allied sciences
523 specific celestial bodies
523.7 sun
523.73 motion of the sun

To satisfy knowledge requirements throughout the college level, our HomeworkCentral.com editors usually did not need to go beyond the third level of detail in the way the Dewey System organizes knowledge.

We did not adhere to Dewey or any other preconceived structure. Our method was to find web pages with superior open knowledge content and connect them to other content, based on their associated meaning. We did the opposite of Dewey, in our case building in a new way from the little subjects outward into networks that were bigger subjects. As explained in Idea 59, many of the little networks we created ended up connected into more than one subject. At least half of the 35,000 subjects enriched more than one bigger topic, doing something impossible in the Dewey System. There, the sun is stuck under the heading astronomy, though it is very important over in ecology, energy, and other subjects too. The Dewey System has developed workarounds, but the network basis for organization is far more elegant.

This all gets very complicated. The point is that comprehensive access to what is generally known by humankind can be achieved within a structure of around 35,000 topics. The end result is the practicality of the virtual knowledge ecology—a network of what is known by humankind, freely available on the Internet.

Returning to the point of this Idea, the knowledge held and expressed by those 35,000 topics is the same for everyone on earth. Students everywhere can use it and share it, so long as they are connected to the Internet and are able to understand the language in which the knowledge is interfaced. Idea 80, "The Grand Idea," develops this concept further.

50 CONTENT FOR SMALL CHILDREN AND OTHER LEARNER LEVELS

A mantra of the education establishment is that learning resources must be at the level of the learner for maximum benefit. Following the mantra means age-level and grade-level materials must be produced to meet the needs of developing children. After all, we must learn to walk before we can learn to run.

There is little doubt that, because of my upbringing, I am at one extreme in my viewpoint on the value of childish learning materials. My parents never limited their vocabulary around their children, and they insisted that we use correct pronunciation and grammar from the time we first learned to talk.

My father's mother, whom we called Granny, paid no attention to my parents' penchant for adult language. My older brother, who did not have much to say as a baby, listened silently for many months as Granny cooed a steady stream of baby talk at him whenever she was around. Finally, when he was over two years old, he responded to her one day with a perfectly pronounced sentence: "What did you say, Granny?"

My ideas about learning-level resources were further conditioned during my years leading the collection of learning content at HomeworkCentral.com, as described in Idea 35. An early lesson I got in that experience was that there is a strong demand for web pages specifically designed to teach small children. Teachers and parents e-mailed us asking for a section for their little ones. The demand was met by collecting web pages with colorful, animated designs using limited vocabulary and large letters to teach children reading and other subjects. We included many web pages in the genre that used games to teach, proclaiming learning is fun. I am not qualified to judge these materials, but I believe it is worth making sure the pages cause true learning, not just fun—that is, if we are counting on the kids using them to learn.

There is nothing wrong with fun, but there is a danger of not helping children realize that learning itself is fun. Figuring out that a ladybug wiggling on a leaf in your garden is cleaning her antenna is more fun than watching a cartoon of a ladybug dancing and singing. At least I grew up thinking that. But then I was a child during World War II, when learning toys were not part of my life—and we had, in fact, few toys. As for cartoons, I actually have a memory from early childhood of thinking the 8 mm *Felix the Cat* cartoon my father used to show us was dumb and boring, an opinion I have not changed. Cartoons became a lot more fun with color and the expressive innovations of the Disney genius.

As I said, I realize my view on this is at the least one-sided. Nevertheless, it does not hurt to think carefully about at what point children should begin to engage knowledge that is interfaced without learner-level filters.

Making a learning website colorful and having the lesson embedded in a game or conveyed by cartoon characters is, of course, an effort to make the experience appealing to children. Doing that is only one kind of learner-level filter, based on age.

Another traditional way of thinking about learning level measures the complexity and course of the knowledge itself. Until recently, I have thought of this as knowledge scaling from simple to more difficult. It made sense to me that there was a linear progression of difficulty in almost any subject. Arithmetic must be learned before moving to algebra, which is needed to understand calculus. Knowing that the earth is a globe and having a mental picture of the placement of the continents allows the geography of nations to come into focus. But is coming into focus linear? I no longer think so.

My point of view has changed on what is happening here. Rather than moving from simple to more difficult, more pieces are being connected. To begin to understand the American Revolution, several major pieces have to be learned: the colonies, what England was doing, the ideas of the Enlightenment, the potential of commerce, and the cast of characters: King George, George Washington, John and Abigail Adams, Thomas Jefferson, Benjamin Franklin, James Madison, Alexander Hamilton, and the rest. I have come to think that pieces of knowledge are not simpler than other pieces so much as they are less connected than other pieces. Connecting pieces causes larger pieces to emerge into a pattern.

To the extent that connectivity of the pieces is the key to learning, the limitless potential for connectivity within the Internet is a fundamental factor in the future of education. The connectivity potential gives us another clue to what kind of learning materials we should be creating: They should be connectible. It turns out that what the learner is doing to learn is connecting things.

The section on *Aggregation* explores the learning muscle that connectivity creates. But for there to be connectivity and aggregation there must be a large ecology full of accessible web pages interfacing knowledge. Specific samples of what has poured into the virtual knowledge ecology to bountifully fill this need are described in the ideas ahead.

Another observation from what happened at HomeworkCentral.com sheds some interesting light on learner-level study resources. Essentially for marketing purposes, we offered visitors to our website three collections of study subjects, one each for "kids," "middle school," and "high school and beyond." The kids collection contained web pages specifically designed for young children. The other two categories both received hundreds of thousands of visits every month for several years. The two collections were identical. To the best of my knowledge no visitor to our website ever noticed and reported to us that the "middle school" and "high school and beyond" collections were the same. (In later years, we inserted a few small differences, but not in the basic knowledge.)

It was obviously psychology and conditioning that divided the traffic to the two identical collections of knowledge. Our systems of schooling have taught us one thing (if, cynics might say, little else): what you know has to do with what level of schooling you have attained. Or, perhaps, the deeper message is that we have been conditioned to accept that there are levels of knowledge you should not expect to attain until you are at least in high school. I know I am swimming upstream against opinion here, but I think learner-level knowledge materials provide a self-fulfilling mediocrity. Every child should be expected to learn what he or she can and is attracted to learn, not some age-appropriate middling amount.

51 DEFINITION AND HISTORY OF THE VIRTUAL LEARNING CASCADE

There were just a few of us who were focused on the scene when the floodgates opened and human knowledge poured into the Internet. That content continues to enter the Internet, refreshing and augmenting what is already there. But in the early days of the cascade, the phenomenon was completely new.

I first used the word cascade in 1996, when I was writing the article that is included in this book as Appendix 1. I still think the word works well to describe what I saw. To me, as my analogies in the article indicate, knowledge seemed to be cascading into the Internet like river water cascading down rapids, over falls, into rivers, and into a great ocean. The root of the word of *cascade* is *falling* and in poetry it suggests the beauty of water rushing off a cliff or happy memories flooding the mind.

Another older meaning of cascade refers to what happens in a phase change between two states of matter. Since I first used it for learning content, I have also found the word *cascade* used in studies of networks. A cascade through a network can occur in many places in the physical world.

In network lingo, things cascade when they reach a tipping point. When enough consumers decide a new color is "in" for the season, garments of that color fly off the racks. When enough people in a community catch the flu, the illness rushes into an epidemic stage. In that sense of the meaning of cascade, I was not far off in my 1996 article, even though I stumbled onto using the word as an analogy for rushing water.

The tipping point for knowledge content that set off its cascade into the Internet happened in the mid-1990s. The timing was, of course, related to the development of the technology, which was in place by 1994. That story is beyond our scope here. I can tell you that by the spring of 1997, when I first saw it, the cascade of what is known by humankind into the Internet had barely begun.

In those early years, everything was an experiment and many different ideas were tried. There was no distinction between open and closed content, though practically speaking the division was there from the beginning. Distance learning was in the process of being conceived and born. Great and small repositories of knowledge—libraries, museums, universities—pondered what to do and tried different approaches. The education establishment dabbled in the digital world, and the education industry looked for ways to acquire markets.

For my own part, I was challenged by my assignment at Homework-Central.com to find and collect those web pages that contained knowledge that would be useful to students trying to learn academic subjects. I was looking for what has come to be known as open content for learning.

In the next two long Ideas, I highlight the great cascade of knowledge as I saw it occur. First by subject and then by source, the accounts include many examples. The Ideas following those highlights the emergence of the open movement within the Internet and in particular the movement toward an open content ecology of learning.

52 EYEWITNESS ACCOUNT OF THE SUBJECT CASCADE

What might be expected to be a simple task—naming and categorizing study subjects—is, in fact, complicated and confusing. To get some sense of the challenge scholars have had over the ages in organizing what is known by humankind, it is useful to visit the *Encyclopedia of Diderot & d'Alembert* website, now being translated from French to English online by a project based at the University of Michigan. Posted on the project website is the "Map of the System of Human Knowledge" used by the authors of the encyclopedia in 1751–1777. There are three main divisions of *Understanding*, each with subtopics:

1. Memory/History
Sacred (History of the Prophets)
Ecclesiastical
Civil
Ancient & Modern: *Civil history, Literary history*
Natural: *Uniformity of Nature (Celestial History, History of, Meteors, Land and Sea, Minerals, Plants, Animals, Elements), Deviations of Nature (Celestial wonders, Large meteors, Wonders of Land and Sea, Monstrous plants, Monstrous animals, Wonders of the elements), Uses of Nature (Arts, Craft, Manufactures)*
2. Reason/Philosophy
General metaphysics
Science of God
Science of Man: *Logic, Ethics*
Science of nature: *Mathematics (Pure: Arithmetic, Geometry; Mixed: Mechanics, Geometric Astronomy, Optics, [Analysis of Chance]), Physicomathematics, Particular physics, Zoology (Anatomy, Physiology, Medicine, Veterinary Medicine, Horse management, Hunting, Fishing, Falconry), Physical Astronomy, Meteorology, Cosmology, Botany, Mineralogy, Chemistry*
3. Imagination/Poetry
Profane: *Narrative, Dramatic, Parable*
Sacred: *Narrative, Dramatic, Parable*

The arrangement of what is known by humankind was quite different only a century after the great French encyclopedia was structured. In 1876, a young American librarian Melvil Dewey invented a hierarchical system that became a standard for his profession. The ten major topics of his Dewey Decimal System are listed and discussed in Idea 49. The Duke University library has a helpful online tutorial on the system, showing how the topics and subtopics flow.

Didrot, d'Alembert, and Dewey all had the same reason for creating subject lists: They had to figure out where to put an article or a book in their encyclopedia or library. One of the amazements of the Internet is that we do not have that problem anymore.

Dewey had to decide if a math book should be put on the science shelf in a library or if it belonged on the bookshelf among the humanities, as had been thought in times past. The answer is that math has a significant place in both areas of human knowledge. On the Internet—but not in a brick and mortar library with limited shelf space—math can be richly connected into both major divisions of thought as well as unlimited others.

Does biology belong with physics and chemistry as a pure science? Is geography a physical or social science? Is architecture an art or technology? Again, Didrot, d'Alembert, and Dewey had that problem. The virtual knowledge ecology does not. If you are studying biology, organic chemistry will connect to biology. If you are studying metallurgy you will be thickly linked into chemistry. The same is true of all areas of knowledge in which biology and chemistry provide information and insight.

Our conditioning to think of categories in hierarchies has made it hard to envision abstractly the omnidirectional interrelating of knowledge on the Internet. But, studying in the networked knowledge comes easily and naturally in practice, as it mirrors the connectivity of our thinking and learning.

In the inherent organization of knowledge itself—whether the medium is an encyclopedia, books, the Internet, or your mind—if you are studying the eighteenth-century history of France, the American Revolution is a subtopic. French history is a subtopic if your main study subject is the American Revolution. Biology, as suggested above, is all over the place: organic chemistry, ecology, global warming, medicine, and paleontology, to name a few places where it is a major or minor topic.

The overlap and interrelationships of study subjects is a powerful argument on its own for interfacing them in a network. In fact, that is exactly what they are doing spontaneously, as the next section on *Aggregation* investigates. In this highlight description, I have neither set up groupings among the subjects nor made any attempt to be comprehensive. I have picked stories to tell that will illustrate several different ways knowledge about subjects entered the Internet and various virtual forms of the knowledge that emerged.

The following is a narration of a still unfolding story of what really happened as material about the subjects mentioned poured into the Internet. Hundreds of thousand of web pages have already been part of the total cascade. Thousands of those web pages have matured, proliferated, and been vetted online.

It is impossible for me to do more than give a few examples of what has happened with study subjects as they have cascaded into the Internet and became openly accessible there for study. The subjects and websites mentioned in the following description are available as links in the "Subject Sampler" at GoldenSwamp.com. The links are listed as well in Appendix 2 of this book. They are also posted as interactive links at GoldenSwamp.com, in the chapter listing for this book on the same web page as the "Subject Sampler." Ideally, as you read the descriptions of the subjects that follow, you will open the links they mention. I have, however, tried to write these short comments so that a reader can get their essence without going online.

ARTS

Paintings and drawings by great artists have flowed steadily into the Internet since the middle 1990s. Some early websites set up for that purpose had images of artworks and brief biographies of artists. In the 1990s, bandwidth was scarce and dial-up connections to the Internet slow. Large images of artworks took a long time to download and display on most computers. Still online in early 2005 is one of the pioneers from those days, WebMuseum.org.

Times changed, and a year or two into the new century, it was becoming routine for museums large and small to flow their collections into websites they hosted and maintained. Curators controlled the interfacing, and the quality of knowledge available to visitors became superb and sometimes sublime. An online leader for several years, the Metropolitan Museum of Art in New York City offers, as I write this, nearly 7,000 objects of art online including virtual representations of everything in its departments of European Paintings and American Paintings and Sculpture. Two other glorious websites for visual arts are those of the Louvre in Paris, France, and the Hermitage in St. Petersburg, Russia. Many, many small museums now have choice online images and exhibits. As broadband and multimedia continue to improve the visual quality of the Internet interface, the future of online arts promises to be magnificent and comprehensive.

The history and theory of music, dance, and other performing arts are increasingly available online. The coming increase of broadband and online audio and video promises a future in which performances will be accessible from the virtual knowledge ecology.

BIOGRAPHY

In the beginning years of the cascade of learning content into the Internet, biography was a favorite to collect into websites for study. There were at least two large collections that were similar in content to biography articles in a printed encyclopedia. A famous person would be listed alphabetically by last name. The biography web collections had the then exciting new feature of being able to also arrange the biography articles by what the people they reported did: movie stars, presidents, inventors, and so forth. Doing so was new and cool.

Early web portals like Yahoo also listed biographies in topic trees. You could follow the tree from biographies, to presidents, to Abraham Lincoln to find Lincoln biographies on multiple websites in a list, and a click on any of them would take you to the biography you chose.

There continue to be biography collections online. There are authoritative biographies for each laureate at the Nobel Prize website, and the White House website has a biography for each president and each first lady of the United States. There are also hundreds—perhaps thousands—of websites devoted to individuals, containing their biographies and work.

It is a reflection of the deepening level of detail and connectivity of open Internet content that biographies can now be assembled from many sources in a few seconds by a search engine for many thousands of historical and living individual people. Search engines have fairly well ended the need to make collections of biographies by name from various sources, as Yahoo once did. A search for "Abraham Lincoln biography" will produce a list of quality biographies for the great man from all over the Internet and is the best method for finding excellent biographies—though it is not yet perfect.

BIOLOGY

An afternoon of exploring networks of online open content can expose a learner to more biology that she is likely to encounter through all the grades of a K–12 education. Biology is the vast subject of life. Its vastness makes impossible more than a brief introduction to biology in a textbook that can be reasonably carried around by a student. Biology includes animals, plants, anatomy, microbiology, cellular and molecular biology, genetics, ecology, paleontology, biotechnology, medicine, and lots of topics related to those and other aspects of life.

There is limitless space online, allowing these fields to be stored, interfaced, and interconnected as never before. Biologists themselves have by and large moved lock, stock, and microscope onto the Internet and in significant number students can visit their work. Open biological content in the Internet has become a significant new factor in the sciences as its practitioners share their work virtually in real time over long distances.

In addition to the websites of active science, a wealth of material is provided to inform the public on health, environmental, and general science news. A great deal of the material of this sort is first rate for use in learning the subjects covered. Following are three examples of the copious smorgasbord of life sciences available online as open content.

A database on scale insects, the Coccoideai, is typical of how biologists have centralized information in minute detail for myriad animals, plants, compounds, and other components of biology. There are 7,355 known scale insect species, of which many are plant pests. A web page called Scale Net is hosted by the State of Israel Ministry of Agriculture and Rural Development. Scale Net interfaces a database that can be queried for details on hundreds of different Coccoideai. In addition, the website provides background, scale families, and photos of the insects. It links to other scale insect and related websites, forming a Coccoideai weblet within the overall virtual knowledge ecology. Although it is hard to imagine a middle or even high school student digging out details of a Coccoideai, a few minutes with the Scale Net is a new kind of opportunity for a student of any age to see real science and thereby get a good idea of what biologists do, know, and find useful. Scale insects are an important subject in applied agriculture, which I learned from my own brief visit to Scale Net.

The "Animal Bytes" pages of the San Diego Zoo website are, like the zoo itself, a showcase for biology. In "Animal Bytes" there are animal categories, habitats, and ecosystems and a section set up by continent. One central habitat/ecosystem page about deserts offers a side bar with clicks to twenty-four animal pages: antelope, bee, beetle, boa, butterfly, camel, cat (small), frog, goat, hummingbird, iguana, jaguar, kingfisher, leopard, lizard, mountain lion (puma, cougar), ostrich, owl, rattlesnake, sheep, toad, turtle and tortoise, and zebra. Each of these pages is an authoritative, interesting account several hundred words long of the animal, illustrated with excellent photographs. Scattered words in the text are highlighted with links to pop-up panels from the "Zoo Glossary." Some of the pages have videos of the animal in its habitat. The "Animal Bytes" are ideal for youngsters and yet they qualify as useful general knowledge for undergraduate college work and for anyone interested in knowing stuff. I learned that frogs have one of two color schemes. The brightly colored ones are toxic frogs, which want to be seen so predators will go away. The mottled green and brown ones are camouflaged so that predators have a hard time finding them.

Several streams of biology merge in a website titled The Ancient Bristlecone Pine, about the oldest living inhabitant of earth. I noticed the website several years ago and am glad to see that, in 2005, its host Leonard Miller continues to care for this little online science gem. Miller works at Sonoma State University and is a special consultant for the Sudden Oak Death Project, fighting an epidemic lethal disease afflicting oak trees. In the website he provides, the bristlecone pines are described historically and biologically. The dendrochronology section explains the methods of tree ring dating that established the age of the tree, and links are provided to laboratories and authorities leading that science.

It would take dozens more examples to be at all representative of the sorts of biological websites already abounding as open content for learning. The tipping point occurred several years ago and caused biological knowledge to go digital and link within the Internet. Undoubtedly, a major portion of what is known about biology at detailed levels has now become available only online. Who would ever want to retype on paper the facts for thousands of genes in a genome every time something new was discovered about a gene? Why should there be a printed manual describing all the scale insects when the Israeli database interfaces virtually everything known about the Coccoideai that everyone in the world who is interested can use?

CHEMISTRY

The many aspects of chemistry are, like those of biology, now represented thoroughly in open Internet content. Somewhat differently than biology could, chemistry lends itself more readily to abstract illustration and animation.

An ongoing flow of open content for learning chemistry is the American Chemical Society "Molecule of the Week," which has been displayed weekly on the society's homepage since 2001. The website archive offers dozens of molecules that have been featured, giving a description and illustration of each. The page with the molecules invites members of the organization to suggest molecules to be featured, which is a way working chemists participate in creating this authoritative content for learning. For an individual student or a chemistry class, the weekly molecule streams quality content at no cost to the learner.

The largest, and certainly among the finest, academic departments of chemistry in the Western world is at Oxford University in England. Its students designed, built, and maintain the online Virtual Chemistry Laboratory. An extensive preuniversity virtual course in chemistry is the first link on the main assets panel. The course present twenty-six subjects. Several advanced topic chemistry courses, tutorials, and resources are listed below the link for the preuniversity courses. Virtual and often interactive experiments are featured on the left side of the homepage. A huge amount of chemistry is available to be learned in the Virtual Chemistry Laboratory, where the accuracy of what is presented is backed up by the authority and prestige of Oxford University.

Case Western Reserve University's Earnest B. Yeager Center for Electrochemical Sciences provides an online Electrochemical Dictionary. It contains over eight hundred terms, as of this writing. The Dictionary web page welcomes additional terms and corrections. It is heartening for the future of science to think about the global gateway the Dictionary provides for student and practicing chemical engineers and researchers. It is a resource they developed and use in common for the help of all and the improvement of the science. The advancement of scientific knowledge depends on sharing among those who work at the frontiers, and the Internet has proven an ideal venue for this sharing. That the content has to be open for this to occur is a given, by definition. Closed and sharing mean opposite things.

COUNTRIES AND CULTURES

Placing content openly online always makes the content global—anyone anywhere can use it. A concern is then raised: It seems important that it is suited for use in various countries and cultures. The concern is about what is called the content's adaptability.

A first consideration of adaptability is language: The online material must be in a language that can be read by students, which is discussed in Idea 43. Another sort of adaptability is appropriateness. An example would be that a student from an underdeveloped area where people are hungry would be perplexed by conservation websites that advocate protecting endangered animals that in his country are considered food. The mindset of the education establishment can be to control what students study to ensure that no offense is caused.

Adaptability issues do not affect basic knowledge itself in a fundamental way and are therefore not a fundamental obstacle to open content. Although ecology raises some issues, the number of basic subjects in which the adaptability of knowledge to cultures is a factor is small. It does not (or should not be allowed to) apply to mathematics, sciences, technologies, current events, languages, or (hopefully) history.

There is a network structural factor that greatly minimizes the adaptability problem. What actually happened as the cascade poured knowledge into the Internet over the past several years is that those websites that the most knowledgeable people approved and respected were linked to by these scholars in their respective fields, and those websites swam to the top at Google. Adaptability is a challenge that, in the main, solves itself in an open network.

Early information about nations and cultures, which began showing up online in 1997 when I was first looking for it, tended to be in the repositioned format of a printed encyclopedia. The "Country Studies" at the U.S. Library of Congress began as the repositioning by the Federal Research Division of the library of the *Country Studies/Area Handbook* printed for the U.S. Army. The studies were intended to focus on lesser known places in the world where the army might be deployed. In 2005, the library has developed this section of its open content to include over one hundred excellent in-depth *Country Studies*.

The travel industry jumped early into the Internet and in a big way. Virtual guidebooks were developed—with a lot of ads or not too many— providing capsule history, culture, geography, weather, and other information for individual countries. An example that is very popular today is the Geographic website. With not the slightest pretense of being material for education, websites like Geographic provide students with far more information quantity and freshness than anything they will find in their K–12 textbooks about the countries mentioned online. If that seems like an overstatement, it is true if only because things change far faster in countries and cultures than printed textbooks can be published and distributed.

The recent emergence of cultural nuggets expressed in Flash exhibits is illustrated by two beautiful examples. "Lakota Winter Counts" from the National Anthropological Archives at the Smithsonian archives displays the tradition of the Lakotas as they recorded nineteenth-century winters on the great American plains in sketches of animals, people, and events.

A 2004 geographical Flash project titled "Life at the End of the Road" provides a nonlinear exploration of the land, sea, and people of Patagonia. The digital nugget is a glimpse of a powerful new learning format emerging from the virtual knowledge ecology.

A big addition to the open content for learning will be the local creation of more content embedding local culture. The potential is strong for a planetwide upflow of cultural knowledge and treasure into digital software like Flash, where it can be preserved and globally shared. The movement is, in fact, already strongly stirring within the virtual knowledge ecology.

EARTH SCIENCES

"World Earthquake Activity" from the U.S. Geological Survey has been my favorite earth sciences website for years, and I have reviewed it several times. The homepage has a map of the world with little boxes scattered around it representing current or recent earthquakes. The size and color of the boxes indicate the severity of each quake and how recent it is. Any child old enough to recognize a map of the world would learn very quickly by looking at the map that most earthquakes happen in some areas, but they do happen frequently and occur in many parts of the world. Older students, or anyone interested, can click on any of the boxes to drill into the pages of the USGS website that hosts the section. As the visitor goes deeper, each level increases the amount and sophistication of the information. An eight-year-old and an earth science professor are both going to learn from these earthquake pages.

The "Plate Tectonics Animations" page from the University of California at Berkeley is another old favorite of mine. Several animations linked there show the movement of continents over the geologic ages. Besides the scientific insight the animations generate, they are a reminder that, geologically at least, what is going on around out planet is all inextricably interrelated.

The website for U.S. GLOBEC "Georges Bank Study" is, as I write this early in 2005, an active, broad program of real science. Having gone to college in the 1950s, I know I could not have imagined then what it would be like as a student to be able to be so close to real science and to follow its activities and progress without being physically on the scene. On Georges Bank, the scientists are looking at zooplankton and fish larvae. Students anywhere are able to virtually track what they see and learn. Kids who do that will know exactly what they would be doing should they choose to become ocean scientists.

GEOGRAPHY

It was probably 1997 when I first spent an afternoon collecting homepages of countries one by one. If someone were to do that today, the websites he would visit would have hundreds or thousands of pages. In 1997, though, not all countries had websites, and many of those that had been put online were only a few pages in size. Usually, the smaller country websites listed the government officials, gave a bit of history, and provided some geography. The afternoon I did the collecting, I learned a lot about geography as I focused on the location of countries I had vaguely (or never) heard of.

One that came into my focus for the first time was Turkmenistan. I was captivated by the country's small but proud website. The site slogan said, "Water is a Turkmen's life, a horse is his wings, and a carpet is his soul." The main, and almost only, cultural feature in the scant pages was about Akhalteke horses. Beneath a photograph of what looked to be a teenage boy on a handsome rearing white horse, the text explained that Alexander the Great's favorite stallion Buccephalus was an Akhalteke. In 2005, the small Turkmenistan website has in part been replaced by the website in English of the Embassy of Turkmenistan, Washington, DC. Seven years after I first saw its predecessor, the 2005 embassy website still had the Turkmen slogan and the same picture of the boy on the rearing stallion.

What was no longer on the Turkmenistan website was the map of the country I found there in 1997. Like many other early websites, this one from central Asia had linked to and displayed a map of itself from the Perry-Castaneda Map Collection at the University of Texas at Austin. The collection at UT Austin has been and remains the quintessential open content map site, contributing widely to other resources within the virtual knowledge ecology. Historical as well as current maps are plentiful and magnificently interfaced online.

Another facet of virtual knowledge ecology geography is something altogether new for learning: satellite images. Something as simple as a visit to a weather website provides a view of part of the earth from a satellite. A search engine will suggest many outstanding satellite images, both live views and photographic images. I date myself when I admit that it still surprises me when I see a satellite image that looks just the same shape as some old-time cartographer made, before getting up that high and looking was not even a pipedream. For a youngster isolated geographically in, for example, the Asian mountains or the jungles of Africa or South America, a visit to a weather website on a WI-FI laptop lets her look down on her actual location and gives her, suddenly, a global perspective.

GOVERNMENT

One of the subjects I taught in high school in the early 1960s was civics. Students were supposed to learn the structure of the local, state, and national governments in which they would become voters when they reached the age of twenty-one. Absolutely everything I was supposed to teach the kids is now readily available online. This content is much richer than what I tried to teach to high school seniors preoccupied with proms and sports while they were trapped in my classroom for forty minutes every day. Today, that information is embedded in context in the websites of the actual governments in which many high school seniors are already voters, having reached the lowered U.S. qualification age of eighteen. If I were teaching civics today, I would use only live open content, such as the home site of the U.S. Senate.

The U.S. Supreme Court can be studied at Northwestern University's Oyez website that has both its own descriptive materials about the justices and the court's history as well as links to the actual ongoing docket and cases.

State and local governments have built websites that have grown comprehensive over the past several years. To find them, enter a search term like "official website of the State of Colorado" and two clicks will take you there. Trying to abstract the kinds of material you will find there into some sort of civics study book or pamphlet will pale as a teaching tool against using the real thing. As I was writing this, I browsed through the Colorado web pages and randomly clicked on the "North Metro Fire Rescue District." A colorful page opened and a jingle started singing "Stop, Drop, and Roll." The music faded and a man's voice said, "Clothing fires are a leading cause of serious burns for children. Teach your children to stop, drop, and roll to reduce the chance of a serious burn." There were five bright icons to click, but I didn't go any further.

Governments of countries around the world have websites. Many are, like those of the branches of the U.S. government, designed for an audience of their citizens. Nevertheless, the government websites of many non-English speaking countries are in part or completely available in English as well the country's languages. The best way to get a sense of this type of open content is to search for the official websites of countries in which you have an interest and see what they are doing.

In 1997, when I rounded up country websites, the ones I found were almost all primarily or completely in English. My guess is that the reason for that was the scant amount of website building going on outside of Western countries and the limiting of software descriptions and fonts to English. Country websites now are primarily interfaced in national languages using fonts for Asian, Arabic, Greek and other languages. Open content is far less limited than it used to be in this way, among many others.

HISTORY

There is, of course, no way to record all of history because that would mean everything that ever happened anywhere would have to be in the record. Still, keepers of history over the centuries have managed to hang on to a lot of facts. In the past two centuries, archaeologists and researchers have dug up a lot more. It is hard to envision how everything known by humankind about what humankind has done could be usefully interfaced without the Internet. Printing, updating, and distributing historical knowledge has been effective without the Internet in only a limited way.

The early organization of history on the Internet tended to reposition bibliographies, making accessible on web pages lists of articles and documents and saying in what book or library they could be found. Without the book or library at hand, the lists were some help but not much. Things got better as many of the lists began to be sprinkled with blue underlined text that could be clicked to go to a facsimile or hypertext version of a document. That was perfect for a scholar or student because he could read the actual document.

The next step was collection of documents as web pages. A much-used website of that sort is *EuroDocs*, which is curated at the Brigham Young University's Harold B. Lee Library. *EuroDocs: Primary Historical Documents from Western Europe* contains at a minimum hundreds of selected transcriptions, facsimiles, and translations. These *EuroDocs* are often viewed through links to collections in libraries, museums, and elsewhere. *EuroDocs* had been visited online in April 2005 nearly three million times since 1996. Awesome though the idea of the collection is as a whole—echoing the ancient dream of the Library at Alexandria—the planetwide dimension of the ability to access specific individual bits of history is conspicuously new. *EuroDocs* is but one Western European reading room in a grand virtual Library of Alexander within all Internet open content—the virtual knowledge ecology.

In addition to the small and specific pieces of history, bigger slices of the human record are represented online in both small and large topics. Wikipedia.org has excellent histories for many eras and countries written by interested individuals and edited by the Internet public as a whole. There is, for example, a Wikipedia history of Zimbabwe that is about five thousand words long, setting out history from ancient times to the present. The Wikipedia article on the French Revolution is about five thousand words long.

Both articles are true wikis, defined as openly created and edited at any time by the hosting website's users. Both articles have an objectivity won by the fact that interested parties of every persuasion are able to edit them.

Web page gems for small historical topics flow steadily into the virtual knowledge ecology. An example, showcasing artifacts from the Chicago Historical Society's collection, is the society's exhibit "Parades, Protests & Politics in Chicago." Surely, as the years roll by, most of the artifacts that have rested in display cases or storage drawers of historical collections across the planet will find their way virtually to accessibility by students who visit the virtual knowledge ecology.

LANGUAGES

The website yourDictionary.com lists dictionaries in dozens of languages and offers a pallet of glossaries for a broad array of study subjects and activities. One listing is a website that catalogs periodic tables of elements in over one hundred languages. The website has some dead links and ads for gambling and casinos—but the insight into language use online is marvelous. My prediction is that, as we go from 15 percent of people on earth using the Internet to nearly ubiquitous computing, two language trends will occur in online knowledge for academic subjects. Basic stuff like the table of elements will show up in dozens of languages, as can already be seen in the table of elements example. Second, the day will come when the echo of Babel will cease and there will be a single language across the planet. But, if software translators come online soon, as they probably will, a single language will be less needed in the foreseeable future. If nothing more, the present availability of multiple languages online shows the diversity of desire to participate in the Internet.

Not only living languages flourish online. Classical languages of many cultures are present. As mentioned in Idea 43, dying languages are also being preserved in online scholarship and oral files. A favorite primer for several years for the earliest human languages is the colorful website Ancient Scripts that introduces writing systems, sounds and phonetics, and historical linguistics.

There are also many websites set up to teach languages, and many of these include open content that is free for would-be speakers to use. Typical of these is MasterRussian.com.

The future promises the coming of more multimedia and interactive language tutorials. The University of Chicago Library has a foretaste in "Kanji Alive," a multimedia, web-based interactive tutorial that presents a unified interface for language fragments to the learner of Japanese.

LITERATURE

Michael S. Hart will without a doubt go down in history as the man virtually responsible for the most free books distributed. He already has 15,000 available at Gutenberg.org and has cranked up his project toward a goal of a million books by 2015. He conceptualized Project Gutenberg in 1971, becoming its first volunteer by typing the U.S. Declaration of Independence and sending it out over the then tiny Internet. Hart's concept was that open computer time could be put to best use by volunteers typing books into digital form. The rest of this remarkable story is told on the project's website.

As described in Idea 42, another virtual knowledge ecology visionary and pioneer volunteer is Aniina Jokinen who created Luminarium. She calls the lovely website a labor of love. Since 1996, when she first put it online, Luminarium has been a favorite for students of medieval, Renaissance, and seventeenth-century English literature. With modesty I find unnecessary, Jokinen concludes her letter to readers with these words from Samuel Johnson: *"In this Work when it shall be found that much is omitted, let it not be forgotten that much likewise is performed."* As time has passed since Jokinen first built Luminarium, the Internet has taken some of the impact out of Johnson's words: Nothing much is ever not found in the virtual knowledge ecology because you can usually link to what might seem to need to be added.

Norton Anthology of English Literature is an exemplary open content for learning website that provides a scholarly sweep across literature in English. The virtual anthology is under the stewardship of the editors of the printed version and is magnificent. In addition to the collection of anthology articles, the erudite overseers evaluate and include links by article subject to websites throughout the Internet where English literature can be accessed.

Smaller websites for smaller literary topics are scattered around the virtual knowledge ecology, linking to various subjects and historical periods. A typical example by Sweet Briar College Spanish professor Alix Ingber is "Golden Age of Spanish Poets." Another is by Dr. Anne Savage of the Department of English at McMaster University. Here, the full text of the tale of *Beowulf* is given in old and modern English. Characters, history, and interpretations are provided.

Literature in languages other than English has cascaded into the Internet, and virtually all human literature appears destined to have its primary source online. Until computing becomes ubiquitous and reading online becomes less clumsy (as discussed in Idea 16), books will continue to be printed. The use of printed books to hold in one's hands to read is, though, a different matter than where the primary source of the literature interfaced by the printed book is located.

Copyright laws have affected recent online literature in a major way since the beginning of the Internet. Project Gutenberg, for example, has focused on having volunteers prepare texts to be placed online. The pioneer Internet literature project has placed more than 16,000 free electronic books online. Gutenberg's focus is on writing that is in the public domain—essentially older works for which the copyright has expired. Some copyright owners have relinquished protection. As described in Idea 104, a trend is being led by CreativeCommons.com to provide a more flexible solution than the absolute protection of copyrights. With all of that going on behind the scenes, massive amounts of noncopyrighted materials have been placed online, including a lot of recent literature. How the issues here will play out is unknowable. That most literature is already available online is a fact.

MATH

When I first began setting up study subjects for HomeworkCentral.com in 1997, the arrangement for most of them was obvious. Science could be broken down into physics, chemistry, biology, and most other sciences fit fairly well under those, if sometimes redundantly. History, I realized, had to be set up in two main ways, chronologically and geographically. But mathematics was a puzzle. I asked several scholars, and they shied away from giving me an answer.

My mathematician brother gave me, as is his nature, an insightful answer. He said that when he was learning math in the mid-twentieth century, it was taught in a sequence so that "lightbulbs went on in your head" as you progressed for example from algebra I to algebra II and on to calculus. But, he reflected, when his sons were learning the new math a couple of decades later, more advanced topics were taught to them early on. In a manner most uncharacteristic for him, he said he did not know which was best.

My brother turned out to be, as he always is on intellectual stuff, correct. He did not know which way was best because many ways to look at math are instructive. Mathematics is not a path or dividing tree, it is a network. That is why a large website where every idea is connected to every other idea to which it relates is ideal for interfacing mathematics. Mathworld fits that description and is very well done. The website is open content provided and kept fresh and current by Wolfram Research, makers of the software Mathematica and related products, which they sell to professional researchers and developers. Undoubtedly the learning that results from their open content at Mathworld leads to recognition and sales. Supporting education because it is good for business is neither new nor degrading to the learning it engenders. Helping the upcoming generation to learn math is good for everybody's business.

Purple Math is a useful small open content website created and maintained by math teacher Elizabeth Stapel. She teaches at Western International University, an online school, and has a lot of useful tips and insights into using the Internet to learn.

Mathematics does not have the enormous number of topics and documents that are generated by the sciences, history, and literature. As the virtual knowledge ecology matures into a self-distilling, richly multimedia environment, mathematics will become a dynamic network modeling the intellectual structure of the subject. Since mathematics is created by the human mind, it seems an ideal candidate to cause a mirroring re-creation of itself in the virtual knowledge ecology.

PHILOSOPHY AND RELIGION

Although philosophy is not studied a lot in schools, and religion is increasingly excluded, it is worth noting that the Internet has been a welcoming habitat for knowledge about both. The pioneering and towering Perseus Digital Library provides the philosophy classics and a lot more. Kant on the Web is typical of the scholarly open content that forms nodes for a web of open content for individual great past thinkers.

The holy books and seminal writings of the world's religions are exhaustively interfaced online. As All About Sikhism typifies, it is possible to drop in on religious websites to learn about their beliefs and practitioners. An example of orthodoxy available as open content for learning are pages from the website of the King of Jordan. There "The Family Tree of His Majesty King Abdullah II of Jordan" sets out his descent from Qureish Fihr through the Kings of Mecca and the Prophet Muhammad, Fatima az-Zahra, and Al-Hassan down through the Hashemites into modern times.

A similar access to religious knowledge is found on the website of the Government of Tibet in Exile. There is a page on the site describing how His Holiness The 14th Dalai Lama was discovered in 1937, two years after his birth, in the village of Taktser in northeastern Tibet. The tests are described by which he was recognized as the reincarnation of his predecessor, the 13th Dalai Lama.

Generations born in the twenty-first century will have no direct experience with the isolation I knew as a youngster from knowledge of the sort I have been describing for philosophy and religion. I would have to have been well along in a germane college major, studying at a university with a library specializing in pertinent resources to have scratched the surface of the knowledge contained in the websites mention here for philosophy and religion. At no college or library could I have had all of the material described at my fingertips, simultaneously, without paying for it.

Both the description of the lineage of the Hashemites's descent from Muhammad and the discovery of the child in which the Buddha of Compassion would incarnate are created and interfaced online by believers in the faiths of the events described. At a profound level, an online visitor is accessing the ideas, experiences, and beliefs directly from their source—absent filters from the visitor's pedagogy and culture. Like so many aspects of the experience the Internet creates, direct knowledge of a panoply of faiths is completely new for almost everyone.

PHYSICS

Physics is massively and minutely represented online by open content for learning. Classical and theoretical physics are thoroughly described and demonstrated in many fine web pages. The Particle Adventure presented by the Particle Data Group of the Lawrence Berkeley National Laboratory introduces fundamental matter and force. Linked to The Particle Adventure is Physics Central, a web page where you can "learn how your world works" hosted by the American Physical Society. Both of these are web pages designed for students, and both recommend more physics pages on numerous topics in the science.

To meet working physicists and see what they are doing, anyone can visit Quantum Diaries. The website follows physicists around the world as they experience the 2005 World Year of Physics.

To take a sample look at a working network of physicists, visitors are welcome to drop in at the website of the Australian Research Council Centre of Excellence for Quantum-Atom Optics. Websites like this one are designed for the use of scientists, not for the purpose of teaching students about their scientific field. The advance of science depends on sharing among scientists and requires researchers interested in the same subject to inform each other of discoveries. For quantum-atom optics, that sort of sharing and informing occurs on this website. Wonderfully, though, the information that it interfaces into the virtual knowledge ecology allows budding scientists to watch and learn—and presumably to join in the discourse when they are sufficiently prepared.

TECHNOLOGIES

The comprehensive and advertising-cluttered website HowStuffWorks contains clear and practical descriptions of the workings of a colossal array of technologies. In recent months, its clutter of ads has been worsened by in-your-face shopping search boxes. Nonetheless, to learn or teach how to fix automotive, electronic, mechanical parts, and other everyday items, HowStuffWorks.com will give you the answer. Two or three clicks apart are articles on picking locks, the basic mechanisms of an air conditioner, and how a nail gun works. The continuing dominance of this website is a tribute to the usefulness and cognitive quality of the open content. Ads and search engines can be ignored if you need to know badly enough how to pick the lock of an inadvertently locked door.

Another quirky aspect of online technology content is that computer technology belongs to the developers and engineers—and the whiz kids. When I was in charge of subject content at HomeworkCentral.com, I was advised by both the graduate student scholars and the tech staff not to try to collect a content section for computer technology. I was told it was impossible to do it well because it changed too fast. With a knowing look I was told time and again that the techies, including students who needed computer technology knowledge, knew how to find it. I was then a little skeptical about that. I am now glad I took their advice because I realize the geeks had formed a wiki that meant they did not need a computer technology section.

The electrical engineers have a website called the IEEE Virtual Museum, which is an outstanding introduction to their field for students and the public. There are exhibits on the basics, like "Socket to Me: How Electricity Came to Be" and "Let's Get Small: The Shrinking World of Microelectronics." An exhibit called "Songs in the Key of E" describes the beginning of electronic music and includes video with audio of the sounds of the early Singing Arc and Theremin.

The website titled Bridges and Tunnels of Allegheny County, Pennsylvania presents a wealth of interesting information. The way the website has been created and maintained demonstrates several facets that make the virtual knowledge ecology a rich and compelling environment for learning. The website is the work of one man, Bruce S. Cridlebaugh, proving, as have many other high value cognitive websites, that it is the quality of the content that is its primary asset. There are a lot of websites where a great volume of people and money have been involved in an effort which ended up conveying very little content through its interface. In the Bridges and Tunnels site, the design and structure of bridges are interfaced in detail, variety, and demonstration through how they are really used. As open content on the Internet, these structural and aesthetic designs are available for study from these pages anywhere in the world. It would not be surprising if one day something quite similar to an Allegheny County bridge spanned a stream or river in Bangladesh, Brazil, or Botswana.

WRITING

To learn to write is to acquire a skill and apply knowledge. An important part of the skill was once penmanship. Increasingly, writing is done by typing on a keyboard or keypad. It is probably a myth—though it seems true as you watch a toddler whiz along punching keys—that babies are now born knowing how to do that. Phone keypads and toys are introducing children very early to the idea of punching keys to get numbers and letters. For kids and adults, there are many effective online tutorials that teach people to write in the sense of mastering the keyboard.

Literacy is another requirement of writing: You have to know the words and how to spell them, at least closely enough for a spell-checker to correct your mistakes. My thoughts on literacy are discussed in Idea 43. The bottom line, I think, is that using the Internet is a way to attain, improve, and perfect literacy. People will acquire literacy for whatever they do on the Internet, just by doing it. I do not mean that as a sweeping statement, but as a simplification. I know some human help is important to advance literacy.

A requisite part of learning to write is mastering grammar and punctuation. There are many guides available online for that. A search engine finds them quickly. Learners can choose the ones that work best for them.

Style and composition begin to move from skill to communication art and aesthetic creation. On the practical side for learning and correcting these aspects of one's writing there are also many guides and commentaries online. An excellent example is Fifty Writing Tools. The author Roy Peter Clark is vice president and senior scholar of the Poynter Institute, a school specializing in journalism.

The ModernWord.com, known first as Libyrinth.com, is edited by Alan B. Ruch, known also as The Great Quail. The website is a delightful center for writers and lovers of literature.

In very recent years, the act and art of writing have burst with great passion onto the Internet as self-publishing and most recently, a cornucopia of blogging. E-mailing and texting on cell phones is becoming a curtailed form of written expression. I, for one, would not have imagined as recently as a year or two ago that individual authorship would profusely emerge from the virtual knowledge ecology—but that is exactly what is happening. The great motivation to learn to write in the future may well be to be able to participate in the online social and intellectual discourse. A lot of people are already working on their writing skills for just that reason.

REFERENCE

Stating that the Internet is like a big virtual library is very common. There is truth in the statement, particularly in the sense of a reference library. There dozens of dictionaries in major languages, dictionaries for dozens of minor languages, and interactive dictionaries that switch words between languages. Supplementing dictionaries are countless glossaries providing a new sort of word reference for specialized subjects. It is an easy matter when authoring a website about a specific topic to include a page in the site with a glossary—a list of words for the subject that might be unfamiliar to the visitor. As a separate web page, the glossary will have its own URL. Someone creating a report in the field can link to the glossary, or to several glossaries, for the topic. This glossary building and networking has become a standard online practice.

Nothing like the glossary phenomenon can occur in a brick and mortar library because glossaries cannot be torn out of paper books and shared. Here are two examples of the level of detail at which word definitions are distributed on the Internet. A classical music glossary NAXOS.com begins with: accelerando, accompaniment, adagio, air, alla, allegro, allemande, alto, andante, anthem, arabesque. The Soils.org glossary has 127 terms beginning with "a" include: abiontic enzymes, ablation till, absorptance, absorption, accelerated erosion, access tube, acetylene-block assay, acid precipitation, acid soil, activation energy, advection, aerate, aerobic digestion, aggregate, agric horizon.

The encyclopedic aspects of the Internet can be thought of in three ways. The roots of the word *encyclopedia* are from Greek: *enkyklios* meaning general and *paideia* meaning education rooted in the word for child, which is *paid*. All of the subjects discussed above are education. The Internet can be compared to a big encyclopedia because the Internet contains subjects that comprise education to look up and learn as is if the student were using a printed encyclopedia.

The second encyclopedic aspect in the Internet is that many printed encyclopedias have been repositioned in cyberspace, as discussed in Idea 7. The basic difficulty of repositioning printed encyclopedias is that the encyclopedia's online version requires constant updating by the editors.

The Internet has experienced a third phenomenon: the birth of a major encyclopedia within the virtual knowledge ecology, the Wikipedia. As explained in the *History* comment, articles in Wikipedia are written by volunteers and edited by the general public. I remember being told by an editor at HomeworkCentral.com about the new and open encyclopedia when it went online in 2001. I thought to my self that it was strange—and had no idea it was a sea change to open content reference publishing. With more than a million articles in the winter of 2005, Wikipedia has fresh, erudite content made up of articles that are watched over by the people across the world, with individual article watchers who know and care about what its open content says.

Most printed journals have put websites into what can be thought of as the periodicals division of the Internet. Many of these journals are not open content and require expensive subscriptions. I hope that changes, and I think it will. There are also journals created for the Internet and published only and openly online. One of the most interesting is the *Internet Library of Science*. This journal appeared in October 2003. Its goal is to provide completely open and unlimited access to the latest scientific research. That openness is a core principle and goal toward the advancement of science that has been in place since the birth of modern science in the seventeenth century. The Internet can fulfill that goal in ways unimaginable by Henry Oldenburg of the England's Royal Society and Benjamin Franklin in founding the American Philosophical Society. The best they had were handwritten letters that took weeks to find their way between working scientists. For the subject of this book, which is the fulfillment of learning by the virtual knowledge ecology, open access to science is a key factor, as it was for Oldenburg and Franklin. Everything working scientists publish openly online as they advance their knowledge is open content for learning by budding scientists across the planet.

The Internet fulfills another of the traditional library roles as an archive of knowledge. A choice example of the archiving of documents from the ages of paper is African Research Central, which is a clearinghouse of Africa primary sources. The website's database links to repositories in African countries and repositories outside Africa. It is interfaced in both English and French.

Finally, the mother of all archives is a project that stores multiple terabytes of knowledge—using the Internet to archive the Internet itself. Since 1996, the Internet Archive has been taking snapshots of websites and archiving them. The only way to get some sense of what is available through the Internet Archive is to browse the website. Everything they have can be accessed at no cost by researchers, historians, scholars, and the general public.

53 EYEWITNESS ACCOUNT OF THE CASCADE SOURCES

A startling truth is that, for all the billions and billions of dollars we spend on education, our students are studying essentially everything but the most vanilla, middling knowledge using materials created outside of the education industry at no cost to the education sector. Before they get to college, students use most of this knowledge outside of school.

With the United States alone spending at least three-quarters of a trillion dollars a year on education, at first blush it would seem reasonable to expect that some of that money has been spent in recent years to place excellent open content for learning online. A small amount has, but almost completely by random offerings by a few departments and instructors at the college level.

There is online tutorial material for sale, and schools are a major customer for the enterprises that make this closed content, selling it over and over again to school after school. School money is also spent on products that, at least in part, simply point to online content that is otherwise open and free. Other businesses buy and digitize content and sell it to school libraries—again being paid for repeatedly by separate subscriptions school by school—and keeping the content they sell closed to general Internet access. Part of the overt or subtle rationale for all of these content-for-money methods is the perceived need for schools to pick, choose, and censor what students have access for study. Much of the for-pay material is the vanilla middling type dictated by standard, and little of it enters the virtual knowledge ecology. The kids tend to find the ecology on their own.

The business of selling closed content to schools is based on the business model of making money by providing the content needed in schools for learning knowledge. It is the same model under which textbook publication has operated for decades. Under this model, education is big business and properly what it sells and buys for its students should be competitive so that students end up with superior products to use to learn.

But problems now afflict the model because the closed digital content being sold to schools is inferior to the open content for learning that has appeared in recent years. This new, open, free, and inexpensively produced online knowledge content should be used, not because it is on some kind of moral high ground by being open, but because it is better knowledge. It is superior because it is available, fresh, up-to-date, authoritative, interactive, increasingly compelling as multimedia enhances it and—most importantly—interfaced in context.

The content that schools purchase from the education industry is marketed as expertly tailored to grade levels and interfaced in effective pedagogically designed lesson plans and courses. It has become the norm to conform the knowledge resources to grade standards, limiting the extent to which a student can follow his intellectual curiosity to subject matter expected to be questioned in tests. The purchased material is touted as safe for students because it is cut off from an Internet wilderness of unsubstantiated sources and tempting or even dangerous diversions.

The big problem, though, with these controlled methods is children are being fed partial knowledge that is often stale—and we are paying billions to do it, when open content is free to the learning consumer.

Several factors make open content superior. One that there is no way for the knowledge entrepreneurs to overcome is the fact, as mentioned in other Ideas in this book, that closed content cannot interconnect and interact in context to relevant knowledge throughout the Internet. Students end up learning isolated facts and disembodied concepts instead of developing conceptual, contextual thinking by experiencing the virtual knowledge ecology.

Another problem with learning materials produced by an enterprise that creates knowledge resources for sale to schools is that the enterprise is necessarily a secondary source. This made sense when, in order to get the content a textbook contained to learners, it was necessary for a book to be printed and shipped for each student who would then be learning what it contained. Now a student anywhere with a wireless laptop receiving the Internet can use his machine to interface directly to limitless learning pages based anywhere on the planet—and quite literally anywhere in the known universe. The Jet Propulsion Laboratory's open content for comets is a primary source tended by scientists who study comets. A textbook's content for comets is a secondary source. In studying the life of Thomas Jefferson, information in a textbook about his Monticello home would be farther removed from the subject than an online visit to Monticello.org.

As described in Idea 40 and below, open content is usually under the active stewardship of experts in their knowledge field and is routinely kept fresh and up-to-date. The multimedia knowledge expression now coming down the pipe is further invigorating open content in ways printed textbooks never will.

As the online knowledge has burgeoned and matured, the education entrepreneurs have continued to dominated K–12 schools. Their printed publications fill children's backpacks. Their online products are purchased as school library subscriptions over and over, multiplying the money spent for them by the number of school libraries in the districts that subscribe. While the schools stick with the old purchasing model, the kids have moved on.

Many precollege students, especially in problem schools, use the Internet very little at school. Those who begin to do Internet research in middle school or high school tend to do it away from school, on their own computers or borrowed computers and on their own time outside of school. When students in the K–12 grades—as well as those in college—do their online research, they are largely using open content originating outside of education. They are accessing what they are learning from the virtual knowledge ecology. Almost none of what they use is created by money we spend for K–12 education. We are moving into a scene along these lines: while computer time on the wired-down, censored computers in schools is rationed and lost to disrepair, parents pay for wireless laptops that their kids use to do homework at home or at WI-FI hotspot like Starbucks.

Perhaps the Starbucks image is hyperbole, but there is no doubt that the next very few years will profoundly challenge the validity of the billions we spend on printed and closed digital knowledge sources to place in schools and the backpacks of our children. That story is beyond the scope of this book. Instead, the following describes the sorts of places the open content comes from to form the virtual knowledge ecology. The sources discussed are where the kid at Starbucks is going to learn stuff.

With no cynicism intended, it is probably true that the lack of education enterprise for open content is simply because it is felt to be not a big money-maker. Creating compelling digital learning content may well emerge as a secondary industry that services a variety of sources like the types listed here. The secondary industry would create multimedia, animation, tutorial interactions, and web pages for these hosting types.

The higher-education sector that receives something like 30 percent of the billions spent on education does contribute to open content. This is explored in Idea 56.

The eight categories of open content sources described below are based on my experience in observing and using the content. They do not provide an exhaustive list of all the places excellent open content comes from, but I think they convey an accurate general picture of where the great content cascade originates.

If it is not the education industry, who does create and pay for what students are using in the twenty-first century to access knowledge? The rest of this Idea is an overview of the several and varied main sources of the open content for learning that forms the virtual knowledge ecology.

ONE PERSON

Of necessity, school courses and textbooks are conceptualized top down, from a large subject covered in the entire course or book, to major sections within chapters, which in turn have subjects and lessons for courses and paragraphs for small subsubjects. If the subject is, for example, world history, it tends to have sections on ancient, classical, medieval, and modern. Each of those would be divided into continents and then countries and so on.

Online study subject content for learning—when it is open content—gets organized the other way around. Little subjects are made into a batch of interlinked web pages that are, in turn connected to other batches, building a larger and larger web of knowledge. The result of this sort of organization is the empowering of one person to make a few interconnected web pages about a subject he knows well. If he makes the best web pages on that subject, virtually everyone else interested in what he knows about links to it, making it part of several or many larger clusters in the virtual knowledge ecology.

Since 1995, Professor Doug Linder of the University of Missouri–
Kansas City School of Law has created and maintained the Famous Trials website. He has collected and organized rich materials for many
trials, creating a thoroughgoing knowledge environment for his subject.

Carey and Jan Cook are a husband and wife team who operate a free
website for learning words using puzzles and other activities. Their website averages 130,000 visits a month. It is called Vocabulary University,
and its domain name vocabulary.com bespeaks its early entry into the
Internet. In 1994, Carey Cook decided to create the website, and the
next year it was online. He works in the investment business in San
Francisco and his wife taught school for a number of years. They operate the website because they enjoy contributing to learning.

Cora Agatucci, a professor of English Central at Oregon Community
College, has been operating the website African Timelines since 1997.
Primarily done for her students, Agatucci's work is open to others across
the Internet and serves as a valuable authoritative resource for African
history.

As I have looked through and reviewed thousands of study subject
web pages over the past nine years, I have realized that many of the best
ones are the work of one person—at least conceptually and in choosing
and organizing the content. Typically, the authors of these websites
know a great deal about their subject and are passionate enough about
the knowledge to interface it online. This is a very different matter than
people building the websites because they are trained as teachers.

When a person who is passionate about a knowledge subject sets
about to create a website, the knowledge is the driving force for the
design, illustrations, and content. This interfaces a different learning
process than a textbook or other reference in typical schooling as we
have known it. In the past, the knowledge resource has played a passive
or secondary role as a human teacher works to convey the knowledge at
hand. An online visitor to Linder's Famous Trials will connect directly
to the knowledge interfaced there. This does not replace human teaching, but is certainly not the same thing. Many of the finest online open
content knowledge nodes are the work of instructors and professors like
Linder. Because he knows his subject so well, he intuitively mirrors the
structure of the knowledge in the way his web pages and their contents
interlink.

Early on in my knowledge-collecting experience, I began looking at The World Lecture Hall for links to place on HomeworkCentral.com and to review in our newsletter. Based at the University of Texas, since its development in 1994–95, the website has invited free content from courses, organized by subject. That content is not at all limited to UT, but comes now from higher education online course materials from all over the world.

Starting in 1998, I began visiting The World Lecture Hall every few weeks to look for subject links. Each time I would go back, a few courses would have been added here and there for chemistry or European history or classical literature and various other subjects. The materials were posted with the name of the source college, course, and instructor. The course syllabus would usually be there, and that was where I would start digging. And there I would find gems!

What I would find would be a diagram, or chart, or set of principles, or animation—in each case the instructor's own concept of how to use the new Internet medium to reinforce his or her teaching of a subject in which the instructor was a devoted expert. Not everything I found was compelling. Some materials were better than others. But they all represented the beginning of a new era of teaching.

The course materials placed in the mid-1990s into The World Lecture Hall were among the earliest open content for learning. Although their source was what is known as the academy—colleges, universities, and their related research and the like—the knowledge nuggets I found at The World Lecture Hall were almost always the creations of individual instructors. Other open content was also beginning to show up online from larger sources within the academy.

THE ACADEMY

Open content for learning whose sources were colleges and universities tended to bubble up from individuals and from departments during the 1990s. To my knowledge, it was not until MIT's OpenCourseware initiative was announced in April 2001 that campus-wide opening of content got under way. The creation of content began much earlier, as the instructor or department kept what was and is produced under the stewardship of the knowledge experts. Open courseware is an access process. Creating the content remains essentially with those who research and teach it, which is a key factor in guaranteeing its authenticity.

There are many college and university departmental projects of major significance in providing open content for learning. They have emerged across a spectrum of schools, with different ones ending up dominant in different fields. There are many examples given throughout these pages of this source of open content based in the academy. Three more are mentioned here as examples representing many, many more that enrich the virtual knowledge ecology.

The University of California–Berkeley's Museum of Paleontology is a magnificent interface to an institution devoted to investigating and promoting an understanding of the history of life and diversity of the earth's biota.

The Douglass Archives of Public Address is a repository of American oratory and related documents built by the Northwestern University scholars and teachers of rhetoric and speech.

Rutgers University is the home of the Nucleic Acid Database, which includes introductory sections to "Nucleic Acids for DNA and RNA" and a "Nucleic Acid Highlights" section.

Many universities create and host tutorial web pages with elementary open content for learning intended for precollege students. Two examples of these are the University of Wisconsin's The Why Files and Drexel University's Elementary Math Problem of the Week.

Academic subject groups that network their knowledge among scholars in their field from many colleges and universities provide another outstanding academy source of open content.

The Advanced Papyrological Information System lists as partners these universities: Columbia, Duke, Princeton, California–Berkeley, Chicago, Michigan, Toronto, and Yale. The collected scraps of ancient writing held by all of these great learning centers are centered into one database. It is a spectacular resource for papyrus scholars, but because the resource is open content, young school students can quickly get a valid idea of ancient writing by looking at the images of actual artifacts. One supposes a youngster in Egypt browsing the images would especially resonate with the relics from his home's vaunted past.

Taking inter-institutional merging around a subject to a new level is a web page based at the University of Arizona called Image Understanding as Multi-Media Translation. Ideas, institutions, images, and words are linked, mixed, and analyzed. The minimalization of ideas into separate web pages, as discussed in Idea 69, gives unlimited configurations of the work of scholars a stunning new richness in research, thinking, and assets for learning.

LIBRARIES

Libraries have responded in several ways as a great deal of what visitors once went to libraries to use has become available online. As they have responded, they have continued to serve a majority, though decreasing one, of people who do not have personal Internet access or do not want to use the Internet at all.

In addition to maintaining their hardcopy collections, small and large libraries have become centers of Internet access, fulfilling the purpose of the profession to provide access to knowledge for patrons and the public. A factor in overcoming the digital divide has been the ability of students who did not have school or home online access to go to a library to use the Internet.

Another way libraries have participated in providing content for learning is in digitizing some of their collected material. The U.S. Library of Congress has offered useful open content for learning exhibits over the years of Internet emergence. Its major digital thrust, however, is to develop preservation techniques and partners for digital material, looking at the burgeoning flow of new materials that are only created in digital formats. Like their early champion, Thomas Jefferson, the librarians of Congress are visionaries.

As libraries have worked toward digitizing hard copy portions of their collections, they have created digital catalogs for close to everything they have. At the grand old New York Public Library, which fills a block on Fifth Avenue at 42nd Street, the giant third-floor reading room was recently restored to its full elegance. At the same time the physical structure was being refurbished, an elegant digital catalog system was put in place so that a virtual visitor from anywhere in the world can locate the contents of the main library and its satellites.

In recent years, the library websites, including the ones mentioned above, have been blossoming with handsome and erudite digital exhibits. In addition to the digitized texts mentioned in Idea 40, the British Library offers exhibits like "Turning the Pages" with several great classics to read virtually.

Another of the growing number of library open content contributions to the virtual knowledge ecology is the republication online by the Brooklyn Public Library of the 1841–1902 *Brooklyn Daily Eagle* in searchable text. For a student of any age, reading through the prebroadcast media's colorful accounts by nineteenth-century newspaper reporters conveys a compelling sense of the vibrancy of history.

MUSEUMS, HISTORICAL SOCIETIES, AND ZOOS

It is the central purpose of museums, historical societies, and zoos to preserve and showcase knowledge. These sectors worldwide have become a truly fabulous source for online knowledge. The following can only touch on a few highlights.

Museums have been placing learning materials online since the first stages of the emergence of the Internet. Because so much of what they collect is visual, they have been able to do much, much more as downloading speed and multimedia tools have gotten better.

In the Idea 52 description of open content for arts, the online collections for some of the major art museums are mentioned. An example on the artistic digital edges is the E-SPACE of the website of the San Francisco Museum of Modern Art.

Over many years, the Smithsonian has placed excellent exhibits online from many of its divisions. A 2005 offering from its Museum of American History, "Whatever Happened to Polio?" has a timeline, a collection of historical photographs, activities for students, and other resources.

"Caught in Oils" from the Natural History Museum in London showcases oil paintings from its collection of animals and of famous naturalists.

Often, small museums offer online exhibits in a narrow, local topic. A choice example from the museum at Hundersingen Germany located on the Danube is a "Time Chart of Celts on the Upper Danube."

The online showcasing potential of historical societies is mind-boggling. Already, the devoted local experts who form these societies are beginning to open their files and storage drawers into the virtual knowledge ecology. A seminal example is an interactive web page called St. Paul Panorama that has been online since 1999. The panorama consists of nine photographs set end-to-end across a web page. The visitor can scroll across the page to see them, and to answer a question for each about a spot-of-interest on the photograph. These pictures were shot in sequence from the top of the town's courthouse as photographer Benjamin Franklin Upton slowly turned full circle to make a photographic panorama of the entire town. He took the pictures in 1857, and now the whole wide world can see the frontier town rising on the banks of the upper Mississippi River.

Zoos are adapting to new online roles of great value in informing the public on animal life and conservation. The New England Aquarium website has several compelling sections of learning content. An interesting example is "Animal Rescue," which describes techniques for assisting animals stranded on a beach and how care is given for those who are being rehabilitated for return to the ocean.

GOVERNMENTS

A major source of open content for learning is virtual material produced by governments as working science and as information for the public in general. There are hundreds of websites operated by national governments and their branches and agencies across the world and by states and regions, cities, and other government units.

An awesome example of working science is the NOAA Satellite and Information Service website. The "Satellite Image of the Day" alone justifies the adjective awesome. There is enough information on and connecting to the service site to provide a student—either elementary or advanced—with weeks of study and learning. Yet, it is the knowledge, not education, that drives this marvelous website. The extensive information about and from satellites is designed for the use of scientists, to design weather projects, and for other purposes not thought of as aimed at students.

Other government website information is provided by experts at the hosting agency or laboratory and is aimed at students. An example of that is the "ABCs of Nuclear Science" page at the Lawrence Berkeley National Laboratory, which in early 2005, had received over 750,000 visits since 1998.

The United Kingdom Parliament website has current goings on, an explanation of how Parliament works and its history, a glossary, and an "Explore Parliament" section aimed at kids.

Typically, the websites of lower levels of government have information about elected and appointed officials and about services. Many websites of this type either point to or have developed geographical and historical content that is excellent for learning. For example, the New York City website includes a long and detailed "History of the New York City Police."

The number and diversity of open content for learning pages that have cascaded from governments into the virtual knowledge ecology is immense. It might seem natural to question whether what governments say on those pages can be trusted. In answer to that, it seems hard to think the science pages would contain false content. Satellite images, earthquake alerts, public health information, and many other types of government data will be vetted by the fact that real-world scientists and citizens are using it. Errors will be caught and publicly criticized.

That is not to say government websites do not promote the causes and images of those in power. It is a lesson in perceptibility for students to evaluate what governments put online about their history and policies. As I write this, an interesting example is the description of twentieth-century events given in its "History of Beijing, China" on the city's official international website. It will be interesting in years to come to see how the paragraph now there may evolve.

From another perspective, it is fair to ask how impartial the textbook authors in different countries are as they compose the histories of other countries destined to be given to students as gospel. In the global age of learning now dawning, students will find more than one view on many subjects as they learn from the virtual knowledge ecology. Because students from everywhere will be sharing the same sources, what is true and what is not seem to have a greater chance of getting sorted out than they have in the compartmented learning venues of the past.

JOURNALS, BROADCAST, AND NEWS MEDIA

The three forms of media in the above title, used to distribute knowledge from predigital times, all have assumed roles in flowing open content for learning into the virtual knowledge ecology. Journals can be open or closed content and repositioned from print or newly created for the Internet. An outstanding leader in creating open content for learning has been *National Geographic*.

Broadcast media has played a varied role thus far. A larger one is coming into view as online video makes halting but steady progress toward practicality. PBS has been a trend-setting leader in using assets steming from its video programs to build a website, but those projects have not yet included moving images in a major way. An example is PBS's interactive story of the "Building the Alaska Highway."

The Annenberg/Corporation of Public Broadcasting online exhibits were also a leader in the initial phase of the evolution of open content for learning. This collaboration has been expanded into Learner.org, with many educational features.

On the news side, the BBC has news and many features for learning like their "Interactive Body." In a broader sense, the online versions of newspapers and television broadcast are all open content for learning, so long as they do not require a paid subscription or a password. Materials for what we used to call current events when I was in school are largely real-time viewing or reporting of events as they happen.

FOR-PROFITS

Habits die hard. The long-standing habit for creating content for students to learn from has been to create and print textbooks, charts, and the like and sell them to schools. As the Internet began to boom, the same model has been tried and adopted in a small way as closed digital content sold to schools. The fundamental weirdness in that model in the

Internet venue is that the need to distribute the content geographically is gone—or artificial at best.

New business models have evolved where high-quality open content for learning is created to the profit of its creator.

WebMD is an example of the model of the open content for learning being the front end of a website for a company making money doing something else. In the case of WebMD, its products are medical business services and practice services. WebMD is a publicly held multimillion-dollar corporation. Its free online content is a marvelous environment for students to use to learn about diseases, medicine, and health.

Another excellent open content source for the same sort of information is the website Mayo Clinic.com. The Mayo Clinic is in the business of treating patients. Mayo Clinic's high-quality online medical open content improves profits by creating awareness and positive perception by prospective patients. The website is funded in part by accepting ads and sponsorships under strict guidelines.

A smaller version of the open content website front end of a for-profit enterprise is All About Tea, with an outstanding collection of historical, geographical, and botanical information about varieties of tea.

The old habits of getting learning content to kids have been hard to break for the education establishment. No so for the kids. I believe the future major role of for-profit enterprises in creating learning content is the placement of their expertise online so that they can profit from the publicity it brings them and for their development of future employees and customers. I call websites like that expertorials.

EXPERTORIALS

The Internet has made it possible for an expert in a subject to create and manage a tutorial that the entire world potentially can study. This fact, and the large presence already of expert-tutorials, expertorials for short, is a significant factor in making the Internet ecology knowledge-rich.

In Idea 52 on subjects, and earlier in this idea, over and over open content examples have been given that are overseen by professors, subject enthusiasts, working scientists, and enterprises explaining their products. Some more examples follow.

Ben & Jerry's has an animated, lighthearted, but information-filled expertorial called "Cow to Cone," tracing the process of making ice cream.

The Carnegie Corporation of New York website includes a lengthy, documented article on how the company's founder Andrew Carnegie provided and encouraged libraries.

The Danish Wind Industry Association has a multipage, animated wind power expertorial in English, Français, Deutsch, and Español.

"Discover Opera" is the name of an open content music learning jewel that is part of the website of the Metropolitan Opera. There are dramatic stories, histories, and suggestions for the newcomer to opera. An illustrated timeline called "Sight & Sounds of Met History" highlights great performances over the decades. Many of the highlights have audio clips, like the one that plays Polish soprano Marcella Sembrich, singing *Lucia di Lammermoor* on October 24, 1883.

A very great deal of money is spent by the for-profit sector on education. Corporations, for example, give millions to education. This money, for the most part, goes to help and improve the schools we now have. Expertorials offer a fresh way to reach the kids, giving them new direct access to compelling learning materials. The for-profit sector will connect to the new generations in constructive ways by placing expertorials on their websites to explain to kids what they know and do.

The question arises as to whether or not Ben & Jerry's or the Metropolitan Opera are objective in what they say. A profit motive for each of the expertorials mentioned above is either obvious or lurking somewhere. In fact, open content from universities, governments, museums, and the rest can never be absolutely free of the profit motive or other selfish purpose. The new and very interesting question is whether the open competition among expertorials is better than an education establishment industry that is paid a very great deal of money to be a secondary, closed, and controlled source for knowledge students are assigned to learn. I think the expertorials are turning out to be a lot better—to say nothing of being essentially cost-free for education!

🔅 54 HOW OPEN CONTENT IS PAID FOR

When schools buy textbooks, videos, wall charts, CDs, and other tangible content containers, they pay the vendor for the purchase. The same is true for closed digital content sold to school libraries or individual online subscribers. Open content—something like radio, and I suppose junk mail—just arrives, and it is free. The content and its delivery costs have been paid for where it originated, at the source.

The receiver's cost to take advantage of the free open content is a device with which to interface the content and the cost to plug into the Internet. Wireless transmission looks like it will make the latter cost disappear.

Looking at what the costs are at the source end of open content for learning, there is a serendipitous synergy spinning this wonderful stuff of knowledge into the virtual knowledge ecology. The parts of the synergy are:

- Subject experts who are enthusiastic to display what they know;
- Institutions and enterprises that possess specialized information and artifacts;
- A technology and medium that is almost without cost;
- The means to build the content from little patterns to bigger ones;
- A connectivity among the content that is limitless and has no cost;
- The constant potential for dynamic connectivity;
- A global audience who can partake of the knowledge for free.

The last of these factors, the global audience, is the most basic piece of the economy formula for open content for learning. When the "ABCs of Nuclear Science" has been accessed a million times, sometime soon, even if the expenditure to create and maintain the tutorial had been a million dollars, the cost-per-use would be one dollar. I cannot imagine how the tutorial could have a total cost at the source of more than a few hundred dollars, making the actual cost per use negligible. There is, in fact, a significant value for humanity is the number of visitors who have learned something about the science.

Certainly, money has to come out of budgets at some level to sustain open content for learning. But the cost comparison to the old way of doing things in education is so out of balance that comparison is meaningless. The cognitive return on investment is astounding.

And there is more. Open content for learning is an amazing win-win situation for its sources as well as its users.

One person can have the satisfaction of hosting and maintaining a website about something she knows and cares about for well under $1,000 a year, including her time. Anyone connected to the Internet can benefit from her expertise.

The academy has a way to let people anywhere connect into and appreciate its knowledge. I feel certain, though this is only my opinion, that open content from a college or university wins interest from prospective students it would hope to enroll, as well as research enhancement through faculty's global connections.

Libraries win by continuing as key players in the stewardship of knowledge, as they have been in the past. Libraries have been outstanding role models for other institutions in transitioning into the digital age.

The governments win by being in touch with citizens in new ways. The public wins from government interfaces by the greater spread of sciences and other information that is useful knowledge for learning.

Like libraries, journals will need to be openly online to benefit from digital connectivity, and they are now trending toward this, some more gracefully than others.

There are for-profits that have led the way in creating expertorials. Doing so is a way of fulfilling corporate community responsibility. These for-profits also win goodwill by interfacing what they know as open content for learning. I hope this trend grows and believe it will. For corporations and other for-profit enterprises, the cost of adding tutorials to their websites is minuscule. The benefit to learning is enormous.

The sources for open content for learning are all of us. We all win from the continuing cascade of what is known by humankind into the virtual knowledge ecology.

55 THE MOVEMENT TOWARD A NEW ECOLOGY OF LEARNING

While the education establishment ogre has succeeded so far in deflecting public attention from the virtual knowledge ecology, a lot of very bright and visionary people—many of them educators—have been doing things that will soon send the ogre off into the gloomy mists of recent educational history.

Like almost everything else about the Internet, the open content for learning that is forming the virtual knowledge ecology has sprung up from the digital grassroots. It is not a top-down movement. There is now, however, something of a movement under way to coordinate opening the content of education institutions to free global use online.

As I mentioned in Idea 36, I was lucky enough to be at the Open Content Meeting of the William and Flora Hewlett Foundation in the fall of 2004, when many of the open content leaders were present representing efforts to open courseware and other learning content within the Internet. These were people at the cutting edge of the open content momentum and were making things happen. A phrase to describe their collective goals emerged from their presentations and discussions. They spoke often of the creation of a new ecology of learning.

The Hewlett Foundation's website page "Open Content" provides an overview of the open content movement and links to the programs the foundation has selected to assist financially. The array of projects of the Hewlett grant recipients is a look at the basic facets of building and facilitating the new ecology for learning now under way. None of the approaches are exactly alike; together, they are a very promising synergy.

When MIT began its OpenCourseWare (OCW) initiative, in April 2001, it proclaimed a vision that other institutions have caught. MIT decided to put the materials used in its campus courses openly online. MIT is far down the road in massively achieving its goal, with materials from over nine hundred of its courses already online. The materials interfaced in this way are being studied by learners across the global Internet and physical world.

MIT's OCW is a model for other universities, such as the Johns Hopkins Bloomberg School of Public Health OpenCourseWare, which had six courses online by spring of 2005.

The Foothill-De Anza Community College District in California is pursuing OCW with support from the Hewlett Foundation. Their project is called Sharing of Free Intellectual Assets (SOFIA).

Harvard University's Open Library Connections Program was

founded in 2002, with the goal of making research materials from libraries and museums across Harvard freely available over the Internet—approaching the content not from the course source but from repositories. Because courses and collections are modularized in their open content form online, they both can be freely linked and are important growing sectors of the virtual knowledge ecology.

Utah State University's eduCommons is an open courseware project that was just getting under way online as I completed this book. Its goals include catalyzing the growth of communities of learners around the eduCommons. That vision reflects the creative momentum from the open content movement to the virtual knowledge ecology. The interconnectivity of knowledge itself and of the people using it arises from the network behavior of the new ecology of learning.

In a purely network-native approach at Rice University's Connexions, a content commons of "knowledge chunks" dubbed "modules" is building up with contributions from the open Internet. Other units of Connexions are software, including a course builder for assembling modules, intellectual property licensing under Creative Commons, and quality controls. As of spring 2005, Connexions had over a million users from more 157 countries tapping into 2,300 modules and courses.

Carnegie Mellon University's Open Learning Initiative has moved into the future of course design. The courses are designed through a combination of cognitive theory and faculty expertise. The open and free course versions are comparable to courses taught at Carnegie Mellon University but do not include the instructor-led aspects of the course, and the student does not get academic credit.

Sakai defines itself as "a community source software development effort to design, build and deploy a new *Collaboration and Learning Environment (CLE)* for higher education." This foresighted effort helps to prepare the way for a future of effortless access and the exchange of virtual human knowledge.

EduTools is a reviewing partner to e-learning activities. Created by universities allied in the Western Cooperative for Educational Telecommunications, the project reviews course management systems, online courses, and research projects.

Two other projects supported by the Hewlett Foundation are not involved in the open content movement as courseware contributors. They contribute crucially in other ways. The Internet Archive, as mentioned in Idea 53, has been archiving vast numbers of Internet pages since 1996. The project's concept is to be a library of the Internet—and following the public library spirit, it is free for public use. I think of it as the library of the virtual knowledge ecology. CreativeCommons addresses the intellectual property issues that come up by making websites open. The issues around the copyright of web pages, the solutions Creative Commons offers, and related topics are discussed in Idea 104.

Coming into view at the Hewlett Foundation meeting in the fall of 2004 was the international aspect of the open content movement. The people attending participated in connecting learners to open content in China, Africa, and India. The sense of their reports was that there is much to be done first to connect people across the world to the Internet and, as that is being accomplished, to adapt open content for global use. There is also a strong desire for people in different locales to contribute to the making of open content for learning. The types of programs described in this Idea are providing models for new waves of open content projects from many sources.

The comment from the group that summed up the consensus for me was "make it and they will come." Open content projects will be adapted into new user groups at greater and greater scale. The blueprint content for global enlightenment is being drawn in the seminal work of open content projects now online or under way toward launch.

The programs supported by the Hewlett Foundation are pebbles causing the virtual knowledge ecology to radiate circles of waves across the breadth of tomorrow's sources for enriching open content of learning. The virtual knowledge ecology is the center around which the new ecology for learning is forming.

56 THE INCREASING LEVEL OF DETAIL

The future of access will include an ongoing cascade of open content that is at an increasingly smaller level of detail. Sweeping survey websites like the venerable Victorian Web are unlikely to appear. The Victorian Web is a grand old lady measured in Internet years. She spreads across fields from literature to history to technology to the arts, and much more. If and when a competitor for a sweeping subject website came along, in all probability it would fail unless it were an improvement over the existing large-topic website in the field. If that happened, the older one would fade, and visitor traffic would flood to the new one. The jargon calls that the *gorilla effect*, and the network theorists refer to the rich getting richer because networks are scale free. In effect, in the Internet world the largest gets bigger. Think of Yahoo, Amazon.com, and Google.

The same effect applies to websites of all sizes, including those at the smallest website scale. If you made a marvelous little website on the type of lace used in the bodices of ladies' dresses in England in the 1880s, everyone on the Internet interested in the topic would use your site. But, if someone created a more thoroughgoing, accurate, and attractive website about those particular laces for that decade, you would lose your traffic.

It is possible to extrapolate from the gorilla effect—big gorillas or tiny ones—that at any level of detail, the most authoritative and instructive website is going to wrest the audience away from all others. That is how Google searches work. The website that gets the most use by visitors goes to the top of the list. Presumably, that means the visitors who are best able to judge the quality of any topic will use it and push it to the top where others will find it. The actual gorilla is the expertise of knowledge peers in the open Internet, and that is a surpassing new way for content to be purified.

As we have looked at before, the routine way to create a textbook for a subject has been to look at the whole of the topic and then break it into a few parts to form chapters to be taught and learned in sequence. Chapters then break down their topic into a few more pieces, set out over the pages in a flow of ideas. Often, a bit more detail is offered as optional extra assignments.

The cascade of knowledge into the Internet works inherently in the opposite direction, from detail up. The Victorian Web is a rare example of a broad subject website. It is, however, essentially a collection of many little piece of Victorian stuff. Some big-picture content was put online in the early emergence of the Internet, mostly by educators repositioning the older method. But, for the most part, as the cascade began, one source added a table of chemical elements, another put some math tables online, museums began to digitize a few specific exhibits, and government websites like NASA and the USGS created a few tutorials here and there for astronomy topics and earth science subjects.

After a decade of the online flow of relatively detailed subjects, just about all subjects are collectively well represented. As the websites for the smaller topics link to each other, they form clusters that collectively represent bigger subjects.

It is quite a change to think of learning a subject from detail outward. Perhaps doing that is what has been called *discovery learning*. In Idea 82, a hypothetical walk in the garden with a child is described. If you are walking with the child, and together you see a ladybug on a leaf, you have come upon a detail that is a node that could be linked to many potential networks of ideas.

Few of us would use this opportunity to teach the child something by launching into a description of insects in general: the number of legs they all have, exoskeletons, and how they produce new generations. Together with the child, you would look closely at the ladybug on the leaf. The child would be likely to notice something and focus on it, perhaps that the ladybug was washing things sticking out of her head. The child would ask you what they were. You could identify them as antennae and say they were important for getting information. Two years later, the child could happen upon a butterfly, notice the insect's waving antennae, and make the mental connection that the beautiful creature was seeking information. Dynamic connections like that are what open content on the Internet allow—something severely limited in static textbooks and curricula.

My prediction is that the great cascade of what is known by humankind has barely begun to pour into the Internet. For one thing, some countries and types of knowledge institutions are farther along in placing their collected knowledge and the expertise of their scholars into the Internet as open content. They will follow a path pioneered mostly in the West, but will be able to do so with much better digital tools and broader band access, promising an ongoing bountiful and beautiful global cascade in months and years ahead.

Once every museum, historical society, library, academic institution, and other keeper of knowledge across the planet has put all of its usually displayed knowledge online, they will next begin to turn to opening their storage drawers and, over time, placing millions more bits of texts and artifacts into web pages. Experts on every sort of subject will place their expertise into websites and will participate in vetting the subjects they know best on other websites.

The result of the ongoing cascade will be a more mammoth and complex virtual knowledge ecology. But the ecology—like, if I may say, the ecology of your brain and mind—has qualities of emergence and connectivity. From the massive virtual knowledge ecology of the child with whom you figuratively walked in the garden, the detail you explained about the ladybug's antennae will arise over the child's lifetime to connect to many thoughts of antennae of different kinds, such as those of butterflies and cell phones. Different as the concept networks are that form from the butterfly and the cell phone, the detail of an antenna serving as a receptor for information is the same. That basic cognitive connectivity abounds in the Internet and is a principal reason the open content is an ecology—because an ecology is relationships.

57 UBIQUITOUS WIRELESS COMPUTING

The global Golden Age of learning now dawning remains invisible to billions of people who have no access to the Internet. Every one of them will be able to see and use the open content when wireless ubiquitous computing is in place.

When the cascade of what is known by humankind began in earnest a decade ago, any hope of everyone using it individually was at best a very distant vision. Now, making that vision a reality is only a matter of time, and probably not much time. It could be accomplished in less years than the decade since the cascade began. The *Action* section of this book addresses how to get that job done.

The factors that have morphed the vision into reality are mostly outside the scope of this book. For the purpose of the virtual knowledge ecology, those changes are relevant in that they will make the open content that forms the ecology accessible to everyone.

In brief, this is what has happened. A computer no longer needs to be wired-down in a single location. Wireless has made a computer both mobile and more a personal device. The spread and acceptance—wild enthusiasm—for cell phones has demonstrated the muscle and benefits of connectivity among individuals. Computers accessing the Internet have become smaller and smaller and thus more portable. Cell phones have begun to access Internet content, and their small screens are increasing in interface sophistication. WI-FI is spreading across cities and popping up in more and more remote locations. Satellites are able to beam Internet access into geographic areas and could one day paint the planet surface into a continuous global hot spot. Everything is moving faster and being displayed more effectively. And it is all getting less and less expensive.

NOTE

1. Lewis J. Perlman. *School's Out*. New York: William Morrow & Co.

4

AGGREGATION

 58 IT TAKES A NETWORK FOR KNOWLEDGE TO EMERGE

The great content cascade of the past decade dumped what is known by humankind into the Internet where each person on earth will soon have access to it in the venue of a virtual ecology. Where did that ecology come from? How did it form from all the stuff that cascaded into the Internet?

The marvelous cognitive explosion described it this section is the story of the aggregating of knowledge into static and dynamic cognitive structures that could only have emerged from chaos. We are learning in our time that order emerges dynamically from chaos and that the emergent order can be a network structure that gives us a roadmap within complexity. The virtual knowledge ecology is an example of that kind of emergence.

The virtual knowledge ecology does not form throughout the Internet but only by connecting and aggregating bits from its open portions. It is the seeming messiness and the absence of planning of this openness that allows the knowledge to aggregate according to its internal meaning, and to do so both as static and dynamic networks. An ecology is a network of relationships—by definition. The virtual knowledge ecology is a network of knowledge expressing the relationships among knowledge that is simulated by computers and computer networks.

The first Ideas in this section are reflections on the virtual knowledge ecology to introduce it as a habitat for knowledge and to look from different directions at what is going on there.

The second group of Ideas briefly sets out theories that shed light on how the mechanisms of the virtual knowledge ecology work and why its underlying connectivity is a marvelous learning environment.

The final Ideas are about practical aspects of using the virtual knowledge ecology for learning.

The *Aggregation* section cannot possibly be a complete, perfect—or perhaps even very clear—explanation of what it seeks to present. We do not yet know what the future that is being created by the new digital learning ecology will be. On the other hand, this ecology is well established and maturing fast. That new ecology is the future venue for global virtual learning.

The seemingly chaotic connectivity within the Internet is challenging and changing many ways things have always been done. Bloggers are impacting mainstream professional journalism. Human swarms are showing up to dominate events. There is new respect for the judgment of crowds. Political campaigns are affected by wireless connectivity at the grassroots. Business is done in virtual meetings. Creative rights are being confronted and shared.

The same connective mechanisms that are changing many other aspects of society are available for the improvement of education but have been too little used so far. It is not enough for school people to condescend to controlling and limiting Internet access for students. The education establishment will not long survive ignoring the natural network powers and gifts of open online content for virtual learning.

I hope the ideas in this section will help to kindle thinking and conversation about the cognitive explosion caused by the new aggregation of minimal bits of knowledge. It is fascinating stuff, filled with hope for a dawning global Golden Age of learning.

59 EARLY GLIMPSES OF THE VIRTUAL KNOWLEDGE ECOLOGY

The cognitive explosion and the resulting virtual knowledge ecology are not theoretical predictions. They have been visible, visited, and used for learning since around the year 2000. They have steadily magnified since then and will continue to do so into the foreseeable future.

My first glimpses of the virtual knowledge ecology occured in 2000, when I was leading our team of graduate students at HomeworkCentral.com. We were collecting links to open content pages for study subjects and organizing them into packets by topic. We were approaching 100,000 links collected and had assembled more than 30,000 packets. Each packet was for a different subject, ranging from volcano mechanisms, to city planning, to European history, to classical art. Packets at the lowest level of our content structure were made up of links. All the levels of packets above the lowest level were made up of groups of packets.

In 1998, when our content department moved into its own space—separate from the business guys and the tech team—I hung a large sign above my desk quoting Stephen Jay Gould and saying: *Like bureaucracy, knowledge has an inexorable tendency to ramify as it grows.*[1] I had been watching the cascade of knowledge onto the Internet for many months, and assumed it was ramifying—branching out into smaller and smaller twigs of smaller topics. I was wrong, and so was Dr. Gould.

I began to catch on when I noticed something that still strikes me as mysterious and is, at the least, counterintuitive. It was something actually happening among our packets and not in the least foreseen or planned by the extremely intelligent and knowledgeable team that was building the HomeworkCentral.com content collection.

An example would be the surprising behavior of a packet of links collected by one of our historians on the subject of the eruption of Mount Vesuvius in 79 A.D., which buried Pompeii and Herculaneum. The packet would keep showing up in different places! Click into the packet comprised of packets on the mechanisms of volcanoes, and the Vesuvius disaster packet would be linked in as an example in the dangerous lava flows packet. In the city planning packet, exactly the same Vesuvius packet would be part of a packet on choosing a city location (not next to a volcano!). The same Vesuvius packet would also show up in European history, perhaps in two or more subpackets, say for ancient Italy and archaeological rediscovery. The classical art preserved beneath the lava also prompted our art editor to link in the Vesuvius disaster there.

Clearly, what was going on was not ramification—not branching. Every time I encountered the Vesuvius disaster packet in a different subject, the Vesuvius packet was a node in a different network from the last one. Each network was shaped by meaning—science, planning, history, art—cognitive stuff.

The part that mystified me, and that I still find counterintuitive, is that all of this is virtual and dynamic. It is not possible to pin down simultaneously the many ideas that issue from the different patterns of connections formed in the subjects. That is very similar to, if not the same thing, as the lack of the ongoing existence of an idea in your brain and mine. In both cases, when connections are active, an idea is happening. But we digress. What is important is that the connectivity is real, visible, and a new medium for interfacing what is known by humankind.

60 CYBERSPACE COGNITIVE EXPLOSION

For all the befuddlement the Internet has caused, understanding its power for change requires knowing just one simple mechanism, which is described in this section. The mechanism is a sort of aggregation resulting from linking little pieces as nodes to cause a network. Perhaps we will one day understand reality fully as the work of a few simple mechanisms. We have learned a lot in the last few years about one of these mechanisms: roles of networks in forming the world we live in. None has more promise than the insight that little pieces put together in different ways make different sorts of big pieces, which is the underlying mechanism and cognitive power of open digital content.

The simple insights into mechanics achieved in an earlier age launched the industrial era. A machine is a controlled means to transmit energy, motion, and forces. It is said that there are only six simple machines: the lever, pulley, inclined plane, wheel and axel, wedge, and screw, and the latter three are actually modifications of the former three. All other machines are combinations of two or more of these simple machines. It would be a stupendous achievement to stumble upon or invent a seventh simple machine or any other simple principle that basic. Actually, stupendous discoveries of simple insights into the workings of reality are dotted here and there over the centuries of human history.

The Ideas in this section are all about an insight like that. It is a newly appreciated mechanism as simple as one of the six simple machines and at least as important. What it does has already been mentioned: It creates completely different new large-scale things by combining smaller-scale parts in different ways. That happens with every machine that is made except the six simple ones—or more precisely, just three of them. It also happens in a lot of other aspects of reality, like making chemical elements, molecules, and us.

Little pieces put together in different ways to make different sorts of big pieces is the underlying mechanism and cognitive power of open digital content. That sounds abstract, but it is sweepingly practical. It is the rudimentary rule of thumb in dealing with the Internet as well as the theory that explains what is going on. The mechanism is the cause of the cognitive explosion.

The Ideas in this section on *Aggregation* all approach this same simple mechanism in different ways and contexts. Reading the Ideas should help reinforce a new way of looking at content organization that is opposite in several ways from the usual approach to education. Materials traditionally published for learning begin with big picture thinking, yet subject matter in reality forms from aggregations of little facts and concepts. Different ways of aggregating the littler pieces—and mixing a few more of them in or out—form new patterns that will convey varied insights. Static resources such as print cannot do that. The Internet does it elegantly.

The cognitive aspect of the explosion is the fact that the bits and pieces of the new networks forming the virtual knowledge ecology are bits of knowledge or networked clusters of bits of knowledge. Knowledge is stuff humans think about, thus cognitive. An idea is a pattern. Different parts of one pattern can be connected to each other differently and to other bits of ideas so that they are aggregated in a new way, and a completely new idea occurs.

The explosion part has to do with the linking. If seven bits of knowledge are set out one by one through the pages of a textbook, the total bits is seven. If those same bits become nodes in an open network, each of them can be connected to any other node to participate in myriad patterns within the network. As I explained in Idea 59, I did not think this up, I watched it happen at HomeworkCentral.com and have been pondering it ever since. What I saw was that, instead of a usual branching tree database where each item in each branch has, as in the textbook, one position, in the open Internet it can have thousands of links. The number of combinations explodes into hundreds and thousands, each combination creating a new splinter or flower of thought. The explosion occurs both statically, in permanent links, and dynamically, as a visitor connects nodes to explore what she is thinking about.

It seems likely that the subtly of thought in the brain is made possible by the same sort of connectivity. A single neuron usually has at least hundreds of synapses to which thousands of other neurons are linked and continually sending a signal by either firing or not firing. In creating the Internet, we may have stumbled on a way to replicate a basic mechanism that supports the infinitesimal cognitive explosions that platform our thought. These events would be biological. As discussed above, at an information-handling level, connectivity is fundamental to thinking and learning.

The digital world of Internet content—when it is open so that it can interconnect freely—seems to mirror the way the mind thinks: All the little pieces are available to connect in any pattern to any or all of the other little pieces. The Internet is the only medium that is or ever has been capable of rudimentary interconnectivity like this. Only the medium of the human mind could do it, until digital venues became large and open.

The cognitive explosion under way within the Internet forms the elegant expanding cloud of virtual cognitive interconnectivity that is the virtual knowledge ecology. The explosion is not scattering bits of knowledge, but is massively proliferating static and dynamic patterns of ideas that can be interfaced on web pages by humans. There is nothing comparable to the digital cognitive explosion in the history of education. It is occurring within a chaos of complexity and emerging as networks. There is no known tidy way to plan or to control this proliferation to get any result approaching so handsome a mirror of what is known by humankind as the one now emerging.

Incredibly, there is a second and complementary mirror of ubiquitous connectivity emerging. This time, the little pieces are individual people. The Internet provides each person piece with the stunning new ability to connect with any and all other person pieces.

Awesomely, both what is known by humankind and humankind itself are massively interconnecting virtually in cyberspace. Bountiful existing knowledge is already liberated into the new cyberspace medium and that emergence continues to bubble up from deeper and deeper levels of detail. The humankind portion is about a quarter of the way toward having everybody connected.

Awesome, incredible, stunning as all of this is, education establishments still spend billions annually on textbooks, make disconnected grades and standards the bottom line, allot knowledge resources by geography and building, block students from the Internet, and hide behind the teaching profession, which they say they protect by maintaining the teachers' nontechnical status (which is meaningless since learning from the Internet is not a technical activity). There are splendid exceptions within education circles and convolutions to this behavior, and to their practitioners belongs the future.

Whether or not the priests of present pedagogy like it, or perhaps ever understand it, the cyberspace cognitive explosion described by the Ideas in this section is the defining event for future human learning.

61 WHY IT TAKES CHAOS AND COMPLEXITY

The cognitive explosion was spontaneous and continues without planning or control. It happens within the chaos of billions of web pages, almost all of which have nothing whatsoever to do with cognitive subjects. Nonetheless, the cognitive explosion has created the virtual knowledge ecology where an elegant mirror of what is known by humankind is coming into sharper and sharper focus.

The chaotic mess routinely horrifies educators. Their instincts and training are founded on order and on inspiring discipline and tidiness in their students' minds. Education is accustomed to dividing knowledge into subjects and linking parts of the subjects into linear curricula that teachers lead their students along in a process of learning.

The prevalent teaching/learning process is organized by separation. Students are separated into grades and not allowed to flow and swarm through knowledge—much less do that through the same knowledge ecology as students elsewhere. The nugget of knowledge of the Battle of the Alamo in 1836 was inserted for many decades into Texas school curricula as a highpoint on the glorious road to Texas's independence.

For students in Mexican schools, the same facts were taught as a step in the history of the United States' grab of territory from Mexico. In recent years, writers of the Texas history curriculum for U.S. students have struggled to keep up with what is thought to be politically correct, which has tended toward hardly teaching anything at all about what inspired the exhortation to "Remember the Alamo!"

Searching up some Battle of the Alamo links from the Internet ecology quickly overcomes the shortcoming of education's segmented, ordered approach. Online, everybody's point of view is represented: Texan, USA, Mexican, official, and anecdotal. With the increasing sophistication of search engine algorithms, the best of the links on the topic are highly likely to be those the inquirer will have found. When he examines the different viewpoints, he is then free to accept or reject any of them and to synthesize his own opinion. This is far different from accepting a point of view from a textbook or teacher, or only to learn some bland and politically correct general facts. The teacher's role becomes a higher one, of coaching her students in thinking carefully and judging thoughtfully.

The network effect is what must be happening in vision, when millions of light rays interface thousands of light-sensitive nerve endings on your retina, which extracts information from that chaos and sends it to your brain, where it is used to create the image you see. Similarly, from the enormous and complex network of genes you carry within you in every cell, information is primarily drawn from only 30,000 genes to continue to replace bits of the physical you, keeping you alive. In the long history of life, as Idea 62 revisits in a fanciful way, little pieces getting together in the biotic ecology have emerged to become earth's rich and varied biosphere.

The network effect is the emergence of order. For these wonderful new cognitive events of our time to occur, it takes the unregimented fluidity of chaos and complexity.

62 THE CAMBRIAN EXPLOSION

Calling the emergence of the virtual knowledge ecology the cognitive explosion is suggested by its striking similarity to an event of colossal global importance very long ago. The following is a fanciful visit to that ancient time of the Cambrian Explosion.

Imagine it is a half billion years ago, and you are bobbing along with a fellow cell chatting about the future. The two of you are science buffs. You each are—like everyone else of your era—just one cell. As you bob and chat, your friend says, out of the blue, I'll bet my ribosome that one day soon there will be creatures made up of lots of cells.

That is impossible, you think, blurting out that he is clearly not only wrong but being ridiculous. For billions of years living things have never been more complex than a single cell. What could possibly come along and glue the cells together? There is no such force. And why would it happen now? What is so special about 543,000,000 BCE? You convince your friend he should keep weird thoughts to himself, and the two of you bob off as you change the subject to chat about some shiny protists that had floated by earlier in the day.

It turns out that the speculative cell's weird thought came true. He predicted what paleontologists call the Cambrian Explosion when, quite suddenly, in terms of earth history, a broad variety of multicelled animals appeared. How? Why then? Nobody knows. Yet, something echoing what the cells did is happening within the virtual knowledge ecology right now to what is known by humankind.

In the primordial Cambrian ecology, gangs of single cells may have hung out together. It can be helpful to the individual to be a member of a gang in the same way one goose has some advantages when she is part of a gaggle. But a gaggle of geese is not a kind of animal; it is a gang of the same kind of animal.

Physically speaking, like a goose, you are a gang of single cells that hang out together. Like a goose, you are very different from a gaggle of geese when you think of yourself as a human being made up of a lot of cells. The unimaginable change to the cell in our Cambrian conversation got under way when gangs of cells were not gaggle-like anymore. They became like a single goose. Somehow, in the Cambrian era, there emerged from the zillions of single-cell creatures an explosion of all sorts of species of different flora and fauna made up of many cells. What happened?

Why it happened is a deep mystery of science, philosophy, and theology. How it played out is the subject of the creationist versus evolutionist wars. Neither is pertinent here. What happened is a key to understanding the primordial virtual knowledge ecology of today and realizing that great and grand changes for the future are inevitable because a gaggle can change to a goose in the virtual knowledge ecology. For what is known by humankind, a cognitive explosion is under way.

Physically speaking, a goose is a goose and you are a human being because your cells are very different from each other, with different cells doing different things. When momma goose took her gander's sperm, each time one sperm connected with one of her egg cells, a separate gosling was initiated. When your parents conceived you, one of your father's sperm entered one of your mother's egg cells. All of us, a goose and you and I, actually start out physically as not one but two cells, and these cells are very different from each other. Once the two get together and their DNA, half from each, binds, the new single cell they start begins dividing into more cells. Quickly, the new cells start forming differently from one another. They become liver cells, and heart cells, and muscle cells, and nerve cells, and soon they become even more specialized with some nerve cells becoming muscle instructors, others participating in vision, and others taking part in emotion and memory.

Looking now at the wonder of the physical bodies of living things, it is sensible to us that the bunch of many different kinds of cells that make up a goose or a human is a whole and understandable thing. As small children, we learned what a goose or a person was—long before we had any concept of a cell. Most educated adults have not spent a lot of time thinking about why our cells make us into one thing.

But to the Cambrian cells, the idea of a multicelled creature was preposterous. If we were to travel back in time, sit those cells down, and tell them: Guys, the future will be crowded with creatures made up of many cells, what would most likely come to their minds would be gangs of cells. So, what is the big deal about that? They would not be impressed. There would be nothing in their world experience to let them understand the step from gaggle to goose.

We would tell them that part of the new kinds of gang found food, and another part of the gang turned the food into energy, and another part served as appendages to fly toward food and away from danger. Cool idea, they might think. Actually, a gaggle of geese is almost like that, with the geese on the outside, inside, front, and back doing different things. We have still not pinned down what makes a single goose different from a gaggle of geese. In what way is a single goose more than a school of cells? How are you more than a gang of cells?

The big difference—at least in my opinion, and certainly for understanding the virtual knowledge ecology—is informational. Somehow, five hundred million years ago, clumps of cells started managing to act as one. A bunch of little things became one big thing. The whole became more than the sum of the parts.

The mechanism of this marvel is an information network. That network is something beyond the structural network formed by neurons and across which it travels. It is the information itself in its dynamic state. It is a flash of danger from an antenna tip that has touched heat sending the information to the insect's wings to beat quickly to back away and fly off. It is the pang of hunger that radiates from an empty stomach to stir a sleeping field mouse to move out of his nest to nibble grass seed to feed all his cells. It is the anticipation of the taste of honey that pushes a bear up a tree to a hive. Danger, pangs, and anticipation are not physical things. They are not static either. They definitely are informational. They are also things our minds can think about and understand: cognitive.

Creatures have ways of conveying information to other creatures. The blue jay who lives somewhere behind my building sounds a shrill alarm when he sights a cat. His signal sends flashes of warning to every nearby bird and mouse, floods the sighted cat with annoyance, and causes my ear to generate an informational surge that leads me to smile. The bird, mouse, cat, and I each experience a cognitive event.

Our ancient human ancestors learned to share information by developing talk. More recently, our kind developed writing as a way to code information that could be decoded by other people by reading it. When we tell other people things in conversation, we rely on our listeners to reconstruct mentally—in their minds—the stuff being articulated from our minds. If you tell me you heard a blue jay warn the yard of an approaching cat, and that the warning told other birds and nearby mice, I would connect the warning, jay, birds, and mice in my mind, forming an idea that would send a signal to my facial muscles to smile.

As you read my little story of the blue jay's warning, do you experience it as something forming and connecting in your mind? Thoughts are dynamic things. Thinking is an active process of connecting, in our jay story, signal to jay, to birds to mice and usually to other ideas stored away in your mind. Perhaps my story brings to mind a blue jay who lived near you long ago, and that bit of memory calls up your pet cat and her adventures in a tree outside of a bedroom where you once slept. Connecting these bits of fact and memory is cognitive activity within your mind.

The vast and open content within the Internet is a virtual knowledge ecology, very much like our human minds, where ideas arise and connect. A cognitive explosion is under way in the virtual knowledge simulated by computers and computer networks participating in the open Internet. The result is the virtual knowledge ecology.

The most minimal bits of information in that virtual ecology are comparable to the single cells of the Cambrian era. Pivotal to the formation of the virtual knowledge ecology is the fact that these bits are freed from static holders such as books. Any bit can be linked to any other bit, making it possible for a limitless number of combinations of static links and of dynamic flashes and patterns.

The Cambrian Explosion was a massive biological experiment within the global ecology of life. Once multicellular creatures began to appear, they began to take many, many forms. Very few of the forms survived the competition. Those that did survive became the progenitors of later life on earth. It has been one of the most fascinating experiences of my life to watch websites embedded with virtual knowledge follow an eerily similar process from which emerge online survivors of the most robust and fit virtual learning resources.

But the bigger observation is the one the bobbing cells dismissed because they had not seen it before. The aggregation of the survivors into larger gestalts, where the whole is more than the sum of the parts, creates something new. In the Cambrian Explosion, a new kind of life appeared. In the cognitive explosion, a new kind of knowledge is emerging.

Emergence is nothing new: Everything there is emerged either through creation or evolution, take your pick. Now that the Internet has caused a sufficient chaos and complexity, network emergence may well be inevitable. Now that what is known by humankind is embedded in that virtual ecology, the emergence of more elegant species of knowledge would seem quite likely.

From gaggle to goose is a pervasive mechanism that we encounter many places in the real world. In the most primordial of all chaos, the universe, soon after creation, reality was essentially homogeneous, as the Bible says, not even light and dark were separate. Over the eons since the big bang caused an incomparably dense mix of quarks and electrons, little bits have linked to make patterns in an unfolding emergence that formed everything. Atoms are composed of combinations of particles, chemicals form compounds, life builds on molecules and our old friends the cells, bodies are made up of organs.

At each of these steps, and the many more in between them, there is a gestalt: The goose is more than a gaggle of her cells and organs; the whole is more than the sum of the parts. Ideas that arise in our minds are gestalts too. They are geese, not gaggles. Pieces connect in such a way that they make sense, and that sense is the informational gestalt.

Comparing these mechanisms to conversational cells and goose to gaggle may seem silly. Doing so helps me think about the topics in the Ideas that lie ahead, and I hope it will illustrate some things for you. Complexity and network theories, Internet phenomena, and cognitive issues can all be frustratingly abstract and obtuse. In all of them, what is pivotal in the ongoing transformation of education is that the virtual knowledge ecology is teeming with gaggles of knowledge that we are able to dynamically form into cognitive geese (ideas) because they are in the open chaos. An explosion occurred in the Cambrian era that ignited life to unexpected flowering across the planet. Something strikingly similar to that is now under way for learning. Like the Cambrian, what is happening on the Internet for education is occurring in chaos, and it is a cognitive explosion.

Knowledge long-trapped in static wads within old mainly print media has been poured into the digital fluidity of the open Internet, where it separates into its smallest component bits. These bits flow freely, like single cells in an open environment, among myriad other types of information bits.

Like the formation of multicellular life eons ago, bits are gathering in gaggles. They are also, quite suddenly, spawning something new: geese. When the Internet began to receive the cascade of human knowledge described in the previous section, gaggles began to be formed: meta-lists, for example, were gaggles of websites for learning about birds.

Like the cell who thought multicellular critters was a weird notion, we have not expected a new sort of knowledge to emerge from the Internet. Yet it has, as the ideas in this section explore. For now, to meet a figurative yet living goose of the virtual knowledge ecology—where her parts work together for a coherent whole—take a gander at Goose.org.

63 HIGHWAY TO NETWORK TO ECOLOGY

The virtual knowledge ecology is an outcome of Tim Berners-Lee's concept of openness in his invention of the World Wide Web—or the web for short. The web is a network, as discussed in more detail in Idea 70. The key for us is the idea of an open network, which was Berners-Lee's immeasurably valuable gift to humankind.

The virtual knowledge ecology inhabits the web plus other openly interconnected portions of the Internet and other digital depositories—together forming a vast open network. The virtual knowledge ecology is the environment in which the open network's open content interacts. The virtual knowledge ecology environment is not the components of the traffic on the information highway. The virtual knowledge ecology is fleeting virtual knowledge that the traffic patterns create for those who use the ecology to learn.

Getting access to content is the well-understood value of visiting web pages where text and images are displayed. The dynamic behavior that can emerge as you connect and aggregate the static text and images is just beginning to be appreciated. The dynamic behavior is little pieces interconnecting in unlimited ways to spark emerging patterns of meaning.

The dynamic behavior is the emergence of fresh new knowledge in the virtual knowledge ecology. The dynamic behavior is a crude—but I am convinced fundamental—way the virtual knowledge ecology mirrors how our brains think. It freely reflects ideas back at us, giving us a new way to learn. Because it exists within the Internet, the virtual knowledge ecology is available to everyone on earth who has Internet access. As more and more people are learning from the virtual knowledge ecology, they are all beginning to find themselves learning from the same virtual page. This does not only create highways among individuals. It also creates human webs of shared knowledge.

What we are looking at in the *Aggregation* section is the second part of the virtual knowledge ecology story. In the first, we saw that what is known by humankind has cascaded into cyberspace. That has caused a second phenomenon that is about to overshadow the first.

When content gets into the open online network, it finds itself becoming part of an ecology. That ecology is not the web, or the Internet, or the open network that operates within the Internet. The Internet and web are made up of chips, servers, wires, strings of glass, and beams of laser light. The ecology absorbing the content does not exist physically. Everything about it is virtual.

Virtual content can be in two or more places at once. We are used to that with broadcast media. Television ratings are based on how many eyeballs are fixed on particular shows at the same time. The content those eyeballs are looking at is virtual—simulated on a screen. The millions of interfaces to it that people are viewing have physical existence only as excited monitor screen phosphors, not as meaningful content.

The travel patterns of television and radio broadcasts are like the airplanes taking off from Chicago's O'Hare International Airport. The planes all start at the same place and end up in different places. More like the Internet are international air traffic patterns of aircraft flying to and from the many airports in countries across the surface of the planet.

The Internet is also like the United States Interstate system with its interconnecting highways and smaller roads and streets. The network for automobile travel is much more irregular, but air traffic and automobile traffic both travel networks. The Internet is a network too.

The early IBM commercial with the little nun saying she could not wait to surf the net caught the adventure of the Internet when it was small. It seemed like ocean surfing to bounce from website to website. Like the fun of traveling in an airplane or car, it was fun to be in one city and then another city. It is unfortunate that the phrase "surf the net" is still around. The Internet experience is different now.

Googling is not surfing—not bouncing from one website to another. Going to Amazon.com to buy a book is not surfing. In both cases, you quickly find that your screen is displaying a lot of related content gathered from many places. Google is still interfacing old-fashioned lists. Amazon's book pages are beginning to capture the natural structure of a virtual ecology. Amazon displays related materials surrounding a book and entices you to click on them. You are seeing a glimpse of the relationships that cause an ecology. The sum impact of everything on the book page is to teach you why you should buy the book.

The underlying and unexpected factor that makes open content in its virtual ecology superior to any previous learning environment emerges from—but is much more than—its powers of access to specific things. The second wonder is its powers of aggregation. Using the Internet is no longer skipping like a stone on the surface of a pond. Users now are deep into a network of relationships surrounded by shifting flows of relevance.

It is time to quit thinking of the Internet as the technology of the highway system because the system focuses on more than its platform. The real action, even for concrete highways, is the dynamic behavior of the traffic as it travels. The open highways of the web are static structures. The web travel patterns are the dynamic and cognitive aggregation that forms the virtual knowledge ecology that offers enlightenment and liberty all across our planet. The static and dynamic aggregation generating the virtual knowledge ecology is the most significant factor in the future of education.

64 THE CENTER OF EVERYTHING

This idea is a look at some actual activity to get a feel for the dynamic centering power a user is given within the virtual knowledge ecology.

When Warner Brothers released its movie *Troy* in the spring of 2004, the British Museum and the movie studio collaborated to put a *Troy* exhibit online. At the entrance of the online exhibit, you must choose between two places to go within the content. One is to learn more about the "Myth of Troy" and the other to visit the collection centered around the Troy theme.

The first option takes you to pages to click through to read a text by the collection's curator. Learning more about the myth in this first option is accomplished in a way similar to reading a book by turning pages. As you always do when read anything, you move down a line of letters and words, translating them in your mind into ideas. There is no center to this first option of the Troy exhibit. Everything goes from left to right, line-by-line and page-by-page.

When you click the second option, you find yourself in a very different situation. You are given the power to put different items into the center of a single collection page.

The centering is done by making choices from two menus. The choices in a menu across the top of the page are Achilles, Hector, Paris, Helen, The Greeks, The Trojans. The menu down the left side offers you choices of periods in history: 500 BC–1599 AD, 1600 AD–1799 AD, 1800 AD–1899 AD, 1900 AD–Present. Each of the periods has further choices of artists from their eras. Poets range from Ovid to Yeats. Shakespeare, Rubens, Beethoven, and many more are listed, with different artists' lists for each of the people listed across the top.

The goal of the Troy exhibit is to show "Immortality Realized" by displaying different artists over many centuries who wrote, portrayed with paint, and created music about Troy. In sum, all of the parts of the exhibit combine in myriad possible ways to convey this theme.

As you interact with the exhibit you choose one of the people across the top and an artist from one of the periods in the menu down the left side. A work of art or image from the movie is then displayed in the center of the visual area, with a panel to its right interfacing information about the item in the center. You find yourself centered on a piece of art that is surrounded by relevant knowledge.

If you click on Achilles, choose the earliest period, and select Ovid, the center image is a poetic profile of Brad Pitt dressed for the movie in his Achilles armor. His head is down, his eyes cast downward. In the right panel is a selection from *The Metamorphoses*, written by Ovid in about 1 AD. It begins: *So, Achilles, conqueror of so much greatness, you are conquered, by the cowardly thief of the wife of a Greek!*

Scrolling to the bottom of the panel displaying the words of Ovid, you find credits to the British Museum and the translator A. S. Kline. Furthermore, there is a link you can click to go to Kline's website for much more under the title "Poetry in Translation," which has many languages.

Leafing through a book, listening to the radio, watching a film or video, and watching television all are almost only a matter of moving along a line—a virtual line that exists in time.

Except in your mind, the point on the line you are focused on is connected only backward in a string of points you have already read. As you read about Achilles' heroics on the beaches of Troy from printed pages, you can remember that in earlier pages Helen was stolen by Paris, causing the war. You cannot know of Paris's lethal arrow into Achilles' heel later in the tale unless you already know the story. The same is true if you hear the story on the radio or watch it on film or video.

There is nothing wrong with linear learning or expression. Novelists use it to hold your interest and build excitement. Storytelling is among the most effective ways to teach. The myths of cultures are thousands of years old. Jesus taught many lessons in parables—stories. Stories are the staple of entertainment industries and a powerful tool of teaching most anything.

Stories happen over time. They are similar to a journey from one place to another and another. Moving the center is a different way of learning and teaching. It is the natural way to teach within a network.

It seems to me that focusing on a center is the essence of how we think. As I focus my thought on Achilles' shame that Ovid is recalling in verse, soon within my mind the thought of the shame is surrounded by recalling deeds of his valor and of his fateful death by the arrow of Paris. I can think of these things together, connecting ideas and centering on one thing and then another as related things shift position around my focus.

Learning from open content within the Internet is a similar experience. Because the different parts of a piece of knowledge are nodes in a network instead of points on a line, I can connect them in all sorts of different ways. Each pattern into which I connect them has a potential for meaning something different—for teaching me something else.

The Internet we can see and touch and hear is a flat piece of glass with light shining from behind. After you use the Internet for a while, you begin thinking of it as space. The screen itself has up, down, and sideways. When you click on a link you tend to feel as if something is coming at you or you are going in.

A big body of theory and practice has grown up around the Internet exploring what is called usability. When a person interacts with a website they are called a user. The usability folks decide in which order menus should be used so that users will get what they want when they click—and get what they will buy on an e-commerce site. Analysis of how users find things is the study of the trip they take.

We get richer results with a shift to thinking about what users connect to and the pattern that emerges dynamically. The page the exhibit assembles when you click on Ovid and Achilles gives you the dejected image of Brad Pitt in his Achilles armor adjacent to the poetic lines from Ovid about the adventures of Achilles. You are no longer moving down a line. You are causing an aggregation. You can see the connections. Achilles' name, the era you are in, and Ovid's name are also highlighted. You are given a pattern of five related items. Although Brad Pitt is in the middle of the page, you can shift the center of your focus by reading the lines from Ovid on the right, centering mental focus on *The Metamorphoses*.

The Internet is not a line. The meaning of its content does not arise over time. The virtual knowledge ecology is a network in which anything can be connected to anything. The virtual knowledge ecology does not have a center. From your viewpoint, though, you are always in the center of the Internet—and of the virtual knowledge ecology while you are there.

The technical, physical Internet is millions of computers connected into a massive network of wires, glass cables, and wireless beams. Every computer is a node in the physical network. Every connection between any two computers is a link in the physical network. There is a wonderful new liberty for Achilles, Helen, and Paris when they are found in a virtual network instead of in a book or film. In the virtual simulation by which computers give them to us, these characters exist as nodes in a network—while in a book or film they are only points on a line. In the virtual network of the Troy website, Achilles, Helen, and Paris become nodes so that they can be centers, with other nodes arranged in patterns around them.

Film editing and writing a novel are both done by putting scenes into a certain order along a line of time or plot. As the Internet matures, we are learning that its greater expressive power is in connecting elements into patterns.

There is nothing new about conveying information by patterns. Maps, diagrams, and charts are indispensable static snapshots for explaining many ideas. The open content of the Internet does much more than a static pattern. It makes possible dynamic patterns that have a limitlessly changeable center that a user can control.

You do not surf the net down a line. You jump onto a center. Think of a Google search. It does not send you down a line. It does everything it can to put you, with one click, exactly in the center of what you are looking for.

Try to imagine what the open Internet would look like if we could see it. The truth is we could not see it even if it were visible. We will get back to that in a minute. Nonetheless, imagine an unimaginable number of identical bits. They are not two-dimensional, on a flat surface. They are a great cloud within the Internet chaos. It is possible to link any one of them to any other one of them. One bit could be linked to any number of other bits at the same time.

Say, one of the bits is a web page about Ovid, another the image of Brad Pitt in his Achilles armor, another a web page with the text of *The Metamorphoses* that displays on the Troy exhibit, another an archeological report of a dig at the ruins of Troy, and another a description of Homer's epics. Each one of the bits would already be linked to many other bits, as we have seen in the example of *The Metamorphoses* link to the translation site.

So far, everything is static. The bits and links are just floating around in the Internet chaos as an enormous cloud. Then you come along. You open the Troy exhibit and click on the early period, Ovid and Achilles. Brad Pitt appears and so does *The Metamorphoses*. You read beautiful lines from Ovid and click on the link to the translator. His website opens in another window. You recall vaguely that the real Troy had been excavated and use your Google box in your browser to search for Troy archaeology. You open one of the sites in the list Google gives you. You Google Homer and get the page about him.

The pattern you created between the bits you used was a dynamic network. It remained in existence as long as you had the windows open on your monitor screen connecting to the web pages (bits). You can make any of the bits of your dynamic network the center of your focus, enriching your understanding by the connections. You may get intrigued by the archeology, center on it and add more links about the finding and preservation of Troy. Or, you may switch the center of the pattern to Homer, or Ovid, or Brad Pitt.

Configure is a word that has popped up more and more in the Internet world. It is a good word. So is reconfigure. A key to configurations in the cloud of open content is that bits link themselves around one bit as the center. When you go out and start connecting related links to Troy, you are doing the same thing. You are configuring links around Troy. This centering, configuring process is the basis of content structure in the Internet in the same way that linear configuration underlies a book or film.

I said that we will never be able to visualize the Internet. Its organization is simply beyond human visualization: Almost any bit within the ecology is the center of many patterns at the same time. What could that possibly look like! Such a structure is not possible in a physical net. The knot, which is another word for node, in a fishnet or a spider web is only the center of the physical strings that move outward from it. A bit, or node, in the Internet is only dynamically a center of the links when they attach to it, and these attachments are always dynamic (existing only in time) and potentially limitless.

It is very strange to think about, but any bit can be the center of more than one—or many—dynamic networks at the same time. One person who was centered on Brad Pitt in his armor could be attaching links about Achilles. Another person using the same picture of Pitt could be using it as a center of an investigation of his various acting roles. In both cases, the single image is a piece in an aggregation configured by an Internet user.

It is, of course, access to materials that makes it possible to link to them. There is new flexibility and power to nudge thinking in being able to put materials together in different ways centered around a subject. What this means for future learning is enormous.

65 SEEING WHOLES

The network effect, and our metaphor in the Cambrian Explosion idea about gaggle to goose, gives us a way to look at how we see. The same sort of grasping of wholes that takes place in seeing happens when bits of knowledge are interfaced on the Internet and connect to emerge as patterns that are ideas.

Always, our field of vision and the splashing of light on our retinas are both complex and chaotic. From them emerge comprehensible shapes and motions that we call seeing. The ecology of the Internet and the ecology of our mind can interface in a way similar to vision—in a dynamic event much like seeing a shape. Perhaps this is a stretch, but I think the two processes achieve the same result: a recognizable whole emerging from a chaos of bits.

When we are in the act of seeing, we are doing something dynamic which, at a simple level, is centering. Look at a forest, and you cannot see trees singly. Look at a tree and you cannot see the forest. Look at the sky, and you see a grand expanse. Look at a bird flying by, and the sky diminishes to context.

While all of this is going on, the retina on the back of your eye is being blasted with light rays. The individual nerve endings that form the light-receiving retina are responding to individual incoming rays. The blast of light is being reduced to dynamic bits of information. A red-sensitive cell will react in a nano second to a stream from a red light frequency that hits it and will send a signal into your brain with information about the location on your retina and the strength and the duration of the stream.

Somehow, your brain is constructing from the streams of incoming bits of information something you apprehend as an image. Smaller parts of the image are connected into something whole that you recognize and give meaning to in your mind.

I am a generalist, not a scientist. I think the general observation here is important and powerful. The image you see starts as little pieces that aggregate into large ones that in turn aggregate into a meaningful whole.

My first glimpses of meaning emerging from parts to become a whole came not from science, but from art. I have spent enormous effort trying to learn to paint. The challenge of doing it well still eludes me, but I have learned a great deal from trying. At one point, I sat back and asked myself how painting managed to express ideas. That led me to a lot of research. The answer that I think is correct I learned from books by Rudolf Arnheim.

Arnheim taught me that the meaning expressed by a painting is caused by the whole, which is more than the sum of its parts. An expressive painting is a gestalt. Both the Metropolitan Museum of Art and the National Gallery in Washington, D.C., have online tutorials showing how the parts of paintings featuring George Washington express a whole idea of the great man. The paintings described by the two museums are different, but the lesson is the same: Meaning emerges from the arrangement of the small parts.

Dynamic vision is endlessly grasping meaningful wholes by aggregating bits and pieces. Because seeing is dynamic—changing continuously over time—the meaning is dynamic too.

As you watch a NASCAR driver speed around a track, the splashing of light on your retina causes constantly changing whole images of cars moving along the track and among themselves. The meaning of who is in the lead emerges and varies. A wreck is a dynamic vision of cars sliding and bouncing into the air. Each image, though a dynamic flash, is an entire picture from which you grasp the meaning of what is happening before your eyes.

One way of understanding the cognitive explosion ignited in the virtual knowledge ecology is simply to realize that parts can openly aggregate dynamically into myriad wholes, causing an ongoing, growing, bountiful feast of meaning. The contrast of this feast to the static and standardized drills of education as usual surely is a root cause for the generation we now have of disinterested and bored school kids. Youngsters today find a lot more action in a digital game joystick than can be scrounged out of a static printed textbook.

66 OPENING THE UNIVERSE OF HUMAN LEARNING

A universe is a whole. That is what the word universe means. All of its parts are part of it, what all the parts comprise together is the universe.

As with most of the underlying ideas here, philosophy beckons because the concepts are interesting and deep. But the practical arena calls us even more urgently, especially in education. Over the past many decades, the practice of education has been dominated by separation. That is now changing and will be caused to change much more by the virtual knowledge ecology.

Schools have been separated into preschool, kindergarten, elementary, middle, high, college, and graduate. Students have been separated into the grade steps through these schools. Knowledge has been divided into subjects, subjects into level, and levels into standards. That is at least nineteen separate universes, counting grades K–12 as thirteen and college-graduate schools as six. Not counted are the subsubjects of the main subjects and the subquestions of the standards of each of the states and other assessment industry sectors. All of this separation is just in the schools in the United States, and many times multiplied in the bigger picture of education as a global endeavor.

The actual universe of human knowledge is a dynamic whole consisting of countless bits of facts and ideas that can be related in countless patterns to mean and teach innumerable ideas. Columbus's landings on Caribbean islands is a key fact in: the story of Spain's rise to riches, the demise of the native islanders, the opening of new worlds of botany, the literature of adventure diaries, the history of sailing, and the opening of the New World. Each of these ideas is formed by different placements of the Columbus event into patterns with other bits of knowledge.

The universe of the Internet is now interfacing the universe of what is known by humankind in a fundamental and fabulous new way. The bits of knowledge are becoming embedded into nodes of the Internet network, freeing them to be interlinked in limitless ways and thus mirror limitless ideas. Education's methods of knowledge separation are starkly restrictive and inadequate in this situation.

It used to be seen as sensible to the pedagogical experts to assign teaching the idea of a cell to third graders, defined ideally as eight-year-olds, and to defer teaching DNA to seventh graders whom the system would expect to be twelve-year-olds. Textbooks would then be bought with the subjects of cells for the third grade and DNA for the seventh grade. Teachers for each grade would be trained for the grade-level material and supplied with the appropriate wall charts to hang in their classrooms. The third- and seventh-grade classrooms would thus be designed as separate universes, assigned to separate groups of students by age.

In the single virtual knowledge ecology universe, where human knowledge now abides in cyberspace, everything about cells can be connected to everything else about cells. A third grader, a seventh grader, a teacher, or an adult seeking education or just interested in a subject can enter at any node and follow its connections in any direction. The universe of knowledge is open to explore and open to all.

Teaching in this open universe of human learning begins by determining which node to enter with your students. To see what that is like and to take a tour of a universe sector, go to one of the most magnificent model and mentor projects for teaching and learning: "The Biology Project" at the University of Arizona website.

As the wonderful new open universe of knowledge is understood and used by more and more people, it will be increasingly difficult for the education establishment to avoid conforming its methods to the virtual knowledge ecology. Doing so will require an about-face from what has been going on for the past decade, as most educators have struggled to shoehorn the Internet knowledge into their predigital ways of doing things.

67 OPEN CONTENT ONLY

The term *open* has been demeaned and played down by the digital powers that be because it threatened their control. Open source was an early use of the word open, meaning the code that operated a piece of software was freely available to and contributed by anyone. Definitions of open source still found around the Internet tend to huff that it is used by hackers.

Open source nonetheless has become a major factor in software development. A struggle is ensuing between those who control the code of established Internet browsers, blog software, and other online functionalities and the open source tech forces who seek to break down perceived monopolies. *Open* has acquired other meanings in reference to the technical aspects of the Internet, including open network and open access.

The word *open* expanded into content with wiki initiatives. As explained in Idea 52, a wiki is a collaborative web location that allows visitors to edit and add content. Thus, the content is open in the sense of collaboration. The foremost wiki, as I write this, is Wikipedia.org, which began in 2001 and now has more than a half million articles contributed from the open Internet.

As the term open content applies to the virtual knowledge ecology, it means unrestricted and free access by anyone connected to the Internet. Huge amounts of Internet content are not open in this sense. This not-open, closed, content does not participate in the cognitive explosion because it cannot be included in aggregation and configuring. Only open content is included in or affected by the dynamic networking that makes the virtual knowledge ecology the global learning resource of the future.

As a hypothetical example, a professor at a university could author a digital animation for a nugget of knowledge for which he is the world's leading authority. He could then place that tutorial online in his department's section of his college's intranet. The website would be password protected so that only students, faculty, and administration could enter its web pages.

The professor's animation would not be part of the virtual knowledge ecology because it would not be open content. This situation follows the long tradition of viewing a college's knowledge assets as property that would attract students. Colleges have always sought to hire expert professors who devise compelling courses. The quality of professors and courses has been crucial in setting tuition rates and keeping the institutions financially viable. Open content would seem to reverse this practice by giving away valuable college assets.

The new factor is that, unless the professor's animation is open content, it will not be part of the interconnected new universe of knowledge and will be cut off from that universe. When a search engine looks for the professor's topic, his work will not be found because the engine's spiders had been unable to crawl the college website and find the animation. The animation cannot be included in aggregations of his topic by his peers because it will be unknown or password protected.

Although the professor could link outward from his animation to pertinent links, his work would never be fully enriched by these one-way links. It would not be included in the global pattern of linking for his subject by incoming links from colleagues and peers. The professor would be forced to continually update links in order to keep his animation at the edge of relevant knowledge—something that would be spontaneously ongoing if the animation were open content and thus in the virtual knowledge ecology.

If the time came when his college placed his course materials online as open content, his animation would enter the virtual knowledge ecology. It would soon be found by the software spiders and begin to show up on search engine results. It would be found as well by other experts in his field and, before long, become connected into the aggregations that are becoming the new basis of scholarship.

The extent that the animation is visited by and is linked to by his professional peers and by students will determine its placement in the returns of search engines. This is the new open peer review of the virtual knowledge ecology. The good news for students is that, wherever they physically study, when they search the Internet, they find the best animation regardless of what campus created it. The bad news for instructors used to making students study their second-rate materials is that their peers in the virtual knowledge ecology will elevate only the finest authorings for all to share, leaving the second-rate stuff to deteriorate in the backwaters.

68 COMPLEXITY AND THE EMERGENCE OF MEANING

Recently I was in Santa Fe, New Mexico, on a vacation with members of my family who live in the western United States. Santa Fe is an old stomping grounds for us. One of my great-grandfathers moved his family there in 1887, and the ever-charming city is a close neighbor by western distance reckoning to our main twentieth-century base in El Paso, Texas.

As I sat next to my brother, who was driving the car north through the outskirts of town on a sightseeing trip, I asked him if he knew where the Santa Fe Institute was located. He shrugged and said he did not, then moments later a large sign on the left of the road announced the entrance to the Santa Fe Institute. I am in awe of the thinking done there and enjoyed taking a passing peek at the building.

The institute is a catalyst for some of our brightest minds of the day who are in hot pursuit of the mechanisms of chaos and complexity. The level at which these geniuses and visionaries ponder such topics is far above my head. I do not have the mathematical or theoretical physics understanding to comprehend a lot of what they say.

Still, a generalist view of complexity is sufficient to understand that out of chaos order does occur: Meaning emerges from complexity. That insight is hugely important in understanding how elegant knowledge can possibly be found in a disorganized mass of information like the Internet. What we can know about emergence from complexity puts us on the path to understanding how an exploding cloud of bits of knowledge can proliferate patterns of meaning. It is beautiful stuff.

Complexity pioneer and Santa Fe Institute science board member John Holland began his 1995 classic book *Hidden Order* with the story of a woman living on the West Side of Manhattan who confidently went to her store to buy a jar of pickled herring. The jar would be there. Why? The answer is the same reason—or at least its close cousin—that a student wanting to know what pickled herring is will get a definitive array of answers in under 0.50 seconds by asking an Internet search engine.

Complexity science tells us that there is great value to the Internet, beyond the ability to access information, and that complexity is a necessity of its gift-giving talents. Complexity science suggests to us that the chaos of the Internet itself is a profound asset for interfacing human knowledge. It is not a bad thing that the Internet is messy and complex—that it is open, liquid, and is full of junk. It is a good thing. Complexity astounds us by producing pickled herring descriptions on demand. The meaning we are looking at seems to emerge on its own. It is the nature of complexity itself that makes the meaning emerge.

We should be thinking in terms of releasing and using that cognitive gift of complexity instead of restricting either the Internet or its users. Open content let loose in chaos causes the most marvelous of all venues for interfacing what we know, surpassed only by the chaos of the human mind.

69 MINIMALIZATION

A highpoint for me of the meeting at the Hewlett Foundation described in Idea 36 was hearing the comments of John Seely Brown and talking with him personally. He was chief scientist at Xerox Corporation, directing its Palo Alto Research Center (PARC) in some of the most radically innovative years leading into our digital age. He continues as a seminal thinker in the field and has nudged my understanding of several ideas deeper and into new directions.

At one point, he urged the group to think in terms of minimalization, which was a new word to me—and one I discovered was not in the dictionary but used by him because it meant what he meant. Later, I asked him privately if minimalization was the same as modularization. He said that it was not, and with a twinkle, "they are closely related but minimalization gets you thinking differently." That it does, and I recommend it to you for pondering.

My pondering about the word led me to realize that modules can be cookie cutters that restrict richness. Modules are parts of bigger things, but they are standard, uniform parts. A course in school is made up of six-week modules or weekly or daily lesson plan modules. A school is made up of grade modules. A textbook is built of chapter modules containing section modules. Testing and assessment design and apply subject content modules.

Minimalization suggests a liberated connectivity at the lowest level of structure. Knowledge to be learned in school that would have been put through a minimalization grinder would be reduced to its tiniest cognitive bits. Those minimal bits would then be free to be linked to each other in virtually any pattern. The richness of thought in your brain probably rests on a similar minimalization, with patterns arising from extremely small and subtle electrical and chemical variances in the action within large synaptic multiples of the one hundred billion plus neurons in your head.

As the next three Ideas on networks delve into, a network is a platform into which these minimalized bits can be embedded as nodes, which can then be interconnected in limitless ways to express cognitive meaning. Your brain contains a neural network where meaning emerges as ideas. The open Internet is a network also able to platform minimal cognitive bits both embedded statically and emerging dynamically.

To look through a window into the connectivity of the World Wide Web—which is an entirely open portion of the Internet—visit Technorati.com, which was tracking over 900 million blogs in the winter of 2005. Click on "Top 100 Technorati" for a list of the current one hundred blogs with the most links to them. The numbers of these links given on the listing, usually several thousand, provide a count of the static connections from other web pages to each blog. The dynamic linking is much more massive, with perhaps an average of around 50,000 visits per day from other websites to each of the one hundred blogs. You are looking here at the most active portion of the blogosphere. The blogosphere is a small portion of the larger Internet.

The virtual knowledge ecology is another entity, like the blogosphere, within the larger open Internet. The virtual knowledge ecology is the interlinked minimal bits of what is known by humankind and the activity of individuals around the world learning from its web pages.

70 NETWORKS

Idea 60 states: *Little pieces put together in different ways to make different sorts of big pieces is the underlying mechanism and cognitive power of open digital content.* The mechanical concept is simple: little pieces connected in different ways.

The structure that results from this mechanism is simple too. It is a network. In network parlance, a little piece is a node and connecting is called linking. A network is a structure that is formed by linking nodes. There are just two components, nodes and links. Only two types of relationships are available in a network: nodes can either link to any number of nodes or not link to any number of nodes. That all seems simple enough, and it is.

But networks have the same sort of practical simplicity that causes simple machines to be so important. The simple machines—lever, wheel and axle, pulley, inclined plane, wedge, and screw—have countless uses. Networks are also in use in a multitude of places. They are found in social sciences, biology, physics, and technology. Their importance is just beginning to be appreciated, and networks are at the hot edge of new science. Therefore, it is not surprising that the Santa Fe Institute has a lengthy section on network dynamics on its website.

The Internet is a physical network that supports a static content network from which emerge dynamic cognitive networks that interface with the minds of human visitors. The virtual knowledge ecology is a portion of the Internet static network and that portion's emergent dynamic networks, which interface to the visitor reflections of what is known by humankind.

To interface with a dynamic network emerging from the virtual knowledge ecology, visit the National Gallery of Washington, D.C.'s, online exhibit called "Rembrandt's Late Religious Portraits." Seventeen small icons across the top of the web page represent masterpieces from the museums where they are housed across the world. The static content network of this web exhibit is the group of nodes that holds a larger image of each painting and descriptive text, other web pages of explanation prepared by the curators for the exhibit, and the interactive homepage with the icons and display component for introductory text. The shape of an emerging dynamic network will be determined by what you click on and in what order you do it to open web pages that then display content as you visit the exhibit.

The cognitive meaning emerges with the dynamic network you cause by clicking. Perhaps you are studying representations of the Apostles of Jesus, so you click the icons to open the images of Paul, Bartholomew, Matthew, James, and Simon. You could then open another browser window to compare portraits of apostles by other painters. If your interest was in Rembrandt's vaunted mastery of painting expressive eyes, you would click to study and compare the portraits with a completely different mindset, looking with extra interest at the depiction of eyes in the artist's portrait of himself as the Apostle Paul. The meaning that would emerge dynamically from those two different explorations would not be the same. In either case, your clicking pattern would become a dynamic content network emerging from a static content network and reflecting ideas to your mind from the virtual knowledge ecology.

Except for being a lot quicker, is using Internet resources in this way really any different than what I did as an undergraduate student back in the 1950s in the stacks of Deering Library at Northwestern University?

Clearly, assembling a bunch of Rembrandt paintings to compare is faster on the Internet than assembling a pile of books with Rembrandt paintings and flipping back and forth among their pages. Also, online access to content is certainly greater—there is more to choose from. This improved access alone greatly increases what one researcher can find and learn in a few hours, weeks, or a lifetime.

If we conclude that the online Rembrandt study in this example is just a sped-up version of what I did at Deering, it is easy to assume that online research is just an improvement in access. There are some who make that assumption and decide too much access is bad for students. From there, the steps are easy to the rationalization and then justification that experts and professionals should decide what students are allowed to look at and learn from. As Idea 75 explains, online content has a very effective mechanism for deciding on its own which content is best—outside censors are not as effective.

There is a marvelous reason beyond access why students experience an exciting new sort of learning within the Internet and its virtual knowledge ecology. In Idea 72, I explain why the cognitive content networks that emerge dynamically from the static content networks we find online are an entirely new and quite wonderful learning medium that is radically different and much more cognitively powerful than the way I learned in the stacks of Deering Library.

First, a look at some inherent behavior that makes networks a favorite medium of Mother Nature for handling a variety of very different content.

71 SMALL-WORLD NETWORKS

The Internet is a network structure, but its pattern is not visible and obvious like the knots and links of a fishnet or spider web. The trillions of nodes interlinked among themselves to form the Internet are also not completely unpatterned, random, or chaotic. The Internet has the internal structure and pattern of a small-world network. The small-world network structure is present in the physical Internet of servers, wires, and beams, again in the static content networks imbedded in the open Internet, and still again in the dynamic networks that emerge from that open content.

Small-world networks were discovered in 1998 by Steven Stogatz and Duncan J. Watts. Albert-László Barabási soon showed that small-world networks obey the mathematical power law, known more popularly as the 80–20 principle. (More about this in Idea 73.) These three scientist/ professors have all written excellent general readership books explaining the widening insights that networks are giving us into how our world works. When I learned about small-world networks in 2003, I wrote my book called *Connectivity* to explain the good news I think the small-world structure of the Internet brings for education and for the defeat of terrorism.

A small-world network is composed of clusters of thickly linked nodes that are connected by relatively few links to other clusters of nodes. This small-world network pattern is why the principle is true that everyone on earth is distanced from each other by about six degrees of separation. The way it works is not complicated. You have a cluster of people whom you know well and to whom you are connected by one degree (you know them personally) or two degrees (say the uncle of the guy who works in the cubicle next to you). The uncle of that guy also has a cluster of acquaintances separated from him by one or two degrees. Because you know his nephew in the cubical next to yours, you are separated from the uncle by only two degrees (1 cubical guy, 2 his uncle). It follows that you are separated from individuals in the uncle's cluster by only three or four degrees.

The "Kevin Bacon Game," which can be quickly found online in several places by a search engine, will illustrate for you how the degrees of separation work within the small-world network of Hollywood movie stars. Members of casts of movies are the clusters in the Hollywood example, and actor Kevin Bacon has been in many movies, thus providing a link to a very large number of actors and actresses in the many casts where he was a cast member. Other cast members in Bacon's casts are one degree separated from him and one degree separated from every member of the cast of every movie they were ever in. So, all Bacon has to do is be in one movie with someone who was in a movie with Humphrey Bogart for Bacon to be separated from Bogart by only two degrees—and by three degrees from anyone in any other movie in which Bogart acted.

This small-world network pattern is found in lots of other kinds of settings. Electrical grids that supply power to a region or country are small-world networks. A sick traveler from an isolated cluster of infectiously sick people can make a first stop on a trip and there infect and make one person sick in a new cluster of her own close connections—and travel on to do that a couple of more times—causing an epidemic to spread throughout the small-world network he traversed. Patterns of the neuron activities in the brain are being studied as small-world networks. There are many more fields being understood in new ways by the growing insights of network theory in general and small-world network theory in particular.

This book is not the place to explore small-world networks in detail. What is important to know for understanding the virtual knowledge ecology, because it is part of the Internet, is that the Internet is a small-world network and so is the virtual knowledge ecology within the Internet.

The small-world network that forms the virtual knowledge ecology is shaped by content openly released into the Internet. The underlying network nature of the Internet liberates the open content to spontaneously pattern itself in clusters by subject, with the clusters connected by a few links to related subject clusters. An example of this content behavior can be examined at a subject cluster called "Seeds of Trade" which is an online exhibit at London's Natural History Museum. Several dozen natural seed products, from aloe, to cotton, to oats, to yam are linked to eleven categories, such as animal fodder, beverages, food crops, and polymers. Each is further cross referenced by continent of origin. Here and there, one of the pages for a specific plant contains a link (one degree of separation) going beyond the museum's "Seeds of Trade" cluster and leading to other clusters such as the Museum's Botany Library. The link beyond may again have links beyond the cluster to which it belongs (two degrees of separation).

The Internet is a small-world network with great clusters like Yahoo and Amazon and small clusters as well. The clusters are connected by relatively few links. This structuring is not caused by the technology that supports the information embedded into the Internet. It is how the information is used that makes the structure happen. The Yahoo website has millions of connections because millions of people decided to connect to it. The Yahoo creators did not begin with enough servers to accommodate their massive traffic today; the traffic pushed them to increase their tech facilities again and again. Amazon has grown in response to the increasing number of customers who wanted to buy books, and now just about anything, online. When it comes to small-world network patterning on the Internet, content rules.

All very interesting, you might be politely thinking, but what is the big deal? This Idea is about theory, and I will tell you my theory about why the small-world network patterning online of what is known by humankind is the biggest of all deals for the future of global learning. The reason: I am convinced that what is known by humankind is itself a small-world network in the individual human mind and collectively for us as a species. The new virtual online medium of the virtual knowledge ecology reflects not only the facts and images of useful knowledge—it reflects them patterned cognitively as they naturally are and as we think about them and know them. The significance of that for education is breathtaking.

I did not think the small-world network nature of human knowledge up as a theory. I observed it playing out at HomeworkCentral.com, in the collection of 35,000 subjects described in Idea 35. Algebra was a cluster, with a few links into the cluster formed by calculus. In the sciences, the cluster of the botany of oak trees had links to the cluster of hardwood forests, to the cluster of lumbering technology, and the cluster of the history of furniture. In Idea 80, at the conclusion this section, I set out what I see as the Grand Idea forming within the virtual knowledge ecology as a virtual reflection of what is known by humankind and to which upcoming generations across the global will go to become educated with that knowledge.

Small-world networking contributes significantly to the Grand Idea. The knowledge offered in traditional education is fractured and separated by grade, textbook hunk, geography, and the happenstance of teachers who are present. By contrast, within the apparent chaos of the overall Internet, order is emerging for the open content for learning. From the complexity of myriad knowledge resources a network is forming. The knowledge content is patterning as a small-world cognitive network that reflects the patterns of knowing and thinking in the medium of human cognition. Breathtaking it is.

72 DYNAMIC NETWORKS

In the stacks of Deering Library, after selecting several books with images of Rembrandt paintings, it was possible to open each book to a painting and spread the volumes out over a table so I could see all of the paintings. If I had looked at them for comparisons of how the great master painted eyes, dynamic patterns of meaning would emerge in my mind as my glance moved around among the images laid out in front of me.

Here is a key question regarding the Internet and education: Is the grasping of relationships by a learner the same if the table that displays the paintings is replaced by a computer screen that does so?

There are some obvious—but perhaps not particularly crucial—differences. The books are heavy in the library and have to be physically assembled, while the images are weightless and can be assembled very quickly online. In both cases, the images can be accompanied by erudite text that elaborates on the painting; the amount of text is variable for the books but unlimited online. There will be instances where the printed images of the painting will seem more true to the artist's vision than the image of light displayed on the screen, but at other times the opposite may be true.

The stunning new advantage of the online cognitive interaction in instances like this example is none of those named above. What is new is the increasingly powerful ways in which we can apprehend, embrace, and manipulate the dynamic network of ideas that emerge from the virtual knowledge ecology. The same sort of dynamic pattern that would emerge in my mind fifty years ago as I glanced over books spread across a Deering Library table displaying Rembrandt paintings now emerges virtually and often obviously and elegantly as a perceivable dynamic network on the computer side of the interface in which a student glances over the same several Rembrandt images.

Something virtual, as we use the definition in this book, is something simulated by a computer or computer network. Over the thousands of years since our ancient ancestors painted marks and colors to simulate the ideas of buffalo, deer, and hunting on the walls of caves, humans have been inventing media to mirror the patterns that form the ideas in their minds. Certainly, the images of the paintings of Rembrandt spread across a table at Deering reflected enough off the paper and ink into my mind to spark the emergence of ideas. The bits and pieces of a story woven through a novel do the same sort of thing, causing dynamic patterns of action to form and connect and excite the mind and sometimes make us cry.

It is the purpose of media to stimulate dynamic patterns in people's minds. The fascinating point I raise here is that it may well be that the new online medium is not only stimulating those patterns. It is actually simulating them—mirroring them—displaying the patterns to reflect them into our minds. How cool is that!

The image painted thousands of years ago of a buffalo is an internal network of colors and lines from which a pattern emerges that we can apprehend as an animal. The bits of the story are scattered through a novel network to tell the tale. A cave wall, however, is not a network but only a flat surface to which paint adheres. A story must be told or read in the dimension of time, so its network strings out over a line. The radio and television media also deliver content in a line of time. The Internet and its virtual network ecology are a network. The mind and known thought are not lines but networks. When images, narration, and knowledge in general nestle into the Internet, they come home.

As the painter sketched out his buffalo on the cave wall, he was guided by dynamic images emerging from the network of his thoughts and remembered network of his vision. When the storyteller records her narration, she ponders the dynamic network of events it encompasses and lays them along the line of time on which they will roll out for the listener or reader. As we look at the buffalo painting or enjoy the story, the dynamic image of their creators arises in our own minds.

Without getting sidetracked into biology and philosophy, it is possible to posit just by common sense that the network medium is the native environment of ideas and thought. Concepts and ideas are patterns of links among nodes—connections among bits of knowledge. When an idea pattern was stimulated by the images in books spread about the library table, I grasped a temporary pattern of relationship connections

such as those between the way Rembrandt painted the eyes of his subjects in each painting.

It is fair to say that the pattern was out there on the table. I could
even have arranged the books to make the pattern obvious. It is also
possible to print an idea pattern like that in a book, selecting the eyes
from several paintings and drawing lines and arrows among them to em-
phasize the patterns. Such a printed pattern would, though, have become static and inflexible, forevermore trapped on the page where it
was printed.

A dynamic virtual knowledge network is a network that emerges from
and dances upon a structural network for as long a time as someone is
interfacing it. We see it when we focus on the buffalo in the painting,
and it is active in our minds as we enjoy a story. It takes two to tango,
and the dynamic network's dancing partner is a dynamic cognitive network in the mind of someone who is interfacing the cave wall, the story,
and now the Internet. We have barely even glimpsed at what the dynamic network is going to do as it tangos with students who visit the
virtual knowledge ecology.

Cognitive functioning is the dynamics of thinking and learning. The
new access to knowledge made possible by embedding it into the Internet gives us a new structure for knowledge—a new location for cognitive dynamics. Static networks of knowledge are accessible online.
The dynamic networks begin to function as you click around in the content that the static ones interface to you, and you think about the connections that are going on.

One of the most significant discoveries of the past decade was the
common existence in the real world of structural networks that support
dynamic functional networks. The name of the network studies section
of the website of the Santa Fe Institute is "Network Dynamics." The
introductory article explains the institute's research: "[It] builds on what
is known as 'emergent dynamics'—the emergence of a system's global
properties and capabilities which are not prespecified by network design and are difficult or impossible to predict from knowledge of its con-
stituent parts."

In other words, static structural networks can spawn emergent networks that are neither prespecified nor predictable. This is what I have
meant elsewhere in this collection by saying that the virtual knowledge

ecology proliferates dynamic networks of ideas. Fresh knowledge happens.

Dynamic cognitive networks emerging from a global network of what is known by humankind is a radical new experience for education. The extent to which it has been unnoticed or ignored in education is shocking.

We individually experience in our minds something similar to the dynamic emergence online of cognitive networks—or perhaps exactly like it—when we think and learn. The dynamic networks occur in our head as thoughts. At its best, a dynamic cognitive event in a fellow's mind occurs when an inventor shouts "Eureka!" celebrating a new idea that has emerged in his head.

The emergent dynamics of functional networks proliferating on the static network of knowledge embedded into the Internet is becoming better and better understood. One thing is crystal clear: There is no excuse for the mindlessly defending pedagogy that clings to the prenetworked times.

73 THE 80–20 RULE

Another interesting insight that has come out of the new network theoretical discoveries is that the 80–20 rule applies in small-world networks. Also known as Pareto's law and the power law, it means that the rich get richer so that the top 20 percent do a lot better than the other 80 percent.

Since the Internet, and (if I am right) the body of knowledge subjects we call academic are both small-world networks, the 80–20 rule should apply to them. It obviously applies to the Internet, as relatively few huge "gorilla" websites contrast to zillions of very small to tiny websites. In the dynamics of the blogosphere as well, there are a few blogs getting thousands of visits and millions getting very few visits.

In my book *Connectivity*, I went into some detail about how the 80–20 rule was visible in the metrics of the knowledge collection at HomeworkCentral.com. The one time we did a site-wide visitor count by subject, about 20 percent of the subjects got 80 percent of the hits. But the other 20 percent of the hits were very evenly distributed over the other 80 percent of the subjects. These percentages are based on about four million pages viewed during one month in the spring of 2000. The visitors were choosing from about 35,000 different subjects, some very general but most very specific and small.

This distribution of interest by the four million page views explains why websites that offer homework study links are usually too limited to satisfy the needs for homework in the real world. The 80–20 principle is at work. The teachers and students using such a website are looking for the 20 percent of topics 80 percent of the time, and in websites limited to the 20 percent of most used subjects, they find something about what they need 80 percent of the time. But the other 20 percent of the time, they do not find the spread of smaller subjects that are 80 percent of academic knowledge. In the virtual knowledge ecology of open content, not only are 100 percent of the study subjects there, but they are richly interlinked. Viewing a general subject page, a visitor is offered links to related major and minor subjects that link in turn to others.

In thinking in terms of the 80–20 rule about the role and importance of the networked knowledge in the future of learning, there is another enormously significant matter, which is the kids. It is easy to think the power law is telling us there is no point in worrying about educating more than the superior 20 percent of children. That is a cynical attitude toward children, yet in a perverse way the distribution of education has long practiced an 80–20 ratio that has little to do with the cognitive gifts of children.

The reality of education today is that only about 20 percent of the world's children—just a rough guess—are being exposed to a quality interface with knowledge that we could think of as giving them exposure to 80 percent of what is known to humankind. That interface is usually a school, and the school is usually filled with children from elite sectors of society. A considerable percentage from the remaining 80 percent of the world's kids receive a fair or mediocre education and many children remain uneducated and even illiterate.

Ubiquitous computing will one day connect virtually every child on the planet to the virtual knowledge ecology, interfacing virtually everything known by humankind. Such a world of learning would follow the 80–20 rule applied to 100 percent of kids, not just to the present 20 percent. That would predict that from all of the world's children the 20 percent most gifted mathematicians, philosophers, engineers, doctors, poets, musicians, painters, athletes, and all the rest could ride the new wave of emergent dynamics from obscurity to leadership for a better world. Why not?

74 THE NETWORK EFFECT

Envisioning the network effect is a not too complicated way of appreciating that order can come out of chaos. Within the open Internet, which is definitely chaotic, patterns abound for useful knowledge. Static, established knowledge is not what emerges, rather the network effect spawns dynamic old and new knowledge from the virtual knowledge ecology. The network effect causing this unique new behavior makes the open content of the virtual knowledge ecology superior to anything education has previously encountered

Everything about learning is dynamic. A thought, idea, or fact cannot ever be completely static when a human being is using it.

For every moment you are alive, an electrical storm roars on within your brain. Anything you are thinking about is a part of the storm. When you are not thinking about a fact that you have lodged in your memory, that fact probably exists in your brain only as minute synaptic changes from which it can again emerge into your consciousness when the necessary dynamic electrical connections create an active circuit that rejoins the ongoing storm of ideas you are thinking about. We know from Idea 72 that emergent dynamics means static structural networks can spawn emergent networks that are neither prespecified nor predictable. New ideas emerge from dynamic connectivity in your brain. I think new knowledge emerges from dynamic connectivity in the virtual knowledge ecology, and it is that emergence that I mean by the network effect on the virtual knowledge.

Daily experience tells us there is a potential in our mind within the ongoing storm to connect ideas to each other to form new ideas. We know that because we do it all the time. If you will now think about the word "orange" an idea of a juice, or fruit, or fashion color this summer, or sunset will emerge within the electrical storm in your brain. If you close your eyes a moment, you can connect the first orange idea to others. If you thought of a sunset, perhaps that will lead to enjoying a memory. Connecting ideas is what thinking is.

Learning is importing ideas into the electrical storm in your brain—say by reading a book or listening to an expert. New ideas, like all the old ones were, are dynamic: active sets of connections zipping about among some synapses. Remembering something new is probably a matter of affecting the synapses that are involved sufficiently to modify them enough so that they will be able later to reestablish the pattern of connections the idea needs. From them, your memory of a romantic sunset would emerge dynamically as you enjoy it once again.

The permanent, static aspect of remembering and learning is thought to be the changes in the synapses. The ideas, when you are using them, are the dynamic signals zipping around among the connections between the particular set of synapses that give rise to the thought.

There are two steps here. The first is access to static ideas. In your brain, you have access to static ideas by activating the connections among the synapses from which they emerge into your storm of thought. Learning builds the amount of ideas you have access to in your brain. The building is done by importing ideas from books, people, and other places, creating first dynamic sets of connections, which then cause synaptic changes that become the static storage of your memory. The second step is the ability to recall ideas from memory into their dynamic form. That happens when you dynamically connect the appropriate set of synapses so that they join the electrical storm in which your thinking is going on.

Ideas are much more than static patterns in your gray matter. They emerge from temporarily activated circuits into a larger dynamic storm. Because thinking is not static, it empowers you to connect ideas within the ongoing dynamic storm in new ways. These brain functions are only now beginning to be understood, but what I have been describing is based on what experts suggest as a general idea of what is going on.

We know enough about how thinking takes place to suggest there could be a resonance with the Internet as the first medium invented by humans to connect thoughts dynamically outside the human brain. The Internet can do it because, like what happens in the synapses when a thought emerges, the Internet connects things dynamically from the bottom up. That sort of connectivity is how the Internet works. We will get back to the brain. Now, more about the Internet.

The content of the early Internet was static. For example, in Project Gutenberg, in which volunteers typed the text of books into digital files, the digital text was put on web pages. If you connected to the Internet back in 1996, you could type in the web address of the project and click there on the titles of books. By clicking on one of the book titles, you would get access to web pages displaying the text of the book you selected. You could then read the book's text on your monitor screen.

That was a big deal if the book was something you could not get in print. Reading a book on a monitor screen turned out to be less comfortable that reading it from printed pages bound in a book that you could hold in your hand. A whole e-book industry developed around handheld reading devices that would hold the text of a book that you could read by displaying its pages one-by-one on its small screen. As Idea 16 mentions, at one point the biggest market for that turned out to be dirty books because it was possible to read them from a machine instead of a book with a printed cover. You could access dirty books without anyone knowing it.

The e-book industry did not reach a highly anticipated tipping point that was expected to see the replacement of printed books by handheld electronic reading devices. There was a general sigh in the industry to the effect that the palm readers might never be attractive enough visually to win readers. But, in the perversity of human nature, by the spring of 2005 reading books on cell phone screens, as idea 16 describes, had become a strong niche market in Japan and elsewhere—belying the arguments that a reading surface had to be large and comfortable for it to be adopted. Readers are gulping miniscule hunks of Shakespeare in Japanese characters from tiny cell phone screens. "Go figure" joins configure and reconfigure in Internet lingo.

Becoming mainstream if not ubiquitous, e-books continue to serve usefully in many fields. Work continues on handheld devices that will be more comfortable to hold and manipulate. When one or more of these catch on, it is likely that books printed on paper will diminish. When a handheld device for reading becomes popular, it will become superior to any other reading venue if it is connected to the Internet because its content will then be interfaced from the virtual knowledge ecology.

As the Internet grew through the second half of the 1990s, it became possible to access more and more information from cyberspace. The Internet came to be compared, correctly so, to a library that stored knowledge. You could go there, using the Internet, to access that knowledge.

Then, something else began to happen as the network effect took hold. The following explanation is a simplification. But the basic mechanism is very real. Content was dumped into the Internet, forming a vast ecology of content. When the content was a massive enough ecology for its complexity to spawn meaningful networks, dynamic content began to emerge in a manner like that described above for dynamic ideas in your brain. Spontaneously, the Internet created new and dynamic content. The network effect was operational for the virtual knowledge ecology within the Internet's massive openness.

In the ecology that is the Internet, an electrical storm rages constantly through its chips, wire, glass, and beams. Patterns of dynamic connections emerging from the storm can reflect ideas. It is all really quite marvelous. I am not suggesting some weirdness such as the Internet turning into a brain. But I know from observation that dynamic patterns of connections can suggest patterns of human thought.

To experience this for yourself, a good example to visit is the website I have been looking in on for several years called "Elephants of Cameroon." The website is an interactive collection of field diaries, records of individual elephants, general information about elephants and their habitat, research data, links to related materials elsewhere on the Internet—and more.

As soon as you access one particular piece of the content, many related connections are in your field of vision. As you then click around through the content that is offered, you are virtually connecting them dynamically. Certainly, this activity is very crude compared to the elegance of the connectivity that is your brain in the act of thinking. But certainly as well, it is more than just access.

The network effect happens as someone who visits the "Elephants of Cameroon" website clicks among the links on the site. There are many other ways to experience that effect. A classic term for it is a gestalt, where the whole is more than the sum of the parts. As the quotation from the Santa Fe Institute in Idea 72 states, the emergent pattern is neither prescribed nor predictable. The knowledge of elephants the visitor interfaces from the pattern of his clicking is new, unique, and dynamic.

The ecology of open content within the Internet, where the network effect takes place, has something about it that goes against our intuition. Nothing, of course, is real. We can take comfort in the fact that an idea in our brain is also not real. You cannot dissect the brain and pick out the ideas, put them in a Petri dish, and watch them interact. When ideas emerge from the Internet, the same thing is true.

The network effect within Internet open content replicates something that happens when you think. Perhaps it does not actually happen on the Internet, but only in your mind. In that case, the patterns of links among elephant stuff on the Cameroon site stimulates the patterns in your brain. It does not matter whether we think of the location as cyberspace or the brain.

Similarly, a fact that is printed in a book you are reading is nothing more than ink on paper until, by reading it, you spark the connections needed among synapses to emerge that fact into your consciousness. When someone else reads that same printed fact so that it emerges in her consciousness, what you think and she thinks can probably never be exactly the same in every nuance. The fact only exists dynamically in each of your brains, making comparisons impossible, at least for now.

Conveying an idea to someone else amounts to firing it up on your brain, sending it dynamically into one or more of your centers of articulation—talking, writing, grimacing—from where further dynamic electrical messaging gets your body talking, writing, frowning, and so forth.

Although we have a very long way to go before we can understand any of this well, one thing is certain: The platform of the electrical storm is very, very complex. Its static platform is composed of billions of neurons that make trillions of interconnections and synapses. That platform in your head supports everything you think or do.

The substance, if you can call it that, of a thought is always a pattern of electrical connections (with chemical events at synapses) that usually emerges for a tiny amount of time—perhaps never to arise in exactly that same pattern again. As the same kind of event occurs when you click around in open content for learning on the Internet, you are experiencing the network effect.

🔆 75 OPEN CONTENT VETS SPONTANEOUSLY

The English verb *vet* has become very much used in our times of confusion and complexity. The word means to examine carefully with the qualifications of an expert and then select what is good and true. One of the most amazing aspects of the open Internet is that content is vetted spontaneously. The vetting is a part of the content's emergence as order from chaos.

Perhaps the most surprising and counterintuitive hypothesis you will read in this book is stated in the following two sentences. Knowledge emerging from the virtual knowledge ecology is the most refined and elegant you will find anywhere. It is higher in authority, accuracy, and currency than its counterpart to be found in any other source.

How can that be? The answer explains how Google gives you the link you want in under .5 seconds. The fact is that, as the virtual knowledge ecology matures, ways to refine content quality will beat Google's, where the search engine must rely on a text search to decide what you are looking for. If you now give Google the word *jaguar*, the search engine does not know if you want a cat or a car. The virtual knowledge ecology has selection criteria superior to text alone.

Educators who complain that the Internet is chaotic and that its content should selectively (by them) be doled out to students do not see the reality or potential of the virtual knowledge ecology. That needs to change or we need to change the leadership for learning.

Internet connectivity in the 2004 U.S. presidential primaries provided a dramatic demonstration of order emerging from chaos—at least from one candidate's perspective. Governor Howard Dean came very close to being nominated for president of the United States because of it. Out of the chaos of millions of Internet users who were potential Deaniacs (mostly young and eager liberals), a network emerged over a few weeks and began to exert influence in the Democratic primaries.

The Deaniac network was formed by connections and visits to Dean campaign websites. A conservative, pro-Bush person might visit a Dean website, but the chances she would link to it or ever visit it again were remote. Dean supporters came by over and over again, linked to the sites, communicated with each other through the site network, and bought campaign supplies there. The network of websites and e-mail connectivity it captured empowered the campaign to enlist and inform supporters. It also moved outside of the virtual world, organizing meet-ups and setting loose swarms of Deaniacs at rallies.

A blogging phenomenon, sparked in September 2004, that analyzed the authenticity of a *60 Minutes* television report was a dramatic demonstration of a network of evidence and logical argument emerging from the chaos of cyberspace. The event was purely about subject matter: Were the date and authorship of letters authentic concerning President Bush's service in the National Guard? In the volatile preelection-day atmosphere, views in the chaos of public opinion were sharply divided. Several networks of proof concerning the letters began to form among the bloggers. There was a lot of commotion in the press about pajama-wearing bloggers not being as well qualified to tell their story as well as established professional journalists were.

Looking only at the network aspects of the event, we can go back and find ordered networks emerging from the chaos of politics, opinion, effrontery, and support aimed at journalists by the bloggers. The connectivity of one set of blogs spontaneously reflected, in greater and greater detail, the falseness of the letters. A second set of blogs connected a network of facts and proof that pointed toward the letters being authentic. Although a lot of emotional and partisan commentary was included in these spates of blogging, the cognitive pattern of linking was very pure. A sufficient case for falsity emerged to force the matter into the older media and, eventually, to a major investigation and television staff departures.

The two blog networks that emerged from the questioning of the letters—like every network within the open Internet—were created by people and based on the meaning each one intended when each link was made. Every time a Deaniac visited a Dean web page, that visit—that dynamic link he created—reflected the high probability of his support for the candidate. The origin of the self-organizing networks of meaning that arose from the Internet can always be traced to the decisions of individual people. These decisions, it turns out, are usually very precise ones, both individually and collectively. An exception would be if a lot of Bush backers had decided for some reason to visit the Deaniac websites—an unlikely possibility and one that the statistical analysis of other factors at the sites would probably reveal.

The ultimate power of blogging activity concerning the letters about President Bush's National Guard service was how the content of the letters was vetted. Bloggers from both sides of the election converged on the challenge of proving whether the letters were or were not authentic. The competition was wide open and global. A network of experts emerged dynamically. Their observations and judgments were interconnected to form a larger picture. Anyone in the world with Internet access could visit and inspect the network, following reports from blog to blog and keeping a newsreader on their desktop to alert them when something new was posted.

The immediacy of the blogs has made order emerging from Internet chaos more obvious, but it has been going on for a long time. I have said that the virtual knowledge ecology has existed since around 2000. That was about the time when the open Internet chaos was large enough and accessed sufficiently for meaningful networks of knowledge to emerge and be vetted for most academic subjects.

The vetting, though, started much earlier. In a sense, it began way back with the birth of the Internet, when a few scholars started connecting pieces of their content on their servers. In 1998, I wrote a review for the HomeworkCentral.com Top 8 newsletter of a website called the Hittite Homepage. As I write this in the spring of 2005, the pages on the Hittite Homepage had last been updated in 2003. Looking at it now, the site is not a lot different than it was when I first saw it, except there are now more links to Hittite resources.

My 1998 review of the Hittite Homepage included this explanation from the site's section on texts: *The Catalog of Hittite Texts (CTH) has become the standard catalog used by Hittitologists in referring to the Hittite text corpus. Because that corpus continues to grow, the need to keep the CTH updated is a current and pervasive problem. The creation of the World Wide Web makes it possible to do this.*

Today, a Google search for the word Hittite returns two different websites titled *Hittite Homepage*. The first is a commercial website for Hittite Microwave Corporation. The second is the same website I reviewed in 1998, as updated in 2003. Several other websites devoted to the ancient civilization are listed by Google below, along with a website promoting travel in Turkey that includes visits to Hittite environs.

The list returned by Google from billions of possible web pages is well vetted. The links recommended on the historical websites you can open from the Google list are still better vetted because they are vetted by the Hittitologists themselves. It is the latter group that comprise the Hittite resources of the virtual knowledge ecology. The microwave website would not have become a suggested link in pages overseen by the Hittitologists.

Of course, Google's vetting was also performed by the links and visits to websites by Hittitologists—that is, Internet users interested in the ancient people. Google spiders got fooled by the microwave site and the travel promotion—though not completely in the second case because travel to Turkey is relevant to the subject. The Google vetting is done by counting the links to websites and evaluating a network, just like the Deaniac web that formed around the governor's candidacy by linking to campaign websites. Google spiders, though, are simply software creatures that only can report text strings, not the meaning of the words the text spells out.

If you click through the Hittite websites that you find near the top of a Google search return, you will see that the more scholarly ones richly link to each other. Those sites are only items on a list when Google interfaces them. The virtual knowledge ecology forms a piece of the network of the history of the ancient Middle East.

The network formed by the interlinked Hittite websites is far superior for education than a list returned by a search engine in two important ways. First, its suggested links have been recommended by the Hittitologists instead of picked by a software spider on the basis of text definition and links. Second, the network is richly connected to related subjects—a cognitive dimension beyond the scope of search engine.

A final point about vetting is yet another way that the education establishment is failing to take advantage of the potential the Internet has for learning. We need to question education's assumption that it must devise and overlay another level of organization, such as curricula and standards, through which to filter Internet embedded knowledge. To what extent should teachers take advantage of the natural aggregation and vetted knowledge by being embedded into the open network of the virtual knowledge ecology?

The Hittitologists and most other scholars of human knowledge have selected and vetted what they know, and placed it openly online where they welcome the visits of students. Why, then, does the education industry get paid to organize knowledge and distribute the scholars' subjects in costly predigital media? Is the point of view of the educator who creates material about the Hittites better or even as well qualified as the scholars of the subject who aggregate and vet it online? Certainly these are major considerations for pedagogues and tax and tuition payers.

76 THE DARWINIAN EFFECT

When scholars like the Hittitologists vet the online knowledge in their field, a process is under way by which the fittest Hittite websites survive and fill knowledge niches. There is no shortage of not-so-wonderful knowledge on the Internet. There is also a lot of well-intentioned online material that is not appropriate for conveying knowledge to students.

An example of the lesser quality material would be a web page on the Hittites by a middle school student. The student would probably include a lot of correct information but he might equally get a D for poor information. A search engine spider would not know the difference between A+ and D stuff, but would duly report a website about Hittites.

In the pre-Google days, before their algorithm began elevating web pages with the most links and visitors, a glut of web pages tended to be listed by search engines for many school study topics. The batch coming up for Hittites would include the middle school web page and almost any other page in the open Internet that contained the name of the ancient people. This range of web pages returned by searches justified earlier concerns by teachers that their students would not know which pages to study.

A way to clarify the built-in network solution to a glut of inappropriate materials Google invented is to realize that only the fittest of them survive to get placed near the top of the search return list. The same thing happens in the Internet ecology. The mechanism has been called the Darwinian effect in biology.

The search engine method invented by Google founders Larry Page and Sergey Brin implements the mechanism of the survival of the fittest and generates search return lists with websites where the most fit is at the top of the listings and those that follow are given in descending fitness rank. The fitness is determined in two ways. Sites are selected as fitting the search words by matching those words. The assumption is then made that the most fit site has the most links to it, so it goes to the top of the list. Exactly how this happens is a fiercely guarded secret.

Less fit sites survive to a lesser and lesser degree by being buried far down the list and many pages away from what the user first see. A middle school website on the Hittites would thus almost certainly be lower on the list than scholarly Hittite sites that are linked to in global research projects.

In the virtual knowledge ecology of open content websites for learning, the survival of the fittest is more straightforward. Scholars for a subject select and link to a website they approve and admire. Academic topics have clusters of links among their scholars in the humanities, sciences, and the rest of the study subjects. The clusters tend to begin with small topics like the Hittites, with those clusters linked to related topics like Elamites and other ancient peoples, forming larger clusters. You can be sure that a website with false information does not survive the vetting by experts in its field. It is not linked into their cluster unless they judged it fit. The network among the clusters of scholars forms a major portion of the virtual knowledge ecology.

77 VIRTUAL CONTENT CREATURES

Non-Internet species of content creatures are books, chalkboards, pictures, wall charts, radio programs, television shows, slide projectors presentations, and CDs. The content of the Internet is delivered by a new kind of content creature—kinds of interfaces from which viewers apprehend the meaning of the content. Basic early Internet species of content creatures are now evolving into new ones.

The first Internet creature for knowledge content was the web page. It was and still is assembled on your monitor screen from instructions that it receives as text through your Internet connection. The assembly of the content is done by your browser, which is a software program specifically for that purpose, such as Netscape, Internet Explorer, and Firefox. If you click on "View" at the top of your browser page and select "Source" a window will open that will display the text that causes the browser to build that page. Those instructions are text written in Hypertext Markup Language (HTML), a computer language. When your browser assembles and displays a web page, it follows the HTML instructions, which tell it what text, images, and links to put where.

Very early on, a new kind of content creature emerged when several individual web pages began to be planned as an interlinked group to convey specific content, thus making what came to be called a website, which was a more complex interface vehicle. The web page and website became the common types of content organization and display.

As the creation and organization of digital content became exponentially more massive, a concept of objects developed and helped to simplify some things. The concept began as object-oriented programming. Its basic idea proved useful in conceptualizing and building digital learning materials. Learning objects evolved.

The object approach is to create an identifiable entity called an *object* that can be inserted in multiple locations in multiple contexts. The learning object approach has been used to populate sections of courses, online digital tutors, and other sorts of knowledge presentations. For online learning content, the efficiency of using learning objects can be very great.

Take the example of the subject abacus. There is an excellent website called ABACUS, The Art of Calculating with Beads. Since that website got top ranking on a Google search I made early in 2005 for the word abacus, undoubtedly it is linked to by many other websites. For those websites in the linked group that are designed for learning, the ABACUS website is serving as a learning object. Among many other outstanding features, the ABACUS website contains an "Interactive Abacus Tutor." The tutor is also a learning object because it could be linked into other learning website. Although learning objects are usually conceived as website assets made for learning, theoretically, every page on the Internet that has its own URL is available as an object to be included in any other web page. That may be a stretch of the usual use of the word object, but the principle is true.

The design and implementation of learning objects is a major subject of twenty-first-century pedagogy, which is beyond the scope of this book. It is pertinent here, however, that learning objects, when they are open content, are radically more economical for education than the interface media they replace. A little checking on the Internet led to a place online to buy a children's wooden abacus for $16.95. The interactive tutor mentioned above is free to use. To provide just one wooden abacus to 100,000 elementary schools for all the children in each school to share would cost $1,695,000. The online interactive abacus is free to use by every child in all 100,000 of those schools—in fact, to every child on earth.

The learning object is a creature of the virtual knowledge ecology. It is effective in the ecology for taking advantage of the new access and network structure of knowledge. Two other ecology creatures have recently become prominent in the practice and speculations about online learning. They are the wiki and the blog. While the learning object is a cognitive presentation that can be scattered among many learning contexts, the wiki aggregates. The blog scatters interrelated ideas.

The wiki aggregates input. As described in Idea 52, the fact that Wikipedia.com is open content means it is open to the collaboration of anyone who wants to contribute to its content. As a content interface, a wiki also brings ideas together from diverse forces, to aggregate those ideas. Interfacing intellectual collaboration is an exciting new phenomenon that is being tried and used in many contexts as this book goes to press.

In 2004, blogging reached a tipping point, and blogs cascaded into cyberspace to create the massive blogosphere. The blog is a creature born in the ecology—cousin to the simple web page and descendant of the diary. As a learning content interfacing creature, the blogs add dynamics to the interlinking that forms new knowledge content. My guess is that a more advanced creature that will have the collaboration of the wiki and the dynamics of the blog will evolve to become a key tool for teaching and learning in the virtual knowledge ecology.

78 WHY AGGREGATED VIRTUAL KNOWLEDGE IS SUPERIOR

The network effect has aggregated knowledge web pages and, for learning, that has turned out to be a very good thing. In a follow-up on Idea

40, we can now explain that content for human learning that has aggregated online retains all the good qualities it has when you find it in print, film/video, broadcast media, and elsewhere. And, as explained in Idea 40, the knowledge accessed online is superior in several ways. Going the next step in what has happened: When the separate web pages forming the nodes of online knowledge are interlinked, they formed webs of related knowledge that is superior, I think, to any knowledge form yet known in human experience.

"Forest of Rhetoric" is an excellent website from Brigham Young University. Dozens of rhetorical figures from *abating* to *zeugma* are listed in a narrow right-side column. General topics are listed in a narrow left-side column. In the wide center panel, the ideas generated by clicking links on either side are displayed. Every small specific idea is related in all sorts of different ways, elucidating the powers and nuances of rhetoric. The website is a strong example of how connecting ideas reveals and amplifies meaning.

There are many examples across the virtual knowledge ecology of websites that interrelate their aggregated pages to ramify and illustrate ideas. Earthquake pages at the U.S. Geological Survey website demonstrate how the connections generate ideas. An interesting entry point to try this process is its interactive "World Map—Clickable to Regions."

Still somewhat rough, the fundamental superiority of online knowledge over older interfacing media is that it is interfaced in context. The context emerges from aggregations not only of pages within a website, like the rhetoric and earthquake material. The context emerges from the potential aggregation with all related open content in the virtual knowledge ecology. Websites and their individual pages can link to limitless other web pages beyond their own sites—so long as the content is open.

A small website portrays the Phrygians, an Iron Age culture from the tenth to the fourth centuries BCE in Turkey. The website places the Phrygians of that period in historical, archaeological, religious, and geographical context. Phrygians.com is maintained by Garance Fiedler, Ph.D., who works at the French Institute of Anatolian Archaeology in Istanbul. He has contributed articles to the website and links from there to many relevant other web pages.

The context available at Phrygians.com is broad and rich. One of the

topics is King Midas and the last meal he ate before he died and was
entombed. There really was a very rich Midas who was king of the
Phrygians. His tomb was found and was excavated fifty years ago by the
University of Pennsylvania Museum of Archaeology and Anthropology,
which now has an open content exhibit online describing what was
found. Phrygians.com describes the great king's last meal and links to
the museum's exhibit. King Midas has thus been found in the rich context of history, archaeology, and the interesting questions of what he ate
before he died. (In case you are curious, forty years after the tomb was
excavated, the meal was determined to have been lentil stew with mari-
nated sheep or goat meat barbecued and flavored with herbs accompanied by barley beer and honey mead.)

King Midas is found at Phrygians.com in a network of maps, photos,
a chronology, articles, and discussions comprising together a fertile context for learning about the king famous for his wealth but otherwise little
known to most people.

The cognitive learning advantages of interfacing knowledge for learning in the natural connectivity of a network structure are stated and implied throughout these Ideas. A summary of Ideas 40 and 78 is that
online knowledge is superior for learning because it is:

- Fresher and up-to-date;
- More authoritative;
- More forcefully expressed;
- Interactive with its user;
- Connected in context.

79 HOW TO FIND SOMETHING ON THE INTERNET

In 2005, the usual answer to how to find something on the Internet has
been to Google it. What you are doing with a Google search is getting a
list to choose from of single nodes that contain words matching the ones
you put into the Google search box. You are also getting at the top of the
list of the links those that are most frequented by the Internet public.

The links returned are from throughout the mammoth open Internet.

A lot of people tend to think of the Internet as something like a great big list because they are so used to the lists search engines display. That impression is incorrect; the Internet is a great big network.

Any item on a Google search return list is just one URL—just the unique address for one page in many billions of interconnected pages. When you click on one of the items on such a list, the page for the URL of the item you clicked opens, and you find yourself looking at one node of the huge network that is the Internet. People who think it is hard to find something meaningful on the Internet tend not to know what to do next after they get to the page that opens up. If the subject of the page that opens is not what you are looking for, the next step is to go back to the list Google displayed and click another link.

A lot of the time, the page that opens has exactly what you want and you do not need to go further. However, if the page contains the information you are looking for, and you want related material, it is best to forget Google for a while and start looking in a different way. At this point ask yourself this question: What kind of network am I in?

Because the structure you are exploring is a network, the node you find is important but so are the links to that node. Most high-quality web pages are a node in a small or large network of related information.

Pursuing the links on a page you opened from a Google list amounts to leaving the text search world and exploring cognitive linking. Cognitive networks are linked up by the connecting of pages, because persons making those links had a reason to do so. The links reflect connections of thoughts; they are cognitive. Exploring this kind of linking is a marvelous new way to learn. It is the way to not only find something you are looking for but to learn often a great deal about what you have found.

80 THE GRAND IDEA

The grandest change the Digital Age will bring to planet Earth and to its inhabitants is the aggregation and universal access to what is known by humankind. We will all be able to interact with our common useful knowledge as we connect to the Grand Idea.

It takes some faith in the good heart of people to expect that huge forest burns will no longer send massive smoke into the atmosphere from remote regions when the people who set the fires truly know the damage they do to the planet we share. In another vein, it does not take excessive optimism to think that when people now politically isolated by tyranny share in planetary common knowledge that they will find a way to shed their yoke. Rather than getting sidetracked into historical and political theory, expecting that knowledge is better than ignorance makes the coming of the Grand Idea enormously hopeful.

Jericho is the world's oldest known town. In its earliest days, around ten millennia ago, its wisest person would contain in his or her head everything known within the world reachable from the town. That knowledge would be of animals, the night sky, town life, ancestral memories, and the few newly acquired agricultural techniques that had allowed the people of the town to wander less and settle in year-round near their growing crops.

Jericho's wise one would ponder those things, seamlessly connecting them in his or her brain into one Grand Idea encompassing everything known in Jericho. There would be clusters of ideas about animals, the sky, and the rest. These ideas would be connected mentally here and there, causing ideas to emerge such as it is dangerous to tend crops alone because lions lurk and killed two Jericho farmers last year.

The Jericho wise one's Grand Idea would not include knowledge of domesticated horses, geometry, or computer programming because those ideas did not yet exist. Neither would the Jericho wise one's grand idea connect mentally to knowledge of hunting and gathering in the forests of America. The American wise ones ten millennia ago would have known nothing of life in a town. There was no knowledge of each other's existence to connect what was known then in Jericho and America.

One of my college instructors taught that Aristotle was the last synthetic thinker. The idea the phrase implied fascinated him: Aristotle knew everything that was known to the humans within his experience. He had read every book and mastered every intellectual discipline. My instructor was intrigued by the thought that Aristotle could synthesize any idea with any other idea within his own mind. I still recall the instructor's wistful tone in which he told us that no one since Aristotle has ever been able to do that again.

Aristotle was not able to relate into his synthesizing the writings of Confucius from two centuries before his time, or early steps being taken in Mesoamerica in agriculture and artistic expression. The knowledge possessed by people beyond his geographically known world was simply not knowable.

A grand vision occurred soon after Aristotle's day for gathering knowledge. Ptolemy II of Egypt founded a library at Alexandria with the goal of collecting every scroll of knowledge from across the world into that one place. The Internet has been compared to the Library at Alexandria. The comparison is a good one. It reflects the events described in the *Access* section in this book.

Though Ptolemy's vision was grand, it could only accomplish half of what Aristotle was able to do in his own brain. By Ptolemy's time, in the century following the one in which Aristotle lived, the notion of everything known being connected within a single mind was not the vision at Alexandria. Aristotle was able to synthesize everything he knew, connecting it dynamically in his thoughts. Such a process could not happen among thousands of scrolls sitting in hundreds of racks filling acres of buildings as was the situation at the mouth of the Nile.

When I was listening fifty years ago to my instructor's musings about Aristotle's synthetic mind, the idea of a virtual place where everything that is known by humankind is interconnected would have been as tough to conceptualize as a flu shot would have been for Aristotle. Viruses and antibodies would have been utterly new concepts for him, just as computer chips and WI-FI would have been in our classroom of college students who grew up in a world without computers.

Yet, something very much like Aristotle's mind now exists within the Internet. It is not complete yet and will continue to receive new content. It is the Grand Idea—made up of everything known by humankind with everything able to be freely connect to everything else.

The Grand Idea and the virtual knowledge ecology in which it abides is not, however, the wise one of our planet. The virtual static and dynamic ideas that emerge are only engaged by human minds—and not comprehended by the machines that simulate them. Because it interfaces everything known, the Grand Idea holds the potential for us all to become learned. None of us will become an Aristotle by importing into our own head all that can be known from the Grand Idea. Yet, by connecting to it, we can access useful knowledge and explore its connectivity without limit.

The Grand Idea is also not the wise one because it cannot think—it is not dynamically synthetic, as Aristotle's mind was when it thought about knowledge by connecting certain things in different ways. In something radically new, the Grand Idea can make you and me and everyone else a synthetic thinker. We can go to where everything known is located and connect anything we want to anything else, forming new and endless patterns reflecting our thoughts. Using the Grand Idea, as it becomes the completed virtual knowledge ecology, any of us can synthesize ideas limitlessly from the vastness of everything known by humankind. Perhaps this is what sitting down for a chat with Aristotle was like.

As I was writing this Idea, I dipped into the virtual knowledge ecology to check the dates in which Aristotle, Confucius, and Ptolemy lived and to verify the age of Jericho and the stirrings of culture in Mesoamerica. I was connecting knowledge to fabricate ideas for what I was writing and synthesizing them with memories in my mind of a classroom five decades ago at Northwestern University. To be able to connect these wide nodes almost effortlessly in a network of ideas for a discussion like this is the gift of the Grand Idea to us all. It will bring global enlightenment that will far outshine the Golden Age of Greece in which Aristotle strolled the colonnades synthesizing knowledge in the isolation of his singular mind.

NOTE

1. Stephen Jay Gould. Foreword. In *Five Kingdoms*, Lynn Margulis and Karlene V. Schwartz. New York: W. H. Freeman and Company, 1998. p. xi.

5

ADAPTING

81 MAKING LEARNING SUIT THE NEW KNOWLEDGE LOCATION

Change creates the need to adapt. Adapt is not the same thing, of course, as adopt. Adopt means to accept and use something new. For more than a decade now, the usual attitude in education discussions has assumed a choice of whether or not to adopt the Internet into the learning process. Now that almost all knowledge in the education venue is online in a manifestation superior to anywhere else, the posture of choosing whether or not to adopt it has become no longer defensible.

Adapt means to make the necessary changes in yourself so that you are suited to something new. This section of Ideas explores how various participants in learning adapt to the new location of knowledge online and its aggregation into the virtual knowledge ecology. Some participants are already well adapted. Others must make some significant changes.

82 THE KNOWLEDGE ITSELF IS NOT ISOLATED BUT CONNECTED

Adaptation in the new era of knowledge embedded into the Internet requires the realization that no knowledge is a virtual island. It is the connectivity itself that is, in a fundamental way, knowledge itself. Looking at this connectivity in action helps us understand what is happening as knowledge bits are now able to connect freely.

Imagine you are walking through a garden and you notice a ladybug on a leaf. The small red creature with black spots becomes, simply by your notice, the center of your thoughts. At that point, one of two things is likely to happen in your mind.

One of the two is to quickly note and dismiss it. Your mind will flood briefly with what you know about lady bugs: She is not going to bite me. She is good for the garden, so don't bother her. By then, a hummingbird has caught your attention. The ladybug is gone from your thoughts and your mind focuses on the hummingbird, or simply wanders along as you walk on through the garden.

Your mind's other option is to focus on the ladybug. When it does, the little bug becomes a dynamic center of a whole lot of other things, and your mind starts to connect into that center. Everything you know about ladybugs begins to emerge in your mind and connect to the sample you are looking at. As you draw closer, your optical processing informs you that her antennae are moving and she is a bit off balance. Then you realize that she is cleaning her antennae with her legs— something you did not know before that a ladybug could and did do. You learned something.

Your realization that she was washing her antennae was a highly abstract cognitive process: An idea arose in your mind. You connected it to an even larger concept that emerged, again in your mind: Ladybugs wash their antennae with their feet. Perhaps that led you to some speculation: How many bugs and what kind use their feet this way? (Writing this made me curious. I did a quick Google check and found that butterflies use their first pair of feet to clean their antenna. The same source said lots of moths and butterflies taste with their feet—something I did not know.)

We can replay the ladybug sighting with a different human cast for a mini-look at the cognitive explosion of the twenty-first century. The new characters are yourself and a seven-year-old child. As you walk together through the garden, the child spots the ladybug—the first one he has ever seen. He asks if the bug will bite, and you tell him not only will she not bite, but that the ladybug is a very garden-friendly creature.

The child comes close to the ladybug and looks her over carefully. The child then asks you what the little bug is doing. You look closely as well, and venture a guess that she is washing her antennae. The child then starts asking you a string of questions. Do all bugs take baths? What are her antennae for? Why is she called a lady? Why is the ladybug garden-friendly?

What the child can learn in those precious cognitive moments of intensely centering on the ladybug is limited to what he can observe and what you know and observe, on the spot, about ladybugs and successfully connect into his thoughts. Before knowledge about ladybugs moved online, your best option for extending what the child could learn beyond what you could tell him on the spot would be to find an expert to ask or to go later to a library and look up more about ladybugs. In both instances, you would have to get the child interested and centered again on ladybugs to relay your new knowledge to him—often not an easy task.

In the incident we have been looking at, we could say that, as the child centered his focus on the ladybug, he was accessing knowledge from three sources: (1) his previous knowledge of bugs, (2) what he saw as he looked at the ladybug, and (3) what you could tell him about ladybugs. It was a dynamic moment—occurring in time and ceasing when the child's focus moved to center on the hummingbird arriving to drink from the plant's blossoms.

The basic idea of the virtual knowledge ecology is that focusing on a bit of knowledge opens the way to connect to other bits, and that what occurs then is more than access. Certainly knowledge has been accessed by the child from each of the sources, but the dynamic event when the access interconnects is the emergence of a pattern.

When an access stream informing you that ladybugs clean their antennae with their feet connects with another stream informing you that butterflies clean their antennae, a pattern forms—that is the occurrence to you of a new idea. If the way seven more bugs clean their antennae were connected, a more complex new knowledge pattern would be created about antennae cleaning in bugs. If how all bugs clean their antennae were connected from multiple streams, a fuller knowledge network of the subject would emerge. The virtual knowledge ecology is where exactly that is happening—fairly roughly now, but inevitably elegant in the near future.

The virtual knowledge ecology is now maturing. Its organization of what is known by humankind is still messy. Nevertheless, it is already quite possible to take a quantum leap from traditional learning experiences to those that will soon become the mainstay of global learning. Let's go back to our imaginary garden for a glimpse of what is to come.

If the garden were a wireless hot spot, and you had your laptop with you, you and the child asking you about the ladybug could sit on a bench and visit the virtual knowledge ecology. As you used a search engine to find some ladybug web pages and began clicking the links among those pages and out from them into related subjects, something will occur that is very much like what your own mind did when you first saw the ladybug. Ladybug concepts will emerge from the Internet around the center idea of ladybug that you and the child are thinking about.

The first burst of enthusiasm for the Internet as a source for learning touted, as we know, an information highway—a phrase that caught well the first value of the Internet. The idea was that you could surf around in cyberspace much as you move around the stacks in a great library. Sitting on your bench in your garden with an inquisitive child and a wireless laptop can still be thought of as traveling the information highway between ladybug destinations.

The information highway model is, however, very limited and superficial. A better model for what is actually going on is a networking of streams of ladybug information. There is nothing within the Internet that is anything like a highway. Like your mind, the Internet is a network from which bits and pieces interconnect in patterns. When related bits connect dynamically around the center of your focus, ideas emerge from the convergence. As we saw, when that happens in your mind, new configurations of bits of information can emerge as completely new ideas.

When I was focusing in my mind on bugs washing antennae with their feet, having learned that about ladybugs, and then connected my new bit of information that butterflies do that too, new ideas began to form in my mind. As you read this, what new ideas occur to you from the ladybug-butterfly feet-wash-antennae knowledge? Just the word *occur* is a clue to how basic this process is to thinking: Ideas occur, they happen.

Educators of the future are adapting to a learning environment of emerging knowledge. It is often a dynamic venue with ideas and learning occurring over time. As you sit on the garden bench with the child, looking together at ladybug web pages, and following links among them and out from them, ideas are occurring to you and to the child.

There are many really interesting questions about this new phenomenon of ideas interfaced for learning from the Internet. These questions raise all sorts of philosophical, pedagogical, information theory, and other issues. None of those need to intrude on this discussion. What we are looking at in this book is the practical fact that the new phenomenon is quite real and very much here, and what that means for learning. The Ideas in this section discuss those points in reverse order.

83 THE EDUCATION TO EXPECT

The core reason for the need to change education is that the knowledge that schools were created to teach has moved onto the Internet. Assuming that this fundamental relocation of knowledge will change how learning occurs, what sort of education can we expect in the twenty-first century?

What we meant during the twentieth century by the word education included many matters other than teaching and learning knowledge. Education came to imply nurture, discipline, articulation, socialization, and the grooming of other aspects of the well-developed mature human being. One good guess about what the future of education may be is to expect schooling to remain in place, with the knowledge expectations removed. School might become the place youngsters go to be nurtured, to acquire discipline, to have opportunities to articulate, and to make friends and become socialized. Athletics might be in that new school mix as well.

In a schools-absent-knowledge-imparting model, many schools would remain pretty much as they are now. There are a lot of schools from which kids graduate as near illiterates, with minimal knowledge of history, literatures, sciences, and the rest. In the new model, the kids would be acquiring knowledge somewhere other than in school.

Another model would be the thoroughgoing use of online knowledge by schools. That has been the practice for some time now in the pursuit of many academic specialties at the graduate level. To some degree, undergraduate studies also engage the virtual knowledge ecology. But by far the most common practice remains directing students to secondary knowledge sources, primarily textbooks, for the cognitive content they are assigned to learn. If computers are used to access knowledge, it is often not from the open content that forms the virtual knowledge ecology. Instead, intranets that are closed to general Internet use are where courses with knowledge embedded in them are positioned by faculty and used only by the hosting school's students.

Homeschooling offers possibilities for transitioning from printed materials to online knowledge. To learn something about Mars, a student studying at home is not restricted to a lesson shared by thirty classmates. He seems more likely to use NASA's Rovers Mission pages to learn, instead of a general science textbook with a page or two on the planets, as his contemporaries would be doing in school classes.

My vision of the future is different from any of these models. I think that within the next five years—if we try to make it happen—the tipping point will come to ubiquitous computing. Our planet will quickly progress toward every individual having a personal mobile computer that will access the full range of the Internet. As the momentum builds, there will be a paradigm shift in focus for learning, and the knowledge on the Internet will become the measure of how, when, where, and what we teach and learn.

When this happens, individual schools will either vigorously engage the virtual knowledge ecology, morph into a new kind of community institution, or be abandoned. Activities we associate with schools, like athletics, bands, clubs, and the like will find other sponsorship. An example would be community theater where youngsters could participate to develop performance skills. High school athletic leagues would be sponsored by minor and major league sports organizations and use their courts and stadiums. If discipline and socialization processes do not have family support, the community will need to step in with programs and buildings. Apprenticing will flourish because kids will have flexible schedules instead of confinement to school most work days. Labor laws will be changed to make apprenticing practical and regulated to prevent abuse.

Reading, writing, mathematics, history, literature, sciences, technology, and other subjects once called academic because they were found in schools will be learned using knowledge from the Internet. Kids will learn on their own or seek out teachers. Teaching institutions will undoubtedly sprout. Teachers will work as individual professionals, both within the institutions and on their own.

A key responsibility of and power held by the education establishment now in place is the assessment and certification it performs. Advancement from grade to grade, the high school diploma, and the college degree are all awarded by schools. Free market online testing and certification will end the education establishment monopoly on announcing who is and is not qualified in areas of knowledge. Mentoring and apprenticing will provide human insight for assessment.

Assessment will be freed from the lockstep grades of our current schools. A fifth grader will be able to take an online test and receive a certificate affirming his mastery of algebra. Certificates of that kind will be incorporated into resumes and job applications and used to apply for apprenticeships or to enter the workforce and advance there.

It is impossible to predict exactly what education will become in ten, twenty, fifty years. It is safe to say we can expect something better than what we now have. The slide into mediocrity, or worse, that education has taken in the past century is being reversed because the virtual knowledge ecology is emerging to offer what is known by humankind to everyone on earth.

84 THE ADAPTATION OF TECHNOLOGY

The underlying technology attracting migration of what is known by humankind into the Internet is the proliferation of a network of computers, all of which can allow every other computer in the network to display, using interfaces humans can understand, content contained in a distant computer.

My website GoldenSwamp.com is a bunch of digital files sitting in a computer—or more precisely a server—in San Diego. I create the posts at my desk in New York City and send them over the Internet by FTP (File Transfer Protocol) to the San Diego server that I pay to host my website. When your monitor displays my website, it is interfacing files your computer just downloaded into its own hard drive or is streaming to your interface directly from the server in San Diego.

At a basic level, and historically, the technology just described did not adapt to or adopt the Internet. The technology of open connectivity created the Internet and will remain fundamentally the same, continuing to connect anything to anything, thereby being the platform of the Internet.

Above its fundamental function, there are four general ways that the platformed open connectivity technology is now adapting to expand the amount and quality of its usefulness. The first adaptation is the switch from wired to wireless connection with the Internet, which adapts to the increasing usefulness and demand for individual and mobile Internet access. The second technological adaptation is the expansion across geography of wireless transmission, which promises to result in wireless access to the Internet anywhere on earth. Third, the first two adaptations of the technology are fueling demand for cheaper and more effective mobile Internet interface devices. Cell phones and laptops are both undergoing adaptations to meet that demand. Fourth, technology is making the all-important adaptation of increasing bandwidth. This adaptation is crucial because it shortens download time. It is also the key to more complex content, using images, video, sound, and remote accessing of web page elements.

The concluding Ideas in the *Action* section of this book delve further into what can be done to speed up the adaptation of technology functions to hasten ubiquitous computing and learning.

85 THE ADAPTATION OF CONTENT

Repositioning the way knowledge has been interfaced for learning before the digital era has not worked very well. Content needs to be adapted to the network medium into which it is being placed to take advantage of the benefits of dynamic aggregation and interactivity.

A clean approach to developing content for learning online would be to start thinking from scratch. To imagine what that would be, step back from analyzing how education has been done for the past century. Suspend the mindset of fixing the schools so they work better. Instead, imagine what things would be like if there were no school buildings, no chalkboards, no pencils and paper, and no industry that ingests billions of dollars annually to produce textbooks. There would only be the Internet abounding in knowledge, mobile Internet access via laptops and cell phones, along with global generations needing to be educated.

How, under these imagined circumstances, should reading, writing, mathematics, geography, history, science, and the other once academic (in "schools") subjects be presented for learning to the uneducated generations? How would the knowledge of these subjects best be adapted to the Internet medium for acquisition by learners?

Reading would already be bubbling up constantly into a student's experience using his mobile Internet access. Even in today's cell phone expansion, practice reading is popping up into the hands of new young people every day. Idea 43 describes why literacy does not need to proceed Internet access. Just as even very small children are beginning to learn to type as keyboards flood into their world, rudimentary reading follows as they eagerly reach for digital toys.

I did the same thing sort of alphabet manipulation in the 1940s with a large set of balsawood alphabet blocks my parents made. But the blocks did not flow into reading as happens with a click or two online. I had to wait for elementary school, where simple *Dick and Jane* books took me to another level. Not until high school was I assigned a book to read in the full range of the English language. Some children are ready far sooner, and they do not have to wait if they use the Internet.

Writing can begin these days with the first text message a kid composes on a cell phone. Children are well aware that spelling corrects itself on a computer interface. Software language translators are on the way. Handwriting may become archaic in a generation or two. Think how relieved scribes must have felt when they could use ink on papyrus instead of bothering with preparing mud tablets into which to write their words with a stylus. We are confronted with children today who keep their opinion to themselves, but they do think handwriting is as archaic as using a stylus and mud. Teaching writing in these circumstances needs some rethinking. When elementary school students are more expert than we are at typing text with thumbs, how do we convince them to pick up pencil or pen? For how long into the future do you suppose we will try?

Arithmetic has already been through one digital conversion caused by handheld calculators. Another is immediately at hand. Interactive tutors abound online for addition, subtraction, multiplication, and division, as well as more complex calculations. Arithmetic tutors are ideal for the new visual and interactive prowess of cell phone screens. Imagine a ten-year-old waiting for a bus in Uruguay, her thumbs dancing on her cell phone keypad as she sharpens her multiplication with virtual flashcards. With fuller Internet access, budding Einsteins can move into higher mathematics at any age, anywhere on the planet.

Old ways of teaching geography—and the books and wall charts they used—are as obsolete as the pre-Magellan concept of a flat world. Geography changes constantly, and online maps can be updated immediately. Students can use satellite images to look at geography in real time. For the historical maps, they can go online to repositories like the University of Texas's "Perry-Castañeda Library Map Collection." The collection's historical maps are previously existing knowledge interfaced in a new medium that allows the material to be studied at any time in virtual form by students around the world. It used to be that for the rare maps in the collection to be examined, students had to come from around the world to Austin, Texas, where the maps are physically housed.

History, unlike geography, is a fairly stable field whose content changes slowly if at all. Education has traditionally supplied students with distillations of the history, generally provided in textbooks. This method is a way of adapting the vast historical record to a medium of units (textbooks) that could be distributed to widely scattered students. In an imagined world where textbooks did not yet exist and the Internet did, it would not make sense to distill historical accounts into textbooks because online access distributes the material to scattered students. When students have online access, it is simple enough and monumentally cheaper to put distillations, if they still made sense, onto the Internet. The distillations method is particularly compromising for this subject to its content because history cannot be adapted to a textbook distillation without losing its richness and ramifications. The Internet easily absorbs bits of knowledge of history and interfaces them in context in an uninterrupted tapestry.

Science content adapts online to learning for each of the reasons mentioned for the other subjects: It is plentiful, tech savvy, interactive, current, and comprehensive. Science studied online is often not even an adaptation but instead the real thing. Websites of open scientific journals, databases, and working groups can be and are used by students to learn from by following along with active and unfolding real science.

Again, pulling back from the notion of adapting traditional education to the Internet, something quite different from is actually happening comes into view. As what is known by humankind flowed into the Internet, the knowledge found a medium that adapted itself to the structure of the knowledge—a process that is continuing, forming the virtual knowledge ecology.

In that process, an archaeologist used the Internet to connect knowledge about the age of his dig to a website about the dating method he used. An expert on Chaucer linked some of his manuscript web pages to the work of a linguist specializing in early English. A student visiting any of the web pages involved encounters connections made to express the meaning of the materials. This is new! It is the medium shaping itself to its content—not the content shaping itself to the medium. No textbook, wall chart, or videotape will ever do that.

86 THE ADAPTATION ACROSS CULTURES

The basic premise underlying this book is that *what is known by humankind* has migrated to the Internet. I have used the phrase what is *known by humankind* in my previous books, as well as in this one, to attempt to pin down a certain meaning out of all the different ones the word *knowledge* raises in people's minds. As explained in Idea 2, I chose the phrase based on this definition of the word knowledge in *Webster's Dictionary*: *the sum total of what is known: the whole body of truth, fact, information, principles, or other objects of cognition acquired by mankind.*

What is known by humankind belongs to every one of us living on this planet. Geometry does not belong to Pythagoras. Francis Crick and James Watson discovered the DNA double helix but have never owned what they deciphered about how genetics works. Although different combatants may believe different versions of a battle, nothing changes what really happened, and the truth of that is no one's property—it belongs to us all. We each have a right to our opinion, but we all have ownership in common and equally of what actually is so.

The virtual knowledge ecology is a common resource of that kind of knowledge—of what is so. The virtual knowledge ecology interfaces the theorems of geometry for all to access. As we move into the future, discoveries made by scientists will pour into the ecology for all to learn. Scholars of history will strive there to refine the facts of battles to get as close as possible to what really happened. The virtual knowledge ecology will develop into a virtual representation of what is known by humankind. It will be our knowledge as a species and as each individual member of that species.

This knowledge absolutely applies across cultures and requires no adaptation by or to cultures. This knowledge will include a great deal of opinion, which is clearly marked as opinion. It is so that medieval intellectuals were of the opinion that the earth is flat. If you are reading this with a philosophical bent of mind, you know of course that all knowledge is inductive. It is induced from what seems to be so. The virtual knowledge ecology will, by definition, be the sum total of what is known at any time, to the best of our collective ability at the time to induce it.

One of the most spectacular changes the Internet has caused is the inability to isolate knowledge. The end of the isolation of knowledge came about as the inverse of the multiplicity of communication. The social ramifications of everybody soon being connected to everybody else are mind-boggling. They are beyond the scope of this book. We are interested in an inverse in the situation in which everybody knows everything because all knowledge is interconnected and can be communicated to all people.

The virtual knowledge ecology is not made up of beliefs that are not held in common. For the Battle of the Alamo, Mexican and Texan children are both taught that it was their side that triumphed for a great cause. Those two opinions are already thoroughly represented on the Internet, but they are not the kind of knowledge that forms the virtual knowledge ecology. What does belong to the virtual knowledge ecology is the substance of what is known by humankind about that historical event, such as the date and place of the battle, the casualty names and count, and the sequence of the siege that occurred.

With geometry, the principles of physics, and the like, what is known is simpler to distinguish from opinion, speculation, and dogma. Just about every now-called academic subject has a knowledge base that is the same in Ethiopia, Ireland, and Tibet. Two main subjects do not. They are philosophy, which is a matter of speculation and conjecture, and religion, which is a matter of belief and faith.

It is fascinating and tempting—though beyond the scope of this book—to explore what effect it is going to have on propagandists and relativists when every person on earth can pop up a screen in his or her hand and check the facts. Conversely, pessimism about the powers of the Internet to convey what is known by humankind to many cultures is unnecessary. The Chinese, Cambodians, Congolese, Canadians, and Chileans all need to learn the same calculus, chemistry, and computerese.

I realize that when I say it is that simple I seem to be forgetting the illiterate impoverished millions across the planet who are spread across cultures and use many languages. The subject of this idea is adaptation. My point is that the day is long past when knowledge can or will be made to fit the culture. Ubiquitous computing will provide every person with a means to learn what is known by humankind. The culture will adapt to being made up of people who all possess knowledge.

Yes, that is a huge change, but human history is the story of adaptation to change. Fortunately, this one promises a global Golden Age of learning that is a lot better than the big change we worried about during the Cold War. This one is global enlightenment instead of nuclear winter.

87 LETTING KIDS REALLY LEARN SOMETHING

As knowledge finds itself at home in the network structure of the Internet, so also youngsters mesh their inquiring minds into the natural network expression of the virtual knowledge ecology. Children do not need to adapt to the new knowledge interface. It reflects the state of nature in their own heads. That natural state is a network.

Kids are innately eager to absorb knowledge into the networks that form in their minds to become what they know. What is known by humankind, the structure of the Internet, and the pattern of what a person

knows are all networks. We do not have to adapt kids to Internet learning, we need only to let them go there so that they can really learn
something.

The schools have essentially become an artificial world of meager, disconnected, and often out-of-date knowledge. Valid knowledge is now
bountiful on the open Internet. Making things worse for school kids is
that learning and thinking are dynamic acts of connecting things in your
head. The content they are expected to learn and think about in established education is largely static and disconnected. No wonder they are
bored.

To the incredible good luck of future generations of kids, the Internet
has come along as a dynamic medium of connectivity. Knowledge cascaded into the Internet during the 1990s. Instead of centering their
knowledge-imparting efforts on the new place where knowledge re-
sides, established education has kept right on using knowledge resource
materials that it buys and controls.

Kids are not adapted to old-school education, and they become less
tolerant of it with every passing month. The immense volumes of fractured, static knowledge students lug around in their backpacks do not
offer the compelling interconnectivity and interactivity of the virtual online world. Print is a static medium and the Internet is a dynamic medium. Nothing will change that. Yet, creating printed textbooks costs us
in the United States alone over $4 billion annually.

Locked away into schools by law, our kids are learning less every year.
What they do learn there is increasingly stale because they are usually
pretty well cut off from the real and fresh knowledge. What students do
get from the Internet at school is isolated, managed, filtered, controlled,
judged, and certified by the education establishment. We pay the education establishment billions of dollars every year to insult the intelligence
of the youngest generation. Meanwhile, the kids occupy their time and
minds with other dynamic denizens of the Internet: music, games, and
messaging.

The time is long overdue to let kids really learn something. Stated
simply: Let them learn from the open content that comprises the virtual
knowledge ecology. We will not improve education unless and until we
center the learning of knowledge in the Internet for the simple reason

that most recent and real knowledge that exists is to be found and best studied in open Internet content.

In contemplating this overdue change that is filled with hope and promise for our kids, the education establishment looms as the ogre. It is a serious matter to say education fails and lets our children down. The key is to remember that what matters is the kids, not the system. If the system is broken, we must have the character and courage to admit that it is and be able to walk away. Our concern is not the system, but the kids. If we will connect them to the Internet, they will find their way to the virtual knowledge ecology, and we will have let them begin to really learn something.

88 HOW KIDS ADAPT TO THE VIRTUAL KNOWLEDGE ECOLOGY

The doleful situation set out in the previous Idea is offset by the fact that the kids are way ahead on getting into the new learning. A lot of kids play the school game and do their real learning online. The school game involves dealing with standards, tests, and grades.

Winning the game is crucial for young people who plan to go on to college and to careers demanding proof that they know something. Schools provide the certification required to move through the grades, receive a diploma, be admitted to a college, and receive a degree.

A lot of learning is done in some schools. Learning happens even in the worst of schools through the sheer will and courage of some teachers. Yet, even in excellent schools and in the classes of the heroic teachers in awful schools using knowledge other than that in the virtual ecology downgrades what is learned. Students in every kind of school setting know that. Open content online has become the primary place they go to learn.

I am convinced this is true—though it would be fiercely denied in many circles. I think it is so for several reasons. My own fierce promotion of the virtual knowledge ecology is based on knowing it is already broadly in use and crucial to learning.

It could be easy to assume that the digital divide means only rich kids in elite schools use the Internet for learning. The lack of open Internet access in even an elite high school diminishes that divide. Students in such an elite school, along with those in below-standard schools and neighborhoods, have to find a way to use the Internet outside of school. Wealthier kids had home computers sooner and now have laptops.

In my experience with students from the full range of the New York City public schools, I have yet to talk with a student who does not use the Internet. Most of the students I get a chance to ask are competitors in high school debate and We the People citywide tournaments. They come from the worst as well as the best schools in New York. They all quote the Internet in their speeches. I have often asked individual students where they use the Internet, and the usual reply is at home or at the apartment of a friend or relative. There are undoubtedly unmotivated students everywhere who do not bother with the Internet, but the word is very much out among the kids that the Internet is the place to go to find out what you want to know.

There is no reason to think that when ubiquitous computing comes online, students everywhere will follow a pattern different from those in New York City. There will be no new print industry born to provide learning resources. The question is, how long will it take to stop spending money on the print industry that used to supply schools with knowledge resources?

Let it be clear what is being said here. Although K–12 schools supply at best limited Internet access for knowledge, their students routinely use the Internet for that purpose. They must play the game of mastering usually printed materials for testing while going independently to the Internet for the full range of whatever they want to know.

The great change to the virtual knowledge ecology is far more obvious in college and higher levels of learning. The time is overdue for the high school and lower grades to accommodate the use by their students of primarily open content for learning.

89 THE GIFT OF THE VIRTUAL KNOWLEDGE ECOLOGY TO TEACHING

If we once again disentangle our thinking from fixing or saving established education, we are left with this definition of teaching: To cause to know. Imagining again that there are no school buildings, established grades by age, standard assessment of subjects, or requirements for attendance or attainment. Computing is ubiquitous—everyone has a personal mobile device interfacing the Internet—and the virtual knowledge ecology is in place, brimming with what is known by humankind.

Education would need to happen. Would there be teachers? What would there be to cause members of new generations to know? Obviously, we cannot answer that with any certainty. My own guess is that there will be two large groups of humans causing students to know.

The first type of teacher will be the remote kind, having little or no primary contact with human students. These teachers will conceive, design, build, and operate teaching machines and software. They will create teaching machines like the flight simulator mentioned in Idea 15 and online learning materials that are forming the virtual knowledge ecology. There is nothing scary or even new about remote teaching. People like Aristotle and Confucius continue to teach from their writings well over two millennia after their deaths.

As the connectivity spreads, broadband access increases, and interface devices become more powerful, the creation of online, interactive, and dynamic teaching software promises to be a marvelous new profession for creative people. The digital expression of what is known in text, still and moving image, sound, and interaction is in its infancy. Great teachers of tomorrow will bring into being yet unimaginable tutorials that will cause billions of people to know.

The second type of teacher will be a professional working directly with students for the purpose of causing them to know. That definition does not include nurturing them, disciplining them, socializing them, or imparting the noncognitive aspects of one or another culture. Perhaps one of the most confusing aspects of the reality of teaching school now is that these many roles are mixed together in all sorts of conglomerations. The mixing is usually not even thought about, but results from teachers are expected.

In the start-over world for education I like to imagine, people who like and are good at the various aspects of rearing children are put to work where their preferences and talents are. Let the nurturers do the nurturing and the disciplinarians enforce the rules. I am being simplistic, but doing each of the jobs well is crucial for children.

A teacher who focused on the challenge of causing kids to know would have a splendid pallet of methods in the imagined world I am describing. She would have her own interest, talent, and dedication. Her knowledge source would be complete and connected to her, to her students, and in context in the virtual knowledge ecology. She could teach full time while with her students. Most of all, her mind and humanity would enhance the teaching to a new level in the history of human teaching. Surely, the virtual knowledge ecology mirrors the mind of a learner because both the mind and the ecology arrange knowledge as networks. But the virtual knowledge ecology is only a primitive echo of the richness of thought offered by a human teacher. Certainly, online interfaces can be designed to interact with a learner, conveying knowledge. But the richness of that interaction pales in comparison to the interaction with a human teacher.

The humanity of a living teacher is a gift the virtual knowledge ecology cannot give to a student. To motivate, inspire, and truly care about the result is a powerful factor in moving a student to knowing. Those are teaching assets that cannot be digitized. It is helpful when your computer congratulates you for getting something right, but not in the same universe as when a human is impressed and tells you so. Under any circumstance, the demand for human teaching will be there.

In our imagined world beyond schools and with ubiquitous learning from the virtual knowledge ecology, there would be a lot of learning done independently of human teachers. I think it is safe to say that is already true of a very great deal of real learning. But without sending kids to school by law and providing teachers to meet them there, another way to get human teachers and their students together will emerge.

My guess is that good teachers will become highly sought after professionals. Many may become independent practitioners, like lawyers and doctors are now. They will probably be found doing their teaching in many settings such as homes, community centers, businesses where apprentices are on hand, churches, and perhaps centers devoted to teaching. The latter is something of a full circle back to schools, but this time teaching in tandem with the virtual knowledge ecology would drive the design.

Certainly, any person with a true teaching gift—who is inherently talented at getting people to know—will appreciate and take advantage of the virtual knowledge ecology. When a teacher becomes suited to having all knowledge at his fingertips and in the hands of his students, there is no adaptation going on. The virtual knowledge ecology is, rather, a wonderful gift to teaching.

90 HOW THE EDUCATION ESTABLISHMENT COULD ADAPT

Across the planet, adaptation of education to the location of knowledge on the Internet will sometimes be very close to starting from scratch. Something similar has been going on with the spread of cell phones into countries where landlines were extremely limited. It has been easier in remote jungles, mountains, and prairies to beam a satellite signal and provide residents with cell phones than to string landlines through wilderness and over very long distances to install telephones at the end of those wires.

In places where education is now extremely limited, the Internet offers a completely new way to provide knowledge. Developing countries are, in fact, likely to set important patterns for countries moving slowly to engage the Internet because of entrenched ways of doing education. In either setting—underdeveloped or entrenched—the bottom line is to adapt the future means of conveying knowledge, which is using the virtual knowledge ecology. On a Siberian steppe, the Australian Outback, a teeming Bombay street, or the Oxford or Stanford campus, a laptop computer receiving broadband WI-FI puts what is known by humankind into the hands of a learner. It is to that new and wonderful fact that "how education is done" will adapt.

In no sense do I mean to discount in this book the efforts under way within education to enrich and tap into the virtual knowledge ecology. As Idea 53 describes, colleges, universities, and those who teach there have been significant sources of knowledge content now available in the virtual knowledge ecology. Also, seminal work for interfacing knowledge as learning objects and for developing other technology concepts has taken place within the academy, but their work is beyond this book's focus on the knowledge itself. Others are far better qualified than I am to describe the interface technology concepts for learning.

Returning, though, to the ogre identified in Idea 53, the education establishment causes delay and missed opportunity for engaging the new knowledge environment. A significant part of the reason the ogre is such an obstructionist might be traced to its vested interests. A lot of profits, jobs, and prestige are threatened by turning to the virtual knowledge ecology as the place to acquire knowledge. Yet, many wonderful people within the establishment give their all to teaching and inspiring youngsters in schools.

Accusations aside, the ogre is confounded by something far more troubling. He may have outlived his usefulness. The virtual knowledge ecology means textbooks no longer should be printed and distributed in hard copy. Nonogre locations like laboratories and historical societies are interfacing better knowledge that the ogre can. The newfangled Internet does not divide subjects by grade, meaning students can stay put until they learn a piece of a subject or zip way beyond where they belong gradewise to learn a lot more. How do you create a standardized test for that?!

Which brings up the most unsettling question of them all facing the ogre. What if getting certified has become the main justification for going to school? Has the ogre become mainly a test-giver? If so, why should he exist? In days gone by, knowledge to learn was found primarily at schools. A grammar school diploma meant grammar and other basic skills had been learned by attending the certifying school. A high school diploma certified a general level of academic learning experience in four years of attendance at classes where knowledge was delivered.

Colleges used to be more specialized in knowledge. Located in El Paso where I grew up was the Texas College of Mines. When the college was established in the early twentieth century, West Texas was a major center of metal smelting, drawing copper, zinc, and other metals from mines in New Mexico and farther west. The college attracted students who wanted to become mining engineers, scientists, and business leaders in the smelting industry. The college has changed over the decades, as reflected in its name, to Texas Western College and now the University of Texas at El Paso. The metallurgical and materials engineering courses there remain strong, but the university has many other schools and departments.

If not already, it will soon be possible to learn everything related to mining—these days part of metallurgical and materials engineering and sciences—in the virtual knowledge ecology. Although the athletic teams at UTEP are still called the Miners, and the university's mascot wears a cowboy hat and carries a pickaxe, the cactus covered hill where the Texas School of Mines once sat is no longer a location of comprehensive mining knowledge. The virtual knowledge ecology is where students across the world will find that.

What then becomes of the education establishment ogre if he can no longer lure students into his dens of knowledge, releasing them in a few years with a certificate and declaring they have learned what they paid him to give them in his lair? Today, his test scores, diplomas, and degrees still entice students into his domain, but online testing will change that before long.

Fortunately for the ogre, he is only a metaphor and does not exist. What does exist is the challenge we all share to change the way education is done. In a democracy, everyone is part of the education establishment. School taxes are paid by nonparents as well as families with kids. Voters choose the elected officials who make education policy. Families provide education's consumers, their children. Employers integrate the products of education—graduates and dropouts—into the workforce. All of us are affected by workforce competence or lack thereof. The origin of that workforce knowledge competence is supposed to be our education establishment.

We can look for answers to how we should do education in the digital future using another analogy. A hundred years ago, the horse-and-buggy industry was decimated by the advent of the internal combustion engine. The result was that the horses got to go out to pasture and the buggy industry adapted. This was an altogether happy change for horses, whose natural lifespan can be more than twenty years but who only survived about four years when they were forced to haul people and goods to provide transportation in nineteenth-century cities. Horses most certainly were overjoyed not to have to adapt anymore to modern transportation.

My great-great-grandfather Stephen L. North was a buggy-maker who adapted to the horseless carriage industry. He was born in the Catskill Mountains of New York in 1827. He was the oldest son of a prosperous farming couple, Uriah and Lydia Schutt North, whose next child Ursula became the wife of famed naturalist John Burroughs. Stephen settled in Leavenworth, Kansas, in 1857, where he dealt in real estate for a decade. In 1867, he and another man established a carriage manufacturing business, employing inmates from the federal penitentiary. What became the S. L. North Company turned out around 275 vehicles a year well into the 1880s.

Family lore reports that the business did very well. The buggies were traded in Santa Fe and Texas for horses, which were then sold for gold in Mexico. Although I cannot document the information beyond what the family passed along over the generations, the story goes that the buggy business ended when the policy at the prison changed, prohibiting the inmates to work at the carriage factory. So, it was not the automobile that put him out of business; but Stephen North found a way to participate in the new industry, which became a source of family pride.

The rest of the family story about Stephen is an insight into the adaptation of one establishment into the next. The story passed down through the family says that he sold his carriage designs to the Fishers, who, so the tale goes, incorporated some of his carriage design ideas into the bodies of early Cadillac cars.

The heritage page of the Fisher & Company website relates that in the late 1800s, a man named Fisher owned a horse-drawn carriage shop in Norwalk, Ohio. There, his sons learned the trade, as incidentally had Stephen North's four sons. In 1904 and 1905, two of Fisher's sons moved to Detroit to work in the horseless carriage shops that were beginning to appear. In 1908, they set up their own carriage business. The company's heritage page continues the story:

In the early years of the company, the Fisher Brothers had to develop new body designs because the "horseless carriage" bodies did not have the strength to withstand the vibrations of the new motorcars. By 1913, the Fisher Body Company had the capacity to produce 100,000 cars per year and customers included: Ford, Krit, Chalmers, Cadillac, and Studebaker. Part of the reason for their success was the development of interchangeable wooden body parts that did not have to be hand-fitted, as was the case in the construction of carriages. This required the design of new precision woodworking tools.

The internal combustion engine literally replaced the power source of transportation, eliminating the use of horses, who had played that role for about four thousand years. The human need for transportation was not replaced. The Internet has literally replaced the knowledge source of education, ending a five-century reign of books as well as fundamentally altering the several thousand-year reign of writing. The human need for education was not replaced.

Stephen North was part of the horse-drawn carriage establishment. Stephen, who had made his money and was beyond his prime when automobiles began to boom, passed along his ideas to the new industry. The Fisher brothers, beginning their careers as the automobiles took over, helped to pioneer the transportation manufacturing methods of the future. There is exciting creative opportunity for people inside the education industry in the coming adaptation to the virtual knowledge ecology. Those who are participating are making key contributions to the Golden Age of learning as it dawns.

6

ACTION

91 EMBRACE THE MAIN IDEA

To help the young global generation connect with what is known by humankind we need to direct our focus, thoughts, energy, and action toward putting the Internet into the hands of each. Education reform is an obsolete notion and as such, a waste of time and resources. We need to embrace the main idea of centering learning into the virtual knowledge ecology.

Ubiquitous mobile computing leads to ubiquitous learning because what is known is primarily available on the Internet, and every individual connected to the Internet is connected to the knowledge. If you have read what I said earlier in this book and do not agree, then I will not convince you. If you do agree, you realize that ubiquitous mobile computing will cause a global Golden Age of learning to emerge.

The following Ideas highlight my suggestions on how we can spur connectivity and thus entice the Golden Age more quickly than it will happen on its own. The first ideas are about the physical connectivity to the Internet. The second concern connectivity within the Internet, encouraging the aggregation that allows the virtual knowledge ecology to form.

92 DON'T TRY TO FIX THE SCHOOLS

The reason for not trying to fix the schools is that doing so is impossible. At least I have concluded that by watching the best people I have known—personally and through following them in the news and in their books—try and try again to little avail. As I have watched this going on for fifty years, things have only gotten worse. If the modern schools Humpty-Dumpty ever was in one piece, we will never put the pieces together again. Frankly, it should be a relief to admit that and turn to doing something else—to a new way for children to acquire knowledge. Many of them have found it already, and it will be a joy to join them in spreading the word and engaging their entire generation.

Within the past few years, the new knowledge venue has emerged on its own. If we cannot fix the schools, there is a great deal we can do to speed up the arrival of ubiquitous mobile connectivity to the virtual knowledge ecology of open content to learning. When that is achieved, the schools may be fixable in new and this time possible ways.

There are, of course, some schools that are good in significant ways. There are a lot of not so good schools and awful schools. There are millions of children who have no schools. The virtual knowledge ecology is a very doable single and simple connection away from every student and potential student in each of those circumstances. Everything about the Internet has and will continue to begin with a single node and then link to other nodes. By focusing on the single nodes—individual children—we will set off action and reaction that will put knowledge into the hands of the next generations.

One evening, many years ago, as I was leaving the meeting of a non-profit group that was trying to fix the schools, an older woman who had sat without comment through the meeting offered me a taxi ride home. I knew she had been a major education reform leader in New York City for many years. I sat in the back seat with her as we rode up Park Avenue and told her how worried I was about the project the group at the meeting was undertaking. She was quiet as I elaborated on the number of children in the New York City public schools who were being left behind or left out completely. What to do about the magnitude of the task had me very discouraged. She finally responded, very quietly, looking toward me in the darkness of the backseat and saying, "You save one child at a time."

One day before too long, I will be an old lady myself, and with the certitude I felt from the woman in the backseat of the taxi, I relay to you that you can save one child at a time. There is a stunning new way to do that: Give the child a wireless laptop and see to it that he or she is in a WI-FI hot spot and thus can enter the virtual knowledge ecology. Whatever education becomes in the future, it will rise as a phoenix around the young global generation embracing what is known by humankind in the virtual knowledge ecology.

93 GET THE VIRTUAL KNOWLEDGE ECOLOGY TO THE KIDS

A negative person could gloomily predict that, because what is known by humankind is now embedded into the Internet, all that has to be done to isolate people is to not let them connect to the Internet. The fact is that it is a lot harder to keep knowledge away in the Internet Age than it was for the book-burning tyrannies of the past. In the past as well, the poverty that trapped people in ignorance often had no solution for bringing knowledge to children.

Stir-fry WI-FI is delivering the Internet to places ranging from remote, disadvantaged Kabul neighborhoods that have no electricity to the upper floors of a Malaysian hi-rise apartment building. The details of how this do-it-yourself access works were described in May 2005, on the Poor Man's WI-FI website. The key technology in the access is a standard Chinese 30-cm stir-fry cooking scoop used as a parabolic dish antenna. Stan Swan figured out that the mesh of the scoop is the right size to receive the 2.4-GHz frequency range and can focus signals on a USB WI-FI adapter mounted about 10 cm away from the center of the scoop. Swan, an Information Sciences and Technology lecturer at Massey University in New Zealand, said in September 2005 that the support website explaining how to use the stir-fry cooking implement to scoop in the Internet had received over one hundred thousand recent visits.

When my mother was ten-years old and living in El Paso, Texas, a visit for her to the British Museum would have been possible. It is something, though, that she never did over the more than seven decades of her life. At age ten, in 1920, her quickest access would have been a four-day train trip to New York City followed by a steamship Atlantic crossing lasting more than a week and a short trip from the coast to London. She probably had access at home in El Paso to some pictures of some of the artifacts housed in the museum through her family's 1911 *Encyclopaedia Britannica*. Now, her great-granddaughters in New Mexico, Colorado, Ohio, and North Carolina can browse the British Museum virtually any time on the computers in their family homes. When those little girls who are toddlers now are teenagers, they will carry a personal device they can take with them, carrying the British Museum and the rest of what is known by humankind virtually in their pockets. Mother, a spirited innovator, would have loved it!

It is awesome that my grandnieces are able already to enjoy the world's knowledge with such ease and efficiency. But far more awesome is the potential now easily within our grasp to provide every child on earth with the same thing. My mother, as a little girl in an American city, with a father who owned a business and prospered, actually could have visited the British Museum. Her family traveled a great deal within the United States, and her horizons were broad as she grew up. But there was no possibility ever to wander among the treasurers of great museums for little girls born in 1910—or until less than a decade ago—who were isolated by geography or poverty.

Now all it takes is a stir-fry scoop to capture a satellite beam carrying the treasures of museums and of all knowledge, to be served to any child anywhere on a computer (the cost of which is plummeting). We can do a lot better than delivering knowledge to children with a stir-fry scoop. The following are some suggestions for action.

94 USE CELL PHONE SCREENS NOW

Many members of the young generations are already connected by their cell phones. These connections are still primarily to networks created by phone companies, not to the Internet. For a cell phone to be an adequately broad device for learning from the open content forming the virtual knowledge ecology, the phone needs broadband access to the entire open Internet.

No one knows if cell phones will morph into the primary mobile Internet devices or whether laptops will continue in the leading role and be modified to do it better. What the device of the future will be is unknowable now. What we do know is that kids have cell phones and cell phones are able to receive and transmit digital materials. To reach the young generation right now, the cell phone is the obvious way to go. All the pieces necessary to provide digital learning assets through cell phones are in place. Someone just has to start making it happen. In fact, they are: The trickle has already begun.

For reading, it is already happening in Japan. Although still a niche market as I write this, there are Japanese cell phone companies that provide novels, classics, and the ever-popular downloadable e-book smut that people are embarrassed to be seen buying in hardcopy in public. This niche market in Japan has shown that reading books on cell phones is doable—and though hard to believe, there are people who prefer to read on the little screens that can only display a few lines at a time. Entire libraries have been put into cell phones in Japan, and users are reading books the phones display at home, in the office, and on the train. Classics are popular, along with leisure reading. Here is an action to take: Find a way to get JRR Tolkien's *The Hobbit* and *The Lord of the Rings* books digitized and available to download into a cell phone for reading.

As I write this in the spring of 2005, an avalanche of multimedia programming is bearing down on the cell phone market. The next months will see a growing gamut of games, videos, and other interactive materials available to download into the phones. In February 2005, Nokia and Macromedia signed a deal to integrate Macromedia's Flash animation software into Nokia phone screens.

The way is wide open to create digital displays, tutors, and practice animations for learning useful knowledge. Someone just needs to build them and get them into the hands holding a cell phone—one child at a time.

95 GIVE EACH CHILD OF YOURS WI-FI

As I have said and implied throughout these ideas, the Internet is an ecology that includes some slime. Small children must be protected from slime wherever it is. As they mature, they must be taught to protect themselves from slime on their own. At the point when you feel a child for whom you are responsible is ready to protect himself or herself from Internet hazards, I urge you to give that child a device that can access the Internet in broadband. In addition, you will need to make certain the child can receive the Internet wirelessly where he or she spends most the most time.

One-on-one computer-to-child makes the computer truly personal. It becomes an extension of the owner's mind, whatever the owner's age. It may seem scary to do that with a child, but doing so is nothing new. There comes a time in a child–parent relationship when it is no longer appropriate for the parent to read a diary kept by the child without being invited. From the virtual knowledge ecology perspective, the reason for a child to have her own computer is not a dark one. The computer becomes an extension of her learning, like the three-ring notebook I had with me at all times in high school.

The personal laptop is much more for students today, replacing from times past pencils, typewriter, bookshelf, file drawer, and art supplies. The most important use for the computer is access to what is known by humankind. Bookmarked links and saved pages from the virtual knowledge ecology become, on her laptop, an extension of the student's personal virtual knowledge and ideas—an important auxiliary to what she knows.

Even if the child for whom you are providing a computer now uses it exclusively at home, he should have a wireless-equipped portable machine, instead of a wired personal computer. The student should have the portability option because taking his device with him is preparation for college and for the life he will lead in the twenty-first century.

In presenting your child with a personal wireless laptop, you do not have to resign yourself to expect him to have immediate or even frequent encounters with slime. If he wants to look at dirty pictures, gamble, or take part in off-color or dangerous chat, he is freed to do so by your act of giving him the computer. But, as in real life in a city, or just about anywhere, the slimy stuff is out there, but you have to go find it. Now, on the Internet it is almost always like getting your hands on printed porn: You usually have to be looking for it.

When I started using the Internet in 1997, slime came up and hit you in the face. That has largely changed. There are a number of safeguards that protect children, including cautions on websites that let them know before they click to enter that the material is adult and not for them. In my opinion, the small risk of running across a pornographic image does not outweigh the loss to a youngster of entering the virtual knowledge ecology. Once he is there, traveling among interlinked open content for learning, his chance of following a link into the slime is very small.

96 GET LAPTOPS TO SCHOOL STUDENTS

The notion of giving school students laptops is not theoretical. In college and beyond, it has been standard procedure for years to require individual students to have computers; the standard is quickly becoming wireless laptops.

Since 2002, the State of Maine has been giving laptops to seventh graders, with essentially successful results, as described in Idea 24. In the State of Michigan 20,357 sixth graders and their 1,200 teachers were being threatened at the end of the 2004–2005 school year with losing the laptops they had been given because of state and federal funding cuts. The kids had done nothing wrong. The program to put the laptops in their hands has been popular and successful. The State of Texas has talked and talked about providing laptops to students since 1998, and some districts have done it on their own. A recent proposal in Texas is to use textbook funding for the student laptops. Good idea!

Providing laptops to students is an obvious thing to do in places where students do not now have school books and libraries. For example, as Mongolians learn English to build the bilingual future they have decided to undertake, providing students with wireless laptops avoids the need to import or publish books. Recruitment of English teachers to Mongolia, now under way, is a sufficient challenge. Vast amounts of English reading and study materials would have already arrived for every student who had a laptop receiving the virtual knowledge ecology.

97 DEVELOP DEVICES FOR UBIQUITOUS MOBILE COMPUTING

So far in these *Action* Ideas, suggestions have been made for using access devices that are already in place: the cell phones the kids have and multiuse wireless laptops not specifically designed for a student. Although the many features that a top-of-the-line business laptop has are fun for a student, for learning they are not all necessary. Less feature-loaded laptops could be provided to more students because they would be cheaper.

The initiative to get 200 million laptops into the hands of children in the next two years, mentioned in Idea 3, is a superlative next step toward ubiquitous mobile computing. The students receiving the computers will be an energizing vanguard, demonstrating the power of the virtual knowledge ecology to achieve learning. Based at the MIT Media Lab, the project will coordinate the development of a new laptop. Project leader Nicholas Negroponte explained the concept of the machine as it stood in April 2005:

> The $100 Laptop will be a Linux-based, full-color, full-screen laptop, which initially is achieved either by rear projecting the image on a flat screen or by using electronic ink (developed at the MIT Media Lab). In addition, it will be rugged, use innovative power (including wind-up), be WI-FI and cell phone-enabled, and have USB ports galore. Its current specifications are: 500MHz, 1GB, 1 Megapixel. The cost of materials for each laptop is estimated to be approximately $90, which includes the display, as well as the processor and memory, and allows for $10 for contingency or profit. . . . The idea is to distribute the machines through those ministries of education willing to adopt a policy of "one laptop per child." Initial discussions have been held with China, where there are approximately 220 million students (for which an order would drive prices way down).

Perhaps the $100 laptop that will be streamed into the learning scene in 2006 and 2007 by the MIT based group will be like the Walkman, which suddenly made listening to music both personal and portable. If so, it will have reached a crucial milestone on our way to the global Golden Age of learning.

Since Sony developed the first Walkman in 1979, the concept of the device has undergone a course of improvements and advancements that is still in progress. Most recently the iPod has had center stage in the trend. But the essential idea of the Walkman is core throughout: personal, mobile music.

I think the $100 laptop project at MIT is coming up with the Walkman-like killer app for learning by interfacing the virtual knowledge ecology. The call to action continues, to think creatively down the long road in distributing and developing devices for personal, mobile learning. For the people who can do it, answering that call to action is of great importance for the generation now entering the world and their youngest siblings. The rest of the kids around the world need the wireless laptops we now have in the meantime.

98 GIVE OTHER PEOPLE'S KIDS WI-FI

Thinking big—on a grand and global scale—may not be the best platform for effective action. Negroponte's one laptop per child proviso wisely works to save one child at a time.

For more than a century, education in the United States has crept steadily from local control to broader and broader programs and authority. When I was a high school debater in the early 1950s, the national debate topic one year was: *Resolved that there should be federal aid to education*. The federal role in education back then was negligible. The affirmative side of that debate won big time over the rest of the century and today, individual children struggle to meet federal assessment goals.

In the wonderful years since the end of the Cold War, countries all over the planet have undertaken large-scale education projects. Funding from the private sector, the World Bank, and other sources have often supported high-dollar, sweeping projects to educate many children at a time. Implementation has often stretched out over years, and usage at the learner level has not actually materialized. Certainly, some programs have worked well, and my purpose is not to chastise the motives or to condemn them all.

However, there is one very doable action: Give a kid somewhere a mobile computer and access to WI-FI. That kid can be in your neighborhood, somewhere else in your town, or on another continent. One of the inherent flaws in public education, which is a form of thinking large, is that many taxpayers are not happy about being forced to educate other people's children. When you act to give a kid a mobile com-

puter, the choice has been yours to do something to help save one child
at a time.

99 PAINT THE PLANET WITH ACCESS

Wireless mobile Internet access devices are useless without a way to
grab a two-way signal transmitting the Internet and send signals from
your computer as you click your mouse to interact with the content on
your screen. The two-way signal came through a wire into which computers were plugged during the early years of the Internet's emergence.

That has changed, so that two-way signals can be used without wires.
The availability of the virtual knowledge ecology calls on us, for the sake
of the world's children, to paint our planet with the wireless Internet
signal. The world's kids need to be able to receive and respond to the
Internet through the antenna of a wireless mobile computer.

Wireless transmission promises to be a diverse jumble, like the rest
of the way the Internet speeds information around the planet. That is a
good thing because no one is going to control major sectors of accessibility. The action I would urge here is that everyone assume a role in
the responsibility to cover the entire earth with Internet access. The
same reason for doing that applies to satellite companies, governments,
armies and navies, businesses, science projects, and you and me sitting
at our own desk. Our reason for openly sharing the signal is that, by
doing so, the kids can then use it. Everybody can then use it, of course,
but that is not a bad thing. The bad guys have already figured out how
to stay in touch wirelessly with each other and the Internet. The rest of
us need to catch up.

Recently, I met with a business partner in a coffee and sandwich
hangout competing with the several Starbucks scattered in the Upper
West Side Manhattan neighborhood. I called the day before we met to
ask the management of the place we planned to meet whether they had
wireless Internet access for my laptop and was told that they did. When
I booted my laptop and tried to connect, about fifteen transmitters were
listed, indicating they were in range of my computer. My partner, who
is a far better tech guy than I am, pointed out that most of the signals
were closed by their owners so that we could not use them. He tried a

few of the others, but they did not have a strong enough signal for the Internet to download well. One loud and clear signal, probably licensed by the hangout where we were, happily let us pay $5 on a my credit card for a single day's access. When I paid the $5, the Internet came in perfectly as we interacted with it for the duration of our meeting.

At other tables in the hangout, numerous people were chatting on cell phones. They were using signals transmitted by wireless telephone company networks. It is interesting that the $100 laptop description says the planned devices will be cell phone–enabled. In addition to offering telephone service using their wireless phones, increasingly, telephone companies are providing optional Internet access through the little phones.

The Internet can also be beamed from satellites, as phone service can be. Satellites beam the Internet to more and more areas of the planet's surface. It is clear that painting the planet with Internet access is doable, and for much of the United States, other Western countries, and large parts of Asia, the signals are abundant. In the rest of the world, cell phone networks are large and spreading. Many efforts are in process to deliver the Internet across the world, and a lot has already been accomplished. If you are in a position to take action to advance this access, it will be important for you to move in and do it.

The frustration my partner and I had at finding ourselves in one of the most WI-FI painted neighborhoods on earth and still having to pay for service demonstrates another need for action. The signal needs to be open, as is the content.

🔆 100 TRANSMIT A LILY PAD

WI-FI is in its infancy. The many signals my laptop received when I met with my partner were undoubtedly mostly from people living nearby who receive the Internet through a cable or DSL line to which they attach a small transmitter. The transmitter's owner can then move around her apartment with her laptop, receiving the Internet without wires. The effect of many small transmitters scattered near each other has been compared to how lily pads spread over the surface of a pond.

Each one covers its own circle and the circles overlap. When there are enough circles, the entire surface of a pond is covered.

It is possible for each of us to act as a lily pad by leaving our own desktop transmitter open to provide a circle of free Internet access. That is unsafe to do, unless you are certain hackers cannot penetrate the protections and firewalls in your computer. However, sharing the signal could be a major force for opening the virtual knowledge ecology if enterprises scattered in a city or country make a habit of, in a protected way, transmitting the Internet from their buildings to the surrounding neighborhoods. In Kabul, Afghanistan, the Internet is now used in many businesses and government offices around the city. Each one of those could be a lily pad, opening a way for students who have a wireless laptop to enter the virtual knowledge ecology.

101 PRESS FORWARD ON LANGUAGE TOOLS

It is not necessary to work out the future of language use on the Internet before acting to get everyone connected. That is doing it backward. As more and more people around the world are using the Internet, the future use of languages online will evolve. For now, three trends are constructive places to take action toward getting the young generation interacting with the virtual knowledge ecology.

Mongolia is coming from one of the three directions by resolving to teach English to everyone in its country. Certainly, a great deal of the active medicine, sciences, technology, and many of the humanities is to be found online primarily in English. The bilingual Mongolians will have access to it all.

The second approach has been to display websites in a few or many languages. International commerce has been a bigger play in this area, with the websites of multinational corporations made available in the languages used in the countries where they do business. Interfacing the same website in several languages is relatively easy to do. Typically, a corporation will not redesign and reillustrate its website; it will just translate the text. Museums and other knowledge showcases often do the same. It would be a very useful action to be encouraged within the entire open content ecology for the content providers to make a habit of interfacing their websites in several languages. As the global usership grows, with more and more people online, demand for multilingual websites for learning will grow, and I hope this demand will be met.

The third trend is still rolling out. There are already software translators into which text can be input in one language and output in another. As these get better and better, they will make learning materials open to people around the world in a potent new way.

102 TAKE OPEN CONTENT INTO THE FUTURE

Throughout this book, I have emphasized that the virtual knowledge ecology already exists and that it is already better than any other resource for knowledge. I would suppose we are at a similar transition point as the automobile industry was when Henry Ford began to roll out the Model-T. By then, the horse and buggy had become obsolete, but there was a lot left to do to perfect the automobile.

The Model-T was superior to the horse-and-buggy because it did the same job better: getting you from where you were to where you wanted to go. A student using wireless, mobile Internet access device in a WI-FI hotspot is embracing what is known by humankind better than he can in any nondigital venue.

The years ahead will pattern something like the improvement of automobiles over the decades of the twentieth century. There will be little conveniences, like a gas gauge with a needle on the dashboard to let you know how much gas is in the tank, replacing the need in the Model-T to carry a short wooden ruler to stick in the tank to find out how many inches of gas were left. There will be bigger improvements, like the automatic transmission that eliminated the need for the foot clutch. Certainly, things will speed up, as they did from the days when "going like sixty" (miles an hour) was a very big deal.

What would interest me most if I had another lifetime to devote to it would be the advances that will be made in the future to the knowledge content itself. As you would guess from many points I have made in these Ideas, I think what is known by humankind will emerge in a stunningly beautiful and expressive cognitive network. Learning and teaching will be compelling adventures. To help the process move more rapidly in that direction, the following are my suggestions. They are approaches and guesses. I expect and hope you will add your own.

🔆 103 ACCEPT OBSOLESCENCE

When I was growing up, everybody wore a hat. Women wore them to their luncheons and tea parties and to church. Businessmen wore hats whenever they walked down the street. In 1961, John F. Kennedy was the last president of the United States to wear to his inauguration a formal tall hat like Abraham Lincoln wore all the time. In the first half of the twentieth century, men in the United States wore brimmed hats most of the time as standard street wear. President Kennedy did not like hats, and seldom wore one after his swearing-in. His generation—men and women—abandoned their hats in the 1960s, and younger generations than theirs are hatless. Along with the hats, a manufacturing industry disappeared. Hat designers, material suppliers, makers, distributors, and sellers no longer had a product they could sell. Felt fell flat.

The difference between what happened to the hat industry and what is happening to the textbook industry is the power of choice at the consumer end. JFK could choose to leave his hat on his closet shelf and go outside bareheaded. School children do not have that choice with their textbooks. There is a large establishment system in place that forces them to use textbooks instead of the virtual knowledge ecology as the place the system directs them to learn knowledge.

In a candid moment, a senior manager of a textbook-related supplier told me, "we have to answer to our stockholders, you know, we are a public company." He was justifying deemphasizing open content study resources because those sources were free. He was telling me that the company had to stick with the old way of doing things so that the stockholders would make money as the company sold content at a profit. He made no effort to tell me the old way was as good as the new one.

Looking around on the Internet, I discovered that there is a diverse and thriving felt manufacturing industry. Few of the companies I looked at mentioned hats, once the staple of the industry. Mentioned among many uses for felt were for making displays, crafts, and toys and for cushioning in the shoe, automotive, orthopedic, and apparel industries.

Certainly, the textbook industry has made adjustments toward the impact of the Internet on schools. This is not the place to analyze that. Motives are not the point either. The matter at hand is what action should these enterprises take? The answer to that is they should accept the obsolescence of textbooks as the vehicle for delivering knowledge to students. That process is, as Davy Crockett once said, "as dead as a beaver hat." Companies that publish textbooks should quit doing that and either publish something else or go into a different type of business.

104 THINK SHARE NOT COPYRIGHT

The bucket Napster tipped over spills a pertinent melody across all sorts of Internet content. The theme is share, and it is very much in harmony with open content. CreativeCommons.org is a key player in both situations. Creative Commons introduces itself on its homepage with these words: *Creative Commons offers a flexible range of protections and freedoms for authors and artists. We have built upon the "all rights reserved" of traditional copyright to create a voluntary "some rights reserved" copyright. We're a nonprofit. All of our tools are free.*

Creative Commons offers different licenses for different levels of sharing online content. If you sign up for one of the free licenses, you can then post an icon on your web page of licensed content. The icon connects to an explanation of how visitors can reuse your content. You can choose a license to let others distribute your content so long as they attribute it to you, and there are various levels of sharing allowing them to derive work of their own from yours. Lawyers at Creative Commons have developed detailed licenses for the different options.

Legal minds and those creating professional creative works are far better qualified than I am to explain this important new movement in creative licensing. Going to the CreativeCommons.org website is an ideal place to begin to explore further.

What I find extremely valuable for the subject of this book is that a Creative Commons license on a web page keeps its status as open content. It remains a part of the virtual knowledge ecology, able to interconnect freely with related content and with students wishing to learn from it. Fully copyrighted materials can also be openly online, but they cannot be copied into other web pages legally without asking and getting permission. Materials with a Creative Commons license can be used, for example, in a teacher's presentation or a student's report, so long as they are attributed to the material's source.

The underlying purpose of copyright has traditionally been to protect the profits of the creator of materials. I am not at all sure that in the future money will be made selling the stuff of the virtual knowledge ecology. The stuff of the virtual knowledge ecology is the shared useful knowledge that belongs to all of humankind. It includes mathematics, science, technologies like agriculture and engineering and computers, history, and the rest of what was once called academic because it was found in schools. In the virtual knowledge ecology, that knowledge networks itself into nodes of the best of it and those nodes are then used by everyone on earth.

What the sharing of a node means is that, for example, millions of students—from Montana to Morocco to Mongolia—would access and study from the same chemical table of elements (a node). Perhaps that table will be the one put online by Los Alamos Laboratory several years ago. Any cost for that table of elements was paid and forgotten long since. There is no profit for stockholders in the sharing of that learning asset, and no cost actually to anyone. When someone else puts a better table of elements online as open content, it will begin to get used by a few people and then more, gradually working its way up to the top of the algorithm that rules the search engines. If the author of the new table puts a CreativeCommons license on it, everyone can share it by simply attributing it to that author. But, if the author restricts it by charging money to use this table of elements, it will no longer be open. That means it will no longer have the value of interconnectivity with related websites. It will also no longer be elevated by public use, and Internet traffic will find another open content table of elements to use.

I suppose since the McGuffey Reader became popular in the 1830s, we have been used to the idea of printing lots of copies of study books and distributing them far and wide. That was as close as students came to studying from the same page as anything has ever been. In the past, most of what has been studied has been what was available on scene: in Montana or Morocco or Mongolia. The materials in different localities were varied and often even contradictory. It takes a while to get used to the idea of students everywhere literally studying on the same virtual page. The phenomenon is actually very real and has begun. To be part of the action in growing and nurturing open content into the future, it is accurate to think sharing, not closed and not copyright.

105 MAKE OPEN CONTENT AND THEY WILL COME

There are kids already waiting, with their stir-fry WI-FI scoops gathering in the Internet. Children of yak farmers on a mountain top in Nepal are moving a cursor around computer screens. In 2006, thousands of $100 laptops will begin flowing to children in countries around the world. All of these children, and many more as time goes by, will be dipping into the virtual knowledge ecology.

The virtual knowledge ecology will not be grown and nurtured by top-down, large-scale programs. The job will be done one node at a time, just as it has been for the past decade. I am convinced that the creative part will and has been done almost completely one person at a time. Even when a large enterprise or university creates the content, there is usually one person who has the idea for a new subject bit and who carries through to get it online. Much can and has been done literally by a single person. The ease and low cost of making web pages has empowered anyone who knows anything to explain it to the entire world. That fact is the principle that released the explosion of blogs in 2004.

One individual in a historical society can, for example, use some of the materials archived at the society to interface some local history online. A biologist who knows a great deal about some particular species can describe and illustrate his knowledge on a web page. This sort of thing is happening thousands of times. If it is something you can do, I hope you will go ahead.

The flip side of how easy it is to put knowledge online is that it is also getting easier and easier to find if there are people who are looking for it. If you build the best open content for any topic, they will come. But they will not stay and send others unless your particular content does the best job in the world of presenting your particular topic. Peer review is open, just like the content, and the world is your judge. This is bad news for mediocre content and good news for the learning public.

106 OPEN YOUR OWN CONTENT

To begin my thought here about the impact of real knowledge on even young children, I started to write something I have said in conversations many times: Michelangelo, one of the greatest artists of all time, was only nine years old when he was apprenticed to painting in the Medici Court. I decided to be sure I was correct, so I entered this text string into the Google search box: "michaelanglo apprentice medici court how old." In its first response Google asked me if I meant "Michelangelo apprentice medici court how old" politely correcting my spelling of the great man's name. I clicked yes and the top website on the return list was Michelangelo.com, an excellent website hosted by a website design enterprise named for the artist.

Checking into the page on his early life, I discovered I had been wrong. Much to the displeasure of his father Michelangelo announced at age thirteen that he had apprenticed himself to the studio of painter Domenico Ghirlandaio. After a year there, learning fresco painting, he entered the sculpture school in the Medici gardens and was soon made a member of the household of Lorenzo de Medici, "the Magnificent."

Before his announcement of his decision to become a painter, Michelangelo had been sent by his father to a grammar school to learn his letters and study Latin. There he made friends with a student six years older than he was. The older boy was studying painting and convinced Michelangelo to do the same. The young man's artistic interests had thus been awakened and honed before he was fifteen by a student mentor, a fresco artist, and the students and masters in the Medici circle.

I was intrigued to discover that Michelangelo himself attributed his engagement with the arts to a much earlier influence. His mother had been frail after his birth and could not nurse him. Instead, he was entrusted to a wet nurse and lived with her family whose trade was stone-cutting. To become what was arguably the world's greatest sculptor, Michelangelo described what happened, saying he had been: *sucked in the craft of hammer and chisel with my foster mother's milk. When I told my father that I wish to be an artist, he flew into a rage, "artists are laborers, no better than shoemakers."*

Toddling about among stonecutters, having a student painter friend, working in a fresco studio, and, least of all, being welcomed into his household by Lorenzo de Medici are remote or impossible experiences in the real world of any child now or in the sixteenth century. But in the virtual knowledge ecology, that can be done virtually by any child anywhere.

Much of the substance of what was once learned from apprenticing is now possible to interface online. Getting that sort of content into the virtual knowledge ecology is a larger matter than moving only the subjects once taught in school—like the grammar and Latin that Michelangelo learned in school. People comparable to the stonecutters, painting students, fresco professionals, and Florence's master sculptors are now in a position to interface what they know openly online. When they do that, a little boy or girl in any spot around the world will soon be able to virtually experience their expertise.

It is worth noting that Michelangelo went to school to learn grammar, his letters, and Latin. He did something quite different to learn to paint: He apprenticed. He learned about the stonecutting that he did later on so gloriously by being around people cutting stone. In moments when I feel like education really should just start over, I realize maybe reading, writing, and arithmetic were all schools were very good at teaching. Way back, the kids in hunter-gatherer tribes learned their knowledge by being around adults and watching them, not by being isolated at a school. Farm kids have traditionally learned agriculture by doing chores and helping with the plowing.

Something that is absolutely new is that you can be like a master sculptor in the Medici gardens whom Michelangelo observed as a teenager. You can be like the stonecutters from whom little Michelangelo absorbed the craft of hammer and chisel. All you have to do is put what you know how to do and how you do it online.

For example, if you are an automobile manufacturer, you can have your web team that is responsible for the corporate site include some pages on the process of building a car. Perhaps they would do an interactive animation of an internal combustion engine. If what they created was compelling enough, it would not be long before kids across the world would be visiting and learning about motors.

The impact on the young Michelangelo of watching various masters at work was more than just inspiring him to want to do the same. He also found out what he had to know to follow in their lines of work. The motor animation would have the same double impact on learners: They both find out what can be accomplished and what they need to understand to join the team. The laws of physics are very much in play in the operation of a motor. Learning those laws is much more interesting with the goal of building a motor than for doing one's homework for a school that is nowhere near an automobile factory.

As mentioned in Idea 53, this kind of thing is happening. I have called the web pages that teach the expertise of their source expertorials. Building them is something enterprises large and small, as well as individuals, could do to add significant enrichment to the virtual knowledge ecology.

107 SPROUT LANGUAGE LILY PADS

Should you have or create an expertorial, make it available in more than one language. This could be particularly meaningful for languages that are not known well among speakers of English. For example, a graduate student from Nepal studying in a university in an English-speaking area and who is fluent in Nepali could easily translate your web pages. I return to Nepal as an example because we know there are village children in the mountains who are using the Internet through WI-FI.

Every language in which your website is interfaced becomes a lily pad covering a small piece of the surface of knowledge and of humanity.

108 RETHINK ASSESSMENT

A cynic could say that, these days, we are paying an establishment billions of dollars annually to assess what children do not know. There has got to be a better way!

It is likely that ubiquitous learning from the virtual knowledge ecology will radically revise assessment, and that has to be a good thing. Although the subject is complex and convoluted, I would suggest the answer lies in bringing assessment closer to the ultimate goal of learning. What is assessed in the long run is what a person can do.

Perhaps, instead of having a testing industry embedded in an education establishment, professions and trades should do their own testing. The Internet opens the way to do that. Medical doctors have become accomplished testers, with rigorous assessments for each of the specialties and at the general level as well. Perhaps they should have a pre-premed assessment test someone could take at the age Michelangelo was when he announced to his father that he was going to be a painter. That sort of test would be a win for the medical profession by being a guide for bringing promising young people into its fold. It would be a winning ticket for the kid who passes it, helping to open her future. It would be a win earlier on for her family as an incentive for her to study and learn what she needs to know to be ready for the test. It would be a win for us all by sorting things out so the best doctors would emerge into practice.

What assessment will be in the future is unknowable. Hopefully, it will be better than what we are doing now—as well as cheaper for the taxpayers, with richer rewards for the kids.

109 BE A PIXEL PEDAGOGUE

The most fascinating connectivity for me in the virtual knowledge ecology is not found among the knowledge assets. Nor is it the connectivity among the ecology of people who come to teach and learn within the ecology of knowledge. There is another beautiful and as yet nearly untapped venue for connecting stuff: It is what is interconnecting dynamically as the user perceives meaning in the content coming from the computer. It is the expressive power of connectivity.

Michelangelo expressed his great artistic ideas by chipping an image out of marble or stroking paint al fresco into drying plaster. He did not use the expressive powers of pigment applied as it is suspended in oil. In 1534, the pope expected Michelangelo to execute his painting of *The*

Last Judgment on the alter wall of the Sistine Chapel in oil. He refused, declaring oil painting to be an "effeminate art."

Like connective expression in the first decade of the twenty-first century, oil painting existed in Michelangelo's time, but the medium needed improvement and was not yet fully appreciated. A century was to pass before Rembrandt unleashed awesome expressive powers from oils and nearly three more centuries before lead paint tubes were invented and the Impressionists moved oil painting outdoors.

Creating images in the pixels of a lighted surface is just one of several new connective expression tools on the pallet of the new digital medium. Text, audio, video, and interactivity are each evocative media. All of the media are available for connective expression in limitless combinations.

I made the comparison to painting in oil because in my adventures of trying to learn to paint, the oils lured me into attempting to use their amazing complexity, from which can emerge profoundly subtle and luxuriant nuances. I spent a lot of time and money, learned a lot, but never painted more than a few square inches that satisfied my efforts. At one point, I had purchased over ninety different pigments. I had, for example nine different greens. Each one had its own hue and character. Some stained the canvas, others sat on top of it, some were transparent, others opaque, and each one mixed with every one of the other colors to produce something different. Perhaps Rembrandt was able to achieve such glorious results because he never used more than a few colors. The variety of colors that overwhelmed me included many that were not developed until after Rembrandt's time, including the brilliant cadmiums the Impressionist wielded so magnificently.

Painting in pixels makes my ninety tubes of different oil colors seem very small compared to the millions of colors available from a computer screen. For two centuries, photographers have been nurturing the art of the still image. The cinematographers have been doing the same for the moving image for more than a century. The radio medium added sound, which has been integrated into the moving picture arts. All of these media are available in the digital realm and can be interconnected limitlessly for expressive effect.

Interactivity is a new expressive medium offered by computers. It is something of a transplant from live human interaction. Communication theorists are undoubtedly working on understanding its muscle.

A pixel pedagogue works with all of the tools on the digital connective expressive pallet to create works of cognitive expression. Carrying that to its logical conclusion, pixel pedagogues create digital works that teach. Such a digital teaching work of expression seems quite different to me than a teaching machine. The expressive piece is something like the software that functions on the hardware in computers generally.

An example of such a digital teaching work of connective expression would be the animation suggested in Idea 106, which presents how a motor works. When a learner is interacting with the animation, and he clicks on a carburetor, something new would occur from the animation that would convey to the learner the role of the carburetor in the workings of the motor.

A great deal of the material in the virtual knowledge ecology is now, expressively, text and illustration modeled from print design, and increasingly moving images, set into web pages. As such, it is extremely valuable because it is accessible.

All of the content now in the virtual knowledge ecology is open content and therefore more valuable cognitively because it can be aggregated and interconnected with related content. As a result, the content in the virtual knowledge ecology is embedded there in cognitive context.

As broadband increases and the gifted pedagogues turn to pixels, a new expressive connectivity will emerge from the virtual knowledge ecology. As happened from the complex interaction of the oil colors and stains of a Rembrandt paintings, meaning will be apprehended in completely new ways. The digital connective expression pallet awaits the pixel pedagogues, some of whom are already at work.

Appendix I

THE CYBERSCHOOL CASCADE*
Written by Judy Breck, August 1996

Winter has gone. The spring sun is warm on the snow pack. Rivulets run and streams edge up their banks. Spawning and hatching are peaking in fresh pools. The first waves of the runoff are reaching thirsty gullies below. Quickly comes the cascade to water the plantings of a new summer.

The advent of Cyberschool would hardly have surprised the two great futurists who envisioned the information age when it was in its infancy.

In 1964, Marshall McLuhan predicted that "the school drop-out situation will get very much worse." He told us then that "TV has provided a new environment of low visual orientation and high involvement that makes accommodation to our older educational establishment quite difficult." And he knew it was not just the tube: "TV is only one component of the electric environment of instant circuitry that has succeeded the old world of the wheel and nuts and bolts."

Fourteen years earlier, Norbert Wiener described the effects of entropy in words that sound very much like the laments of those who try to improve the schools. Wiener said that as entropy increases, the systems affected "tend naturally to deteriorate and lose their distinctiveness, to move from the least to the most probable state, from a state of organization and differentiation in which distinctions and forms exist, to a state of chaos and sameness."

*Submitted to *WIRED* October 1996 and March 1997, not accepted

The Cyberschool cascade is vacating teaching and learning from the entropy-exhausted education establishment into what Dr. Wiener called an enclave "in which there is a limited and temporary tendency for organization to increase. Life," he continues in his classic *The Human Use of Human Beings*, "finds its home in some of these enclaves." Cyberschool is the education enclave existing within the consequences of digital technologies. Dr. Wiener put "cyber" into our language because, as he said, "there was no existing word for this complex of ideas, and in order to embrace the whole field by a single term, I felt constrained to invent one." It follows that we should use his invented word to name teaching and learning embedded in what has been set loose by information technology.

Big changes in human history often follow a pattern of something new being done and then unexpected things happening. Writing was probably invented just to keep track of how many oxen and skins of grain were bought and sold; no one expected the invention of love letters and novels. Columbus expected a way to get to China; he did not anticipate locating half of the world and causing lung cancer. The invention of digital technologies caused Cyberschool; its origins are not in the mountains of well-intentioned anguish, talk and work which have gone into trying to fix schools.

In the late-490s BC, Buddha, Confucius, and Pericles were all alive. Not since then, until now, has there been such a time when changes were being set in motion which would cascade around the world and down the centuries. The cyberspace phenomenon is generating all sorts of surprises, and the Cyberschool portion of this larger cascade is pure serendipity. A consortium implementing digital technologies in dozens of small public schools in Manhattan calls itself *The Eiffel Project* because:

> As the Eiffel Tower showed the world a century ago how architects could use new materials to break existing architectural constraints, now digital technologies loosen long-lasting constraints on education which have shackled many with limiting opportunities. Digital technologies are for education what iron and steel, reinforced concrete, plate glass, elevators, and air conditioning were for architecture.

BEFORE THE MELT

During the second millennium BC, communication in and among the ancient lands around the east of the Mediterranean Sea was simplified and multiplied by the alphabet. This invention of phonetic symbols reduced from hundreds to forty or less the number of signs needed to write, and opened up literacy. Long before that, the powerful scribal caste of Egypt, an elite protected by the many years of training required to master hieroglyphics, had developed twenty-four symbols to represent consonant sounds. The scribes never made the transition to using the marks as an alphabet—over tens of centuries, as Egypt slid from the greatest power in the world to becoming a breadbasket for Rome. It was not the asp who ended the glory on the Nile, it was a software glitch.

Connectivity in cyberspace has sprung teaching and learning free. Cyberschool may never have occurred without the advent of the Internet; institutional resistance to computerizing from a classroom-based initiative had been effective. Yet whether digital resources and pedagogy can "work" in teaching is a question that has been thoroughly answered "yes" by prescient early mushers among the winter snowbanks.

Bill Atkinson got things started by inventing wonderful Hypercard. In 1990, Kristina Hooper, director of Apple Computer's Multimedia Lab, wrote:

> Hypercard is fundamentally designed to address how people think rather than how processors might work effectively. We can now design pedagogical surrounds with tools designed to be compatible with mental activities.

The first generation of students who were supplied with Apples in the classroom have graduated into the workforce. Thousands of instructional software programs have been authored, produced and used—most of them to drill and practice lessons. Many are available online or on disk and CD. A durable example of these early Cyberschool lessons is a terrific and popular program which may never be much bettered in teaching typing. Why would a teacher wish to waste time competing with Mavis Beason's Typing Course 2.0 CD plus Correct Grammar 3.2? (*How would you* correct your students' grammar while drilling typing!)

Children with developmental disorders are moving beyond their handicaps because their computer teacher can exercise inhuman patience and is incapable of embarrassing kids with nuances of frustration. Lew Robins' "Everybody Can Read" software does a better job of this teaching than parents or teachers, and is helping children for whom hope for literacy had been abandoned.

A Cyberschool star is the New Laboratory for Teaching and Learning at the Dalton School, a 1,300-student private school located in New York City. This very well-funded computer technology education project began in the fall of 1992. Without the usual financial constraints, bright and able people began five years ago to fulfill the vision of a school where computers did a lot of teaching. As the teaching software at Cyberschool becomes more sophisticated, a major change is that more kids are beginning to experience good teaching. This is fun and complex to think about. There are those who believe human teachers are superior to machines. Malcolm Thompson, a masterful human teacher at Dalton, has developed software lessons in science which he has his students learn using a computer before they take the course he teaches in person. He explains that he does so because the kids do better in his course because of what they learned working through the lessons on the computer. Perhaps he will create more lessons where a computer teaches his entire course. Will that be bad? If he does, and his courses go online, anyone anywhere could access them and learn some science, and Thompson's teaching gift would have a pretty important role.

The spring melt began with the expansion of the Internet and World Wide Web. The founders of the Dalton program could not have foreseen how things have spilled out into cyberspace. Really cool now is how, at Dalton, teaching, studying, assignments, and homework zip about the Internet from teachers to students and back—and beyond to and from websites all over the world.

Last year the Council of the Great City Schools and Scholastic Network cosponsored a study of online use by students. Scholastic New Media executive vice president Ruth Otte reported that online communications help students to "become independent, critical thinkers, able to find information, evaluate it and then effectively express their new knowledge and ideas in compelling ways." This study of five hundred fourth and sixth graders showed that those with online access achieved significantly higher scores on measures of information management, communication, and presentation skills than those who had no online access. Enrolled in Cyberschool for this study were students in Chicago, Dayton, Detroit, Memphis, Miami, Oakland, and Washington.

AWASH IN WIRING

The Cyberschool surge roaring through the rocks right now is the multiplication of wiring. Wiring the schools is part of the great plug-in, but there are other more important hook-ups in progress. Control of access for children has moved beyond the authority or capacity of the education establishment, and is making "establishment" a fading adjective for education. Kids are getting plugged in at home, in libraries, at community centers, at jobs, and legion private franchises are budding. Crashing in behind the unrolling wire are waves of more affordable computers, settops, and a dozen good ideas for cheaper and more personal access devices. The fact is that schools have to get wired to log on their clientele.

CLEARING THE DAM

Obstacles of government regulations, evaluations and mandates to curriculum selection are debris floating and bobbing into the distance. Another total surprise, this is brand new. Resources are becoming so much greater on the Internet than anything in a particular school, that homework and classwork are already inextricable from Cyberschool. Beyond just all that information out there, lessons and curricula are being put onto websites and accessed at home, school, and elsewhere. Although private companies are the publishers of textbooks and curricula, major sales to schools traditionally have been made by lobbying—and legislative approval in a key state ensured sales (not competition) in other states. The cataracts of new and changing information make the designation of a certain textbook over several future years absurd. The power of a state legislature to mandate a single curriculum makes no sense either, because it is impossible to anticipate or control the resources of Cyberschool. It can only be good news that, as the technology push has made producing teaching software a national priority, the shackles of government control have dropped away. As Milton Friedman has said:

> No one can predict in advance the direction that a truly free-market educational system would take. We know from experience of every other industry how imaginative competitive free enterprise can be, what new products and services can be introduced, how driven it is to satisfy the customers—that is what we need in education.

PADDLING AROUND

The cascade is gliding across the parched prairie of late twentieth-century schooling. It is great fun to look about in the Cyberschool shallows of what is quickly becoming oceanic. Genentech, Inc.'s Access Science website *www.gene.com/ae* is up-to-date and updateable. It shows how Cyberschool has made containment of a knowledge domain in one book or one place obsolete. More is already available at Access Science than any textbook ever contained. Like the mind, Genentech AE reaches out to touch—for example, The Nanoworld Image Gallery www.uq.oz.au/nanoworld/images_1.html, where a magnified flea inks down to fill the screen. Below the flea, signed by the Center for Microscopy & Microanalysis, The University of Queensland, is this message: *The image files contained on this page are currently gaining some order, as more images come on-line a greater semblence of order may appear. We trust that some of these images will assist you in teaching or general education.*

The Whole Brain Atlas, www.med.harvard.edu/AANLIB/home.html offered by Harvard Medical School had had 110,000 visits by the beginning of March 1997. This multilevel model and chart of the brain is sophisticated science which is a useful reference for doctors and medical students (from Cambridge, to Cairo, to Canton). This site has made printed charts on classroom walls and in books obsolete because they just cannot teach the three-dimensional structures as well. Available as a marvelous Cyberschool tool, the Atlas is undoubtedly playing a role in interesting high school and grade school children in anatomical sciences and the practice of medicine. The Whole Brain Atlas is to wall charts what the electronic calculator is to the slide rule.

Neuroscience for Kids weber.u.washington.edu/~chudler/neurok-.html is maintained by Eric H. Chudler, Ph.D. at the Department of Anesthesiology of the University of Washington. With great stuff for young students, the site displays this wisdom from Dr. Seuss:

> You have brains in your head.
> You have feet in your shoes.
> You can steer yourself any
> direction you choose.

Changing the rudder toward the liberal arts brings us to lessons and resources in every subject. "Grammar" provides a screen full of sites, offering definitions of parts of speech, and uses of punctuation, and several kinds of practice exercises. The contents of libraries and bookstores are increasingly accessible. The Smithsonian has so much out there already that it defies summary. Historical resources are plentiful and colorful. A request for nineteenth-century American history produced a large list, including *Mountain Men*. Linked to it is *The Santa Fe Trail Page* www.tsjc.cccoes.edu/sft/sft.htm a site in formation by Trinidad State Junior College in Colorado. The pages for topics are promised only, and bear labels like: "Independence, Missouri—Under Construction—Jocelyn Montoya."

IT IS RAINING HARD UPSTREAM

William Gibson was asked recently if he thought the World Wide Web had become what he had envisioned when he coined the term "cyberspace." Gibson replied in terms of the spawnings and hatchings:

> It is cyberspace the way radio was cyberspace in 1906. I don't think many people have come up with anything particularly appropriate to do with this medium yet. Whatever the Web is now, it's some kind of larval version of something else. Those periods in technology always fascinate me.

To anticipate the metamorphosis education is enjoying, we need to expect pedagogies that will be entirely new. They will not displace the marvelous resources already flooding into Cyberschool. They will use these sources more, use them better—and initiate things a nascent modern we cannot yet discern. They will make our learners knowledge-rich, and make the pedagogical inventors rich in the old fashion money way!

On February 26, 1997, the New York New Media Association held a founding meeting of an Education Special Interest Group (SIG). One hundred and fifty people showed up, representing major players like Scholastic, HarperCollins, Disney, Random House, McGraw-Hill, Infoseek, Prodigy, Teachers College, New York University School of Education, College Board, plus dozens smaller businesses in Manhattan's Silicon Alley. It was a very intense crowd; no one laughed at the speakers' jokes. When Julian Alssid, founder of the SIG, announced that the meeting would begin ten minutes late and urged people to turn around and say hello to one another, they took him seriously. Within a few seconds the animated conversations lifted a roar across the room. When the program had been presented the imperative was tidal: create content.

Seybold NY Seminars' Advance Program Guide for their April 23–25, 1997 Exposition describes why most of the Cyberschool software next waves cannot now be described:

> Each new communications medium has been defined by those media that preceded it: photography in terms of painting, film in terms of theater and television in terms of radio. The Internet has emerged as a unique hybrid that does not have a single direct ancestor. Although we feel the need to find a coherent metaphor within which to define it, this may not be possible or even relevant.

When Johann Gutenberg made the use of moveable type practical, its natural technical extensions were the book and various forms of pamphlets. Type, and the books and pamphlets it prints, are all technology (in today's parlance, "hardware"). The first thing this technology caused was the accessibility of existent literature. Beginning with the Bible, materials preserved over the millennia by chisel and pen were printed in multiple copies on paper, bound in volumes, and distributed broadly.

Next came software. Five hundred years ago, technology cause the fresh potential market for books, evolving another species of inventiveness. Completely new forms were devised for the information structure of print: the novel, the encyclopedia, the newspaper, the magazine, the textbook, the brochure, and the mass mailing (to name a few). So far, the software written for digital technologies largely mirrors print, graphics and video without transforming them very much. An encyclopedia is put on CD-ROM as a database with links: Encarta. The drawings and sounds from a movie are arranged as games and burned to a CD/ROM: *The Lion King*. Here, digital hardware is displaying and manipulating book and movie materials, and this is meaningful because it makes these helpful and entertaining things available literally to the world. But there is more to be done!

To get a sense of what inventing a new kind of communication can be like, a useful exercise is to rent videos together and watch first a pre-1935 Disney cartoon and then *Snow White*. During the half decade between the making of the films you will watch, the artists at Burbank invented cartoon communication for the moving picture—a medium much used by the Disney people and many others ever since to the enjoyment of all! Most striking in this exercise is the primitivism of Disney's pre-1935 offerings.

In all probability, digital teaching software award winners of today will seem just that primitive five years from now. Tutoring innovation still minimally uses the radically new tools of interactivity, hyperlinking, and the convergence of input from sight and sound over time. The creation of digital tutors presents artistic, pedagogical, and intellectual challenges. Some very smart people are working at it and some good things have begun to come down stream. Several totally new methods of digital tutoring may be invented. Although voices clamor for guidelines for them, ranging from "fun" to "multicultural," software that endures like Snow White will do so because it teaches.

The ideas for teaching at Cyberschool issue from parental instinct, the teaching gifted, and old and new pedagogical theories. Monopoly need not be feared because there is too much to be done. The territory for homesteading is vast. As they settle in, the new pedagogies—those here and those to come—will have enormous impact. A century ago a similar cascade, of medical advance, had begun: sterilization, anesthesia,

X-ray, surgical specialization, elimination of diseases, antibiotics, organ replacements, and gene therapies. Life expectancy was doubled and good health became routine. The Cyberschool cascade will be just as important for the human mind.

STEERING THE CURRENTS

Charting routes through Cyberschool allows description of discrete paths for study unimaginable without the Internet. Undoubtedly this will lead to profitable competition among curriculum designers. The big browsers are already providing proto-curricular indexes in their education and home schooling sectors. There is no limit to how this curricula design of the future can be specialized for: Muslim preschoolers, gifted adolescent poets, basic academic drills for dumb jocks, anything! Families and institutions will be able to choose what their children learn. Cyberschool imposes no common denominator.

SWIMMING AND SINKING

Competitive testing will keep it all within view. Job applications will begin to replace emphasis on graduation information with a "Test Scores" section requesting the applicant's scores on certified online tests. The competition will become intense among testing companies because employers will learn which tests are effective, and will hire people based on their scores on the better tests. Among the obvious tests to be created is one for fourteen-year-olds newly in the job market. Here, a kid will take a digital test—at a computer at a test center, online from home or school, or using a writeable CD to mark with answers. The test-maker will grade the test and certify scores on verbal and number literacy, general knowledge, and advanced abilities. Teenagers with low scores will get messenger jobs, while the ones with high scores can be apprenticed in professions like medicine, engineering, and the law. As this testing becomes commonplace, employers will play a major role in preparing young people of all abilities for the workforce. Competitive testing will also become a realistic incentive for kids to study and learn.

DOWN TO THE SEA IN CHIPS

Cyberschool is not culture-forming. For all the hype and dark predicting by the media, cyberculture is a very difficult thing to imagine. Maybe people in chat groups feel a shared interest, but you can't go much further than that. Fostering a culture is, however, the way American schools have been controlled over recent generations. The football team and cheerleaders, school spirit, correctness about race and creed, and the many rites of passage culminating in graduation so dominate schools that academics are a nuisance. A school's culture is an institutional common denominator to which all are supposed to conform. Both dropouts and the nerds at the top of the class are cultural misfits. Because there is no culture there, learning at Cyberschool is a sea change from what we are used to in America. Instructional designers at Utah State University explain:

> Groups don't learn, individuals learn. Learners may be part of a group while learning, learners may learn from one another, and the social context of a learning environment may provide support for its members; nevertheless the change in cognitive structure and the acquisition of knowledge and skill is an individual event.

Learning without school culture should not seem scary. People do it by reading books, by thinking on our own, by talking with people who know stuff. Cyberschool removes the cultural barriers to the acquisition of knowledge and skills.

Cyberschool is omnischool: it is universal and unrestricted, replacing education as we have known it. Unattached from school buildings, Cyberschool admits everyone, without regard to age, sex, race, tribe, nation, or persuasion. Eventually, the Cyberschool cascade will subside into the vast, user-friendly enclave of human knowledge where young and old may learn, at their individual pace and preference. Those who teach will have at their keyboards undreamed of sources to ply their gifts. Crowded, regimented classes will disappear in the onrush of new places and ways to teach and learn at Cyberschool. Thus, the teacher-learner relationship will become more direct, more human. Cyberschool will have increasing links from learners to the learned, and ways will be refined to enhance the personal interplay.

Cyberschool is already one of the great achievements of our species, and it is not even very sophisticated yet. In a time when tribal sensitivities are deepening and multicultures are demanding their perpetuation, cyberspace is the domain of the individual. A kid caught in a dismal family, neighborhood, or school can jump into a chip, to go out to the ocean and find a far horizon. We are all that kid, in one way or another. The cascade washing over the world is giving each of us the captaincy of our own mind.

CYBERSCHOOL SOURCES NOT CITED IN THE TEXT

Marshall McLuhan. *Understanding Media*. McGraw-Hill, 1964.

Norbert Wiener. *The Human Use of Human Beings*. Avon Books, 1967.

The Eiffel Project. Project Abstract distributed at February 27, 1997 meeting of the New York New Media Association Education SIG.

Sueann Ambron and Kristina Hooper, Eds., *Learning with Interactive Multimedia: Developing and Using Multimedia Tools in Education*. Microsoft Press, 1990.

"Everybody Can Read": "The Infinitely Patient Computer." *New York Times*. September 27, 1996.

Dalton School. Personal visit to seminar there November 1996. Malcolm Thompson described the astronomy software at the seminar.

Ruth Otte, et al. "Breakthrough Study Shows Online Use Increases Student Learning." PRNewswire, October 16, 1996.

Milton Friedman. *Washington Post*, February 19, 1995.

William Gibson: "Father of Cyberspace Sires Techno-Naive Web Sites." *New York Times*, March 12, 1997.

Utah State University. "Reclaiming Instructional Design," by M. David Merrill, Leston Drake, Mark J. Lacy, and Jean Pratt (Teachers College course materials).

Appendix 2

URLs FOR WEB PAGES MENTIONED IN THE IDEAS

This list can also be found at GoldenSwamp.com in the *Subject Sampler*. There, the links can be clicked to go to the websites without having to type their URLs into your browser address box.

Section 2: Attitude

Idea 7. The Internet Is a Big Encyclopedia

AvianBrain. http://avianbrain.org/index.html

Idea 9. Children Need Culture Comfort

Forest of Rhetoric. http://humanities.byu.edu/rhetoric/silva.htm
Aristotle's Rhetoric. http://www.public.iastate.edu/~honeyl/Rhetoric/
Rhetoric of Mencius. http://www.hkbu.edu.hk/~ringoma/water.html
Crow's Nest. http://www.u.arizona.ed u/~tkinney/resources/rhetoric.html

Idea 12. Knowing the Bad Stuff

The History Guide. http://www.historyguide.org/europe/lecture10.html

Idea 15. Attitude: Technology Cannot Replace Human Teachers

PBS: Auschwitz, Inside the Nazi State. http://www.pbs.org/auschwitz/
New York Public Library e-Books. http://ebooks.nypl.org/4EF9EC0F-E89B-
    44AD-96CA-8400CD1172B6/10/121/en/Default. htm

Idea 16. Attitude: Books Are Better

Mark Twain in His Times. http://etext.lib.virginia.edu/railton/index2.html
Tertullian. http://www.tertullian.org/
Information Please Almanac. http://www.infoplease.com/
Pearson: Education Timeline. http://www.infoplease.com/aboutip.html
United States Congressional Directory. http://www.gpoaccess.gov/cdirectory/
    index.html
Zipcode Look-up. http://zip4.usps.com/zip4/welcome.jsp
infoplease.com. http://www.infoplease.com/index.html

Idea 19. Attitude: Control Internet Access to Protect Children

Seattle's Woodland Park Zoo: Multimedia. http://www.zoo.org/multimedia/
    index.html
BabyCenter. http://www.babycenter.com/refcap/preconception/
    gettingpregnant/7056.html

Idea 21. Attitude: Education Must Retrieve Control of Open Content

University of Washington: Tsunamis. http://www.ess.washington.edu/tsunami/
    index.html

Idea 22. Attitude: The Education Industry Creates Superior Content

California Turtle and Tortoise Club. http://www.tortoise.org/

Idea 23. Attitude: Curriculum Standards Rule

Understanding Genetics. http://www.genetics.gsk.com/understand.htm

Idea 24. Attitude: Wire the Schools Not the Kids

Maine Learning Technology Initiative. http://www.state.me.us/mlte/index.htm

Idea 27. The College Level Clearer Course

University of Virginia: Electronic Text Center. http://etext.virginia.edu/
Most Unwired College Campuses. http://www.intel.com/personal/products/
   mobiletechnology/unwiredcolleges.h tm

Idea 28. The Extra-Education Little-Noticed Morph

Macromedia: Authorware Showcase. http://www.macromedia.com/cfusion/
   showcase/index.cfm?event = finder&productid; eq1519&loc = en_us
Sun   Mircrosystems: Online   Courses.   http://java.sun.com/developer/
   onlineTraining/

Idea 29. Distant Learning Is Many Things

Famous Artists School. http://www.famous-artists-school.com/index.php/

Idea 30. Responses of Various Countries

Nokia: China. http://www.nokia.com.cn/

Idea 31. The Accurate Attitude about Technology

HowStuffWorks.com: Bits and Bytes. http://computer.howstuffworks.com/
   bytes.htm

Idea 32. Can Pedagogy Be What It Teaches?

Astronomy Picture of the Day (APOD). http://antwrp.gsfc.nasa.gov/APOD/
  astropix.html
Theban Mapping Project. http://www.thebanmappingproject.com/

SECTION 3: ACCESS

Idea 36. Hewlett Foundation Initiative

William and Flora Hewlett Foundation: Open Content. http://www.
  hewlett.org/Programs/Education/Technology/OpenContent/
  opencontent.htm

Idea 38. What Knowledge Is

American Philosophical Society. http://www.amphilsoc.org/about/

Idea 40. Why Knowledge Accessed in the Virtual Knowledge Ecology Is Superior

Nature: Nature Genome Gateway. http://www.nature.com/genomics/
  index.html
  The United States Library of Congress. http://www.loc.gov/
British Library: Treasures in Full. http://www.bl.uk/treasures/
  treasuresinfull.html

Idea 41. Open Content Only Is Accessed from the Virtual Knowledge Ecology

The History Guide. http://www.historyguide.org/

Idea 42. Why Open Content Is a Bargain

Library of Congress. http://countrystudies.us/russia/10.htm
Los Alamos Laboratory: Periodic Table of the Elements. http://
  periodic.lanl.gov/

Chemical Elements: Interactive Periodic Table of the Elements.
www.chemicalelements.com/
University of Sheffield in England: Web Elements Periodic Table. http://
www.webelements.com/
Luminarium. http://www.luminarium.org/lumina.htm
Learner org. http://learner.org/
Journey North. http://www.learner.org/jnorth/

Idea 43. Literacy and Language

Nepal Farmers. http://news.bbc.co.uk/2/hi/technology/3744075.stm
Starfall. http://www.starfall.com/
Nepali Times. http://www.nepalitimes.com/issue241/index.htm?
BBC: Napali.com. http://www.bbc.co.uk/worldservice/index.shtml
Louvre Museum. http://www.louvre.fr/louvrea.htm
Neuroscience for Kids. http://faculty.washington.edu/chudler/neurok.html
HowStuffWorks. http://www.bbc.co.uk/worldservice/index.shtml

Idea 44. The Container Is Not Its Content

Hermitage Museum: Leonardo da Vinci's Madonna and Child (Madonna
Litta). http://www.hermitagemuseum.org/html_En/03/hm3_3_1b.html

Idea 45. Direct, Individual Access

Jet Propulsion Laboratory: Mars Exploration Rover Mission. http://
marsrovers.jpl.nasa.gov/home/
Library of Congress: Thomas. http://thomas.loc.gov/

Idea 46. Search Engines as Access

Elephant Information Repository. http://elephant.elehost.com/
PBS: Elephants of Africa. http://www.pbs.org/wnet/nature/elephants/

Idea 47. Repositioned Old Kinds of Access

PBS: Nature. http://www.pbs.org/wnet/nature/index.html
PBS: Kalahari Explorations. http://www.pbs.org/wnet/nature/kalahari/
kalahari.html

Idea 52. Eyewitness Account of the Subject
Cascade

University of Michigan: Encyclopedia of Diderot & d'Alembert. http://
    www.hti.umich.edu/d/did/
Duke University: How the Dewey Decimal System Works. http://
    www.lib.duke.edu/libguide/fi_books_dd.htm

Arts

WebMuseum. http://www.ibiblio.org/wm/
Metropolitan Museum of Art, New York. http://www.metmuseum.org/
Louvre Museum, Paris. http://www.louvre.fr/louvrea.htm
Hermitage Museum, St. Petersburg. http://www.hermitagemuseum.org/

Biography

Nobel Prize: Biographies of Laureates. http://nobelprize.org/
White House: Biographies of Presidents and First Ladies. http://
    www.whitehouse.gov/history/life/

Biology

Scale Net. http://198.77.169.79/scalenet/scalenet.htm
Animal Bytes. http://www.sandiegozoo.org/animalbytes/index.html
Ancient Bristlecone Pine. http://www.sonic.net/bristlecone/home.html

Chemistry

American Chemical Society: Molecule of the Week. http://www.chemistry.org/
    portal/a/c/s/1/acsdisplay.html?DOC = HomeMolecule%5ca
    rchive%5cmotw_archive.html.
Virtual Chemistry Laboratory. http://neon.chem.ox.ac.uk/vrchemistry/
Electrochemical Dictionary. http://electrochem.cwru.edu/ed/dict.htm

Countries and Cultures

United States Library of Congress: County Studies. http://lcweb2.loc.gov/frd/
cs/continent.html
Geographic. http://www.geographia.com/
National Anthropological Archives: Lakota Winter Counts. http://
wintercounts.si.edu/
Life at the End of the Road. http://endoftheroad.org/

Geography

United States Geological Survey: World Earthquake Activity. http://
earthquake.usgs.gov/recenteqsww/index.html
University of California at Berkeley: Plate Tectonics Animations. http://
www.ucmp.berkeley.edu/geology/tectonics.html
U.S. GLOBEC Georges Bank Study. http://globec.whoi.edu/globec.html
Embassy of Turkmenistan, Washington, D.C. http://
www.turkmenistanembassy.org/turkmen/history/horses.html
University of Texas at Austin: Perry-Castaneda Map Collection. http://
www.lib.utexas.edu/maps/

Government

United States Senate. http://www.senate.gov/
Northwestern University: *Oye.* http://www.oyez.org/oyez/frontpage

History

Brigham Young University's Harold B. Lee Library: EuroDocs. http://
library.byu.edu/~rdh/eurodocs/
Chicago Historical Society: Parades, Protests & Politics in Chicago. http://
www.chicagohs.org/history/politics.html

Languages

YourDictionary.com. http://www.yourdictionary.com/diction1.html
Ancient Scripts. http://www.ancientscripts.com/

MasterRussian. http://masterrussian.com/
University of Chicago Library: *Kanji Alive*. http://kanjialive.lib.uchicago.edu/
main.php?page = overview&lang = en

Literature

Project Gutenberg. http://www.gutenberg.org/about/
Luminarium. http://www.luminarium.org/lumina.htm
Norton Anthology of English Literature. http://www.wwnorton.com/nael/
welcome.htm
Golden Age of Spanish Poets. http://sonnets.spanish.sbc.edu/
Beowulf. http://www.humanities.mcmaster.ca/~beowulf/main.html

Math

Mathworld. http://mathworld.wolfram.com/
Purple Math. http://www.purplemath.com/

Philosophy and Religion

Perseus Digital Library. http://www.perseus.tufts.edu/
Kant on the Web. http://www.hkbu.edu.hk/~ppp/Kant.html
All About Sikhism. http://allaboutsikhs.com/home.php
King of Jordan. http://www.kingabdullah.jo/homepage.php
The Government of Tibet in Exile. http://www.tibet.com/

Physics

Berkeley National Laboratory: The Particle Adventure. http://
particleadventure.org/particleadventure/
The American Physical Society: Physics Central. http://physicscentral.org/
Quantum Diaries. http://www.slac.stanford.edu/
Quantum-Atom Optics. http://www.acqao.org/index.html

Technologies

How Stuff Works. http://www.howstuffworks.com/
IEEE Virtual Museum. http://www.ieee-virtual-museum.org/index.php
Bridges and Tunnels of Allegheny County, Pennsylvania. http://
  pghbridges.com/basics.htm

Writing

Fifty Writing Tools. http://www.poynter.org/content/
  content_view.asp?id=61811
ModernWord.com. http://www.themodernword.com/themodword.cfm

Reference

Classical music glossary NAXOS. http://www.naxos.com/NewDesign/
  fglossary.files/bglossary.files/g_ab.htm
Soils.org. http://www.soils.org/sssagloss/a_browse.html
Wikipedia. http://en.wikipedia.org/wiki/Main_Page
Internet Library of Science. http://plos.org/
African Research Central. http://www.africa-research.org/
Internet Archive. http://www.archive.org/

Idea 53. Eyewitness Account of the Cascade Sources

Jet Propulsion Laboratory. http://deepimpact.jpl.nasa.gov/
Monticello. http://www.monticello.org/

One Person

Famous Trials. http://www.law.umkc.edu/faculty/projects/FTrials/ftrials.htm
Vocabulary University. http://www.vocabulary.com/index.html
African Timelines. http://web.cocc.edu/cagatucci/classes/hum211/timelines/
  htimelinetoc.htm
The World Lecture Hall. http://web.austin.utexas.edu/wlh/

The Academy

Museum of Paleontology. http://www.ucmp.berkeley.edu/
Douglass Archives of Public Address. http://douglassarchives.org/
Nucleic Acid Database. http://ndbserver.rutgers.edu/
The Why Files. http://whyfiles.org/
Elementary Math Problem of the Week. http://mathforum.org/elempow/
Advanced Papyrological Information System. http://www.columbia.edu/cu/
    lweb/projects/digital/apis/
Image understanding as multi-media translation.
http://vision.cs.arizona.edu/kobus/research/projects/words_and_pictures/
    index.html

Libraries

Library of Congress of the United States. http://www.loc.gov/
New York Public Library. http://www.nypl.org/books/
British Library: Turning the Pages. http://www.bl.uk/onlinegallery/ttp/
    digitisation2.html
Brooklyn Daily Eagle. http://www.brooklynpubliclibrary.org/eagle/

Showcases

San Francisco Museum of Modern Art. http://www.sfmoma.org/espace/
    espace_overview.html
Whatever Happened to Polio? http://americanhistory.si.edu/polio/
Caught in Oils. http://www.nhm.ac.uk/library/art/caught_in_oils/
Time Chart Celts on the Upper Danube. http://www.dhm.de/museen/
    heuneburg/en/zeit_frame.html
St. Paul Panorama
http://www.mnhs.org/places/historycenter/exhibits/territory/territory/
    panorama /panorama2.html
New England Aquarium: Animal Rescue. http://www.neaq.org/scilearn/randr/

Governments

NOAA Satellite and Information Service. http://www.ssd.noaa.gov/
Satellite Image of the Day. http://www.osei.noaa.gov/OSEIiod.html

ABCs of Nuclear Science. http://www.lbl.gov/abc/
United Kingdom Parliament. http://www.parliament.uk/
Explore Parliament. http://www.explore.parliament.uk/
    parliament.aspx?searchstring=k
History of the New York City Police. http://www.ci.nyc.ny.us/html/nypd/html/
    3100/retro.html
History of Beijing, China. http://www.ebeijing.gov.cn/About%20Beijing/

Journals and Broadcast Media

National Geographic. http://www.nationalgeographic.com/
Building the Alaska Highway. http://www.pbs.org/wgbh/amex/alaska/
Learner.org. http://www.learner.org/exhibits/
Interactive Body. http://www.bbc.co.uk/science/humanbody/body/interactives/
    3djigsaw_02/

For-Profits

WebMD. http://www.webmd.com/
Mayo Clinic. http://www.mayoclinic.com/index.cfm
All About Tea. http://www.tealand.com/AllAboutTea.htm

Expertorials

Cow to Cone. http://www.benjerry.com/fun_stuff/cow_to_cone/
Carnegie Corporation of New York. http://www.carnegie.org/sub/about/pessay/
    pessay98.html
Danish Wind Industry Association. http://www.windpower.org/
Discover Opera. http://www.metoperafamily.org/metopera/discover/

Idea 55. The Movement Toward a New Ecology of Learning

William and Flora Hewlett Foundation: Open Content. http://www.
    hewlett.org/Programs/Education/Technology/OpenContent/
    opencontent.htm

MIT OpenCourseWare ("OCW"). http://ocw.mit.edu/index.html
Johns Hopkins Bloomberg School of Public Health OpenCourseWare. http://
   ocw.mit.edu/index.html
Sharing of Free Intellectual Assets (SOFIA). http://sofia.fhda.edu/
Harvard University Open Library Connections Program. http://ocp.hul.
   harvard.edu/ww/
Utah State University eduCommons. http://parrot.ed.usu.edu/Index/
   ECIndex_view
Rice University Connexions. http://cnx.rice.edu/
Carnegie Mellon University Open Learning Initiative. http://www.cmu.edu/oli/
SAKAI: Collaboration and Learning Environment (CLE). http://www.
   sakaiproject.org/cms/
EduTools. http://www.edutools.info/. Internet Archive. http://www.archive.org/
CreativeCommons. http://creativecommons.org

Idea 56. The Increasing Level of Detail

Victorian Web. http://www.victorianweb.org/

SECTION 4: AGGREGATION
Idea 62. The Cambrian Explosion

Goose.org. http://www.goose.org

Idea 64. The Center of Everything

Troy. http://www.thebritishmuseum.ac.uk/troy/
A. S. Kline. Poetry in Translation. http://www.tonykline.co.uk/

Idea 65. Seeing Wholes

Metropolitan Museum of Art. http://www.metmuseum.org/explore/gw/
   el_gw.htm
National Gallery in Washington D.C. http://www.georgewashington.si.edu/
   index.html

Idea 66. Opening the Universe of Human Learning

University of Arizona: The Biology Project. http://www.biology.arizona.edu/default.html

Idea 67. Open Content Only

Wikipedia.org. http://en.wikipedia.org/wiki/Main_Page

Idea 69. Minimalization

Technorati. http://www.technorati.com/

Idea 70. Networks

The Santa Fe Institute. http://www.santafe.edu
National Gallery of Washington D.C. Rembrandt's Late Religious Portraits. http://www.nga.gov/exhibitions/2005/rembrandt/flash/index.shtm

Idea 71. Small-World Networks

London Natural History Museum: Seeds of Trade. http://internt.nhm.ac.uk/jdsml/seeds/

Idea 72. Dynamic Networks

The Santa Fe Institute: Network Dynamics. http://www.santafe.edu/research/networkDynamics.php

Idea 74. The Network Effect

Elephants of Cameroon. http://www.fieldtripearth.org/div_index.xml?id=3

Idea 75. Open Content Vets Spontaneously

Hittite Homepage. http://www.asor.org/HITTITE/HittiteHP.html

Idea 77. Virtual Content Creatures

ABACUS, The Art of Calculating with Beads. http://www.ee.ryerson.ca:8080/
~elf/abacus/
Wikipedia. http://en.wikipedia.org/wiki/Main_Page

Idea 78. Why Aggregated Virtual Knowledge Is Superior

Brigham Young University: Forest of Rhetoric. http://humanities.byu.edu/rhet-
oric/silva.htm
United States Geological Survey: World Map—Clickable to Regions. http://
earthquake.usgs.gov/recenteqsww/
Phrygians.com. http://www.phrygians.com/

SECTION 5: ADAPTING

Idea 83. The Education to Expect

NASA's Rovers Mission. http://marsrovers.jpl.nasa.gov/home/

Idea 85. The Adaptation of Content

University of Texas: Perry-Castañeda Library Map Collection. http://
www.lib.utexas.edu/maps/

Idea 86. The Adaptation Across Cultures

Merriam-Webster Unabridged. http://unabridged.merriam-webster.com/
cgi-bin/unabridged

Idea 90. How the Education Establishment Could Adapt

Fisher & Company Heritage. http://www.fisherdynamics.com/heritage/
heritage.htm

SECTION 6: ACTION

Idea 93. Get the Virtual Knowledge Ecology to the Kids

Poor Man's WI-FI.
http://www.usbwifi.orcon.net.nz/
Massey News. 19 November 2004
http://masseynews.massey.ac.nz/2004/Massey_News/nov/nov22/stories/
08–21–04.h tml

Idea 97. Develop Devices for Ubiquitous Mobile Computing

$100 Laptop. http://laptop.media.mit.edu/

Idea 104. Think Share Not Copyright

CreativeCommons.org. http://creativecommons.org/

Idea 106. Open Your Own Content

Michelangelo.com. http://michelangelo.com
Early Life 1475–1504. Michelangelo.com. http://michelangelo.com/buon/
bio-index2.html

INDEX

ABOUT THE AUTHOR

Idea 35, *The Author's Vantage Point*, describes Judy Breck's ten-year participation in the emergence of online knowledge. For presentation at the 2006 FlashForward conferences, she has developed a topic "Connective Expression" about creative laws and practice of the new digital network medium. She maintains a website and blog devoted to the emergence of online education at GoldenSwamp.com, and *109 Ideas* is her fourth book on the subject. She is webmaster for the Justice Resource Center, a project of the New York City Board of Education. She serves as an advisor to the World Bank Development Gateway, where she has written two articles and contributed editorial assistance.

An inventor, Judy Breck holds U.S. Patent #4,360,836, issued in 1982, for a method for protecting viewers' eyes from video monitors. With the tech chief at HomeworkCentral.com as coinventor, she created the system (patent applied for) that organized and interfaced knowledge in the medium of the Internet and was used by the then largest open collection of online study subjects. From 2003 to the present, she has worked with a coinventor on a centering object for online content network nodes, as described at TheCOB.com.

She attended Texas public schools, primarily in El Paso, completed a political science major at Northwestern University, and received her bachelor of arts from the University of Texas at El Paso. In 1968, a job on the national staff of Richard Nixon's presidential campaign brought her to New York City, where she has remained.

Other books by Judy Breck include *The Wireless Age* (2001), *How We Will Learn in the 21st Century* (2002), and *Connectivity* (2004).